ENOS MILLS'
COLORADO

OTHER TITLES BY THE AUTHOR

Frederick Chapin's Colorado:
The Peaks About Estes Park and Other Writings

Mr. Stanley of Estes Park

In the Vale of Elkanah:
The Tahosa Valley World of Charles Edwin Hewes

The Ways of the Mountains:
Thornton Sampson, Agnes Vaille and
Other Tragedies in High Places

Early Estes Park Narratives

America's Switzerland:
Estes Park and Rocky Mountain National Park,
The Growth Years

ENOS MILLS'
COLORADO

—

James H. Pickering

BOWER
HOUSE

DENVER

BowerHouseBooks.com.

Cover Design and illustration by Margaret McCullough
Field, built by Enos Mills in 1908. Courtesy National Park Service

Library of Congress Cataloging-in-Publication Data
Mills, Enos Abijah, 1870–1922.
Enos Mills' Colorado / [edited by] James Pickering.
p. cm.
Includes bibliographical references.
ISBN 978-1-55566-367-4
1. Natural history—Colorado. I. Pickering, James H. II. Title.
QH105.C6M55 2005
508.788—dc22 2005019338

10 9 8 7 6 5

Contents

Preface

I have lived with Enos Mills for most of my life. Our relation-ship began during the summer of my 9th year, when I was my-self miraculously transported from suburban New York to Estes Park, Colorado. For two all-too-short weeks my home was a turn-of-the century log cabin on the slopes of Twin Sisters Mountain looking out on the towering East Face of Longs Peak across the Tahosa Valley. It was here, among stands of lodgepole pine and shimmering aspen, in a world of mountain bluebirds and shy mule deer, scampering chipmunks and chattering pine squirrels that I first heard of Enos Mills.

The Tahosa Valley's most famous resident had been dead for more than two decades, but his legacy was still very much ap-parent, most visible in the small tin-roofed homestead cabin which stood below us on the lower slope of the Twins and in Longs Peak Inn directly across the road. Though it had been sold that winter by his widow, Mills' famous mountain inn was still in operation, as were its two equally historic neighbors, Columbines Lodge and Hewes-Kirkwood Inn. To reach Mr. Davis' red-roofed stable where we rented our horses, we had to pass by the Inn and its complex of cabins and outbuildings. What we did not know was that three short years later, on June 9, 1949, the main building of Longs Peak Inn would be de-stroyed by fire, never to be rebuilt. Enos Mills was also very much present in the stories which the adults told about life in the Tahosa Valley in earlier days. They talked about Enos Mills' efforts to establish a new national park in the Estes Park region, efforts which I later learned earned him the title "Father of Rocky Mountain National Park." They also talked about the darker, more controversial side of their former neighbor, and of the quarrels of the Tahosa Valley in which he had played such a central role, quarrels which even then still lingered in memory. In time I would learn, and write about, this aspect of Mills' character and personality. As a boy I simply felt their presence in the talk of my elders.

Back in the East, I read—and was delighted by—Enos Mills' nature essays. They spoke of a special place that I had come to know and love. As a teenager I could also readily identify with the youthful and optimistic narrative figure which Mills presented to my imagination, and as for the animals and birds, mountains and lakes, trees and plants that he described with so much pleasure, well, I had seen them too, at least in summer dress. Later, when I came to know the world of Enos Mills in other seasons, my appreciation for both man and writer only deepened.

Years later, with a wife and family of my own, it was natural—I suppose inevitable—that I would want to introduce them to the world of Estes Park and Enos Mills. Our first summers in Estes Park were spent, like so many other families, in a small two-bedroom cabin at the Y Camp, and it was there, from books taken out of Jellison Library to read around the evening fire, that I first began to absorb the history of early Estes Park that would in time become a major preoccupation. My interest in history, I would later discover, mirrored Mills' own. Enos Mills was still in his early twenties, when, inspired by the stories of old-timers like his uncle, the Reverend Elkanah J. Lamb, a resident of the Tahosa Valley since 1875, he began to gather up the facts and legends of local history which he published in 1905 as *The Story of Estes Park,* a small volume which would grow by accretion through several more editions during its author's lifetime.

Had my academic career taken a different course I might well have been tempted to research and write a full-scale biography of Enos Mills, much in the way I have done for his contemporary and friend Freelan Oscar Stanley. Such a book, I came to realize early on, was badly needed to help understand this complex and fascinating man. But my full-time involvement in university administration precluded such sustained efforts. The inclination was there; I simply lacked the time. In terms of Mills himself, such circumstances were clearly fortuitous. Alex Drummond, who brought to the task an extraordinary sensitivity to Mills and his world, has written a far better book than I could have done. His *Enos Mills: Citizen of Nature* (1995) is clearly a definitive biography, capturing the essence of the man, and providing the long needed prism through which to view accurately and appreciatively his work.

For my own part, I decided to pursue my interest in Mills in a different, and more manageable, way with the help of the University of Nebraska Press by bringing back into print facsimile editions of his first four volumes of collected essays, *Wild Life on the Rockies* (1909), *The Spell of the Rockies* (1911), *In Beaver World* (1913), and *Rocky Mountain Wonderland* (1915). This project yielded an unexpected dividend. In researching Mills for the introductions, I began to correspond and share questions and insights with Alex Drummond. That correspondence, carried on periodically over many months, has since deepened into an important friendship, one, I fancy, that Enos Mills himself would both understand and approve of.

In recent years my return to the professorial life has given me time to research and write more fully about the growth and development of Estes Park and Rocky Mountain National Park. In these full-length historical studies, in which I have tried to trace the history of park and town in the context of the development of western tourism, Enos Mills remains an important, indeed dominating, influence and presence. As readers of my most recent book, *America's Switzerland: Estes Park and Rocky Mountain National Park, The Growth Years* (2005), will discover, for example, having worked so tirelessly to establish Rocky Mountain National Park, Enos Mills was personally responsible for the decade-long political controversy involving police jurisdiction of park roads that dominated the 1920s, and at one point even threatening the continued existence of the park itself. Try as I might, it would seem, I cannot shake Enos Mills.

When Johnson Books suggested the possibility of a new collection of Enos Mills' essays, I was of course immediately interested. With his essays now part of the public domain, yet unavailable in annotated editions, here was yet another way of bringing Mills and his accomplishments to another generation of readers. None of us, alas, will ever have the opportunities enjoyed by several generations of Mills' patrons at Longs Peak Inn who could stroll with their exuberant host to nearby beaver ponds and listen by firelight to his after-dinner talks delivered from the split-log staircase adjoining the Inn's living room. But we can, if we pay close attention to his essays, hear the voice of Enos Mills speaking to us, telling his stories of bears and beaver and of the magnetic "spell of the Rockies," stories which link us to the natural world around us and of our need to understand, appreciate, and protect that world so that those who follow may have similar adventures. To that end *Enos Mills' Colorado* is dedicated.

James H. Pickering
Estes Park, Colorado
Houston, Texas

Introduction

He is of the brotherhood of John Muir: larger, freer, simpler, than our eastern states naturalists,—for wide as Thoreau's thoughts swept, we must allow that not all the phenomenon on earth can be found in Concord, and joyously as Burroughs or Torrey or Dr. Abbott noted things, they were all parochial in comparison. Mills is to the Rockies as Muir to the Sierras; and there are no more interesting books than theirs in respect to nature in the large.

— Springfield Republican *(1915)*

My chief aim in life is to arouse interest in the outdoors.

— *Enos A. Mills (ca. 1917)*

For the first quarter of the twentieth century the names Enos Abijah Mills (1870–1922) and the Rockies of Colorado were virtually synonymous. Making the most of his base of operations, a rustic mountain inn at the foot of fabled Longs Peak, Mills wrote some sixteen books and scores of magazine and newspaper articles, bringing the attention of the nation to the animal life and other natural wonders of the Rocky Mountain West. When not writing or personally entertaining guests at Longs Peak Inn with fireside talks or accompanying them on interpretive nature walks to nearby beaver ponds, Mills was crisscrossing the country, first on behalf of forestry and the need to protect the wilderness and later, in the years after 1909, on behalf of his own special project, the creation of Rocky Mountain National Park.

Mills' essays are for the most part now overlooked and neglected, and the writer himself, beyond, perhaps, Colorado, largely forgotten. This is unfortunate, for in his own time, as the quotation from the *Springfield Republican* suggests, Mills' writings were widely compared with those of John Muir and John Burroughs, the best nature writers of the day. This was even true of the eastern establishment press, which prided itself on its sophistication and lack of parochialism.

Though his perspective and style would mature over the years, Mills discovered early in his career that his talents as a writer lay in his ability to use incidents drawn from his own personal experience to tell a good story in a dramatic way. It was this ability as a storyteller, coupled with the easy readability of his prose, that appealed most strongly to his middle class audience and accounted for much of his contemporary popularity. The straightforward tales Mills told of his wilderness adventures with snow-slides, wild beasts, and even wilder weather were interesting, exciting, and fun—good reading on a quiet afternoon. They were also accessible to the average reader in a way that the more discursive and transcendental writings of a John Muir or a John Burroughs were not. Mills also chose his publisher well. Boston's long-established Houghton Mifflin Company, which included among its authors "the two Johnnies," Muir and Burroughs, was America's foremost nature publisher. That Mills' first books bore the Houghton Mifflin imprint virtually guaranteed that they would be noticed, read and reviewed.

There were other reasons for Mills' popularity. As one reviewer of his first book, *Wild Life on the Rockies* (1909), put it, there was the charm of "the author's personality"—the intrinsically attractive character of the narrator that Mills establishes in the mind of his reader. "I had many experiences—amusing, dangerous, and exciting," Mills' narrator announces in the first pages of his opening chapter. "There was abundance of life and fun in the work. On many an evening darkness captured me and compelled me to spend the night in the wilds without bedding, and often without food. During these nights I kept a camp-fire blazing until daylight released me." The persona that Mills sets before us is impossible not to like: his wide-eyed boyishness and sense of wonder and astonishment, his abundance of good will and friendly spirit, his tight nerve in tough places, his capacity for new experiences, adventure and fun. Equally important is the narrator's ability to summarize the important bond or "spell" linking man to the natural world that for Mills gives the pursuit and enjoyment of nature its final (and moral) meaning. At times this persona moves to the center stage to tell an action-packed, hair-raising story of his adventure on some isolated mountain height. (He was, like most of us, it seems, unusually prone to accidents and mishaps, another endearing quality.) At other times, the Mills persona is more reticent, content to retire to the sidelines and allow nature and its creatures to occupy the full focus of our attention.

Mills' popularity among his contemporaries was also attributable to the fact that he was an all-purpose naturalist, an approach he first put to use and then matured during his early years as a Longs Peak guide. "I can't say I have any particular system in nature study...," he told Colorado journalist Arthur Chapman late in life. "It's just trying to make the most of what offers." While guiding Mills developed what he afterwards referred to as "the poetic interpretation of the facts of nature." Nature, he insisted, was not to be discussed in the "dead language" of scientific information, but rather in terms "of its manners and customs, its neighbors and its biography." Such attitudes found their human embodiment in the wilderness avatar that Mills called the "nature guide." "A nature guide," he explained in *The Adventures of a Nature Guide* (1920), is

> a naturalist who can guide others to the secrets of nature. Every plant and animal, every stream and stone, has a number of fascinating facts associated with it and about each are numberless stories. Beavers build houses, bears play, birds have a summer and winter home thousands of miles apart, flowers have colour and perfume—every species of life is fitted for a peculiar life zone. The why of these things, how all came about, are of interest. Touched by a nature guide the wilderness of the outdoors becomes a wonderland. Then, ever after, wherever one goes afield he enjoys the poetry of nature.

The interpretive nature guide, as Mills himself was very much aware, was a latter-day version of the frontiersman, whose qualities, especially his self-reliance and rugged individualism, were widely associated in Mills' day as in our own with the quintessential American character. "Our late lamented frontier is forever gone," Mills writes, "and so, too, is the picturesque frontiersman, the trapper, the stage driver, and the audacious and heavily armed scout. The work of a guide is very much like that of a scout with shooting ability omitted and an array of nature information added. . . . there are numberless opportunities for helpful service and there will come frequent calls for heroic deeds."

Mills' nature guide, like Daniel Boone, Kit Carson, Davy Crockett and other worthies of the historic frontier, is pragmatic and resourceful, well-schooled in woodcraft and nature lore, and sufficient unto himself. He is also a rather amiable eccentric, a basically shy and detached observer who courts the solitude of nature, but stands ever-ready, like Natty Bumppo of James Fenimore Cooper's Leatherstocking Tales, to help when needed. Mills courted for himself the identification with the heroes of the frontier, pointing out to his guests at Longs Peak Inn a decaying log-cabin nearby over which he erected a crude sign reading "Kit Carson Cabin Site."

This simple and commonsensical approach to the wilderness and "its big principles" summarized Mills' approach to nature writing as well. Stripped to their essentials, his essays and articles, with their palatable mixture of scientific information, field observations, and personal anecdote, were only nature guiding in a more refined, better organized, and more compact form. Readers caught the flavor at once. "No student of natural history may say his library is complete," Arthur Weld of the *Waterloo Reporter* told his readers in November 1909, "if a copy of Enos A. Mills' *Wild Life in* [sic] *the Rockies* does not adorn the shelves." Mills' achievements as a naturalist, moreover, were substantial. *In Beaver World* (1913) was the first important work on the animal since Lewis H. Morgan's study of 1865. *The Grizzly: Our Greatest Wild Animal* (1919) deliberately set out to correct long-standing myths and misconceptions about the grizzly that were leading to the extinction of a species that he considered "the greatest animal on the North American continent, if not the world." Of equal, if not greater, importance was the influence he exerted through his books, articles, and public appearances on the views and attitudes of thousands of Americans, many of whom he converted into lifelong support-ers of conservation and national parks.

To be sure, Mills' work as a naturalist can be faulted on any number of scientific grounds—grounds which, of course, are far more visible in our day than in Mills' own. Mills was fortunate. He largely side-stepped the acrimonious controversy begun in 1903 by John Burroughs who in an *Atlantic Monthly* article ac-cused a number of well-known nature writers, including the popular Ernest Seton-Thompson, of exaggerating, anthropo-morphizing, sentimentalizing or otherwise falsifying animal be-havior. Burroughs' article initiated a debate that came to be known as the "nature faker" controversy, a controversy that dominated nature writing circles during the very period when Mills himself was establishing himself as an author and student of the out-of-doors. Though Mills was aware of the danger of being lumped together with those who wrote what Burroughs called "sham natural history," and was careful enough to de-nounce such writers in an essay of his own, Mills occupied what Alex Drummond has rightly perceived as "the radical end of the spectrum on matters of animal behavior." As Drummond con-tinues, "His portrayal of the forest as a dynamic community of animals—responding to their environment and to each other, often forced by circumstances to exercise their 'wits,' to modify instinctive patterns with resourceful invention to meet the unex-pected, and learning through experience, curiosity, and play—was a bold departure from the mechanistic view of Burroughs and the scientific majority he followed."

From the perspective of the modern naturalist, Mills can be faulted for any number of reasons, including an over-reliance on unique and unsynthesized events as the source for his under-standing of animal behavior as opposed to a statistical or exper-imental approach. His chief short-coming, however, as Drummond suggests, was Mills' tendency toward the anthropo-morphic treatment of animal life. Beginning with his first pub-lished collection of essays, *Wild Life on the Rockies* (1909) Mills was willing, if perhaps at times unconsciously, to attribute to an-imals the ability to think. Such "utterances" did not go unde-tected, and as one reviewer noted, they "of course, put Mr. Mills in the 'reason' school of American nature writers, as opposed to the 'instinct' school of which John Burroughs, the Sage of Slabsides, is the official mouthpiece."

It is unlikely that Mills arrived at his anthropomorphizing through any careful, systematic weighing of the abstract, theoretical arguments for or against attributing mental states to animals. More likely, in the beginning, he simply followed his "gut feelings," much in the way that many modern pet owners do with a favorite dog or cat, without taking into account the scientific arguments that could be raised for or against his position. The problem with wandering so near "the danger zone," as he so clearly does in many of the essays, was that Mills, who took great delight in correcting popular misconceptions about the natural world, not only risked straining his reader's credibility but undermining the very scientific understanding of nature he so wished to encourage. To be sure, the question of animal rationality is by no means a closed case in even current scientific circles, and Mills, interestingly enough, succeeds in raising some of the very issues that biologists today find to be of interest. Moreover, the long hours Mills spent in the field "watching and waiting," carefully observing, photographing, taking measurements, and drawing diagrams, together with his willingness to study animals in their natural environment anticipates the development of modern ethology in the 1930s.

Though more than three-quarters of a century has now passed since the death of Enos Mills, his writings remain interesting and important documents in the history of early twentieth-century American conservation in the West. That they are now generally neglected has, finally, less to do with the intrinsic value of his work than it does with the vagaries of changing literary tastes. As American conservationists have increasingly come to recognize, Enos Mills' achievements as a writer and wilderness champion are real, important, and need little in the way of apology.

The facts of Enos Mills' life can be easily summarized. His is a fascinating story. Born on a farm in the hill country of eastern Kansas in 1870, Mills came west as a boy of 14 to seek his health among the mountains of Estes Park, northwest of Denver, where his father's cousin, the Reverend Elkanah J. Lamb, was running a small guest ranch as a way station for those intent on climbing the peak to supplement his small ministerial salary. Building a homestead cabin of his own on the lower slopes of the Twin Sister Mountain close to the Lambs, the young Mills threw himself into the mountain world around him. His health dramatically improved, so much so, in fact, that he was soon able to support himself by working winters in the mines at Butte, Montana. There he earned enough money to indulge himself in the out-of-doors during the summer months, becoming a climber and mountain guide whose cat-like agility, stamina, and skill few of his contemporaries could equal. In the summer of 1902, Mills purchased Longs Peak House from the Lambs, which he rebuilt after a disastrous fire in 1906 and transformed into Longs Peak Inn, one of the most distinctive and best-known resorts in Colorado and the West. He also began to write, making use of the mountain world around him, first for the Denver papers and then for many of America's large-circulation magazines.

For all his success as a mountaineer and inn-keeper, Enos Mills' reputation would have remained largely a local one had it not been for two critical events during the first decade of the twentieth century that catapulted him to state, regional, and national attention. The first was his appointment in 1902 as Colorado's official State Snow Observer, a career Mills followed for three successive winter seasons. It was a highly romantic calling, and Enos Mills—as the Colorado "Snow Man"—quickly captured public imagination as he wandered in high places up and down the Continental Divide measuring the snowpack in anticipation of the spring runoff to follow. By the time he retired from the post in the spring of 1906, the Enos Mills legend had been well and permanently launched. He had become an intrepid, solitary, wilderness explorer of heroic dimensions, the survivor of storm, avalanche, and death defying mountain-top adventures.

The second important event of the decade followed closely and extended Mills' reputation to the nation at large. He agreed to accept the invitation of Gifford Pinchot and join Theodore

Roosevelt's Forest Service as an independent, salaried lecturer. From January 1907 to May 1909, Enos Mills crossed and re-crossed the nation promoting the cause of Progressive forest conservation and the recreational and spiritual uses of the wilderness. It was this national platform that prepared him for the major challenge of his career: the six-year fight for the creation of a new national park in the Estes Park region—an assignment he later came to refer to as "the most strenuous and growth-compelling occupation I ever followed" and "the achievement of my life." Other individuals and groups helped, and helped mightily, but it was Mills' persistence which was largely responsible for the passage of the bill creating Rocky Mountain National Park, signed into law by President Woodrow Wilson on January 26, 1915. The "father of Rocky Mountain National Park" they called him, and the epithet was well-deserved.

The final seven years of Enos Mills' tragically short life should have been ones of happiness and contentment. Though he finally married in August of 1918, at the age of 48, and the next year became a father, these years were marred by events of controversy and acrimony with Mills himself at the center. Most Americans tended to equate Enos Mills with the affable and generous spokesman for nature they encountered on the lecture platform or in the pages of his books and articles. There was, however, another, darker side to Mills' personality. Quick to take offense when opposed, surprisingly thin-skinned and often contentious, Enos Mills was in fact a difficult man to get along with. Exacting in his standards and expectations, Mills demanded the same of those around him. Unwilling to compromise on issues, ideas, or approaches on which he felt strongly, Mills aggressively rejected out of hand challenges to his own authority, all-too-often converting reasonable disagreements into personal disputes which alienated Mills from friends and supporters, neighbors, and even members of his own family. Flashes of the highly temperamental Mills had been visible during the stressful days of the park campaign when he had lashed out at his opponents, including his former employer, the U.S. Forest Service, which he suspected of secretly opposing its creation. Now he took on another government bureaucracy, the new National Park Service, an agency which, ironically, he had enthusiastically helped create to guard the nation's parks.

The issue which consumed his final years was the decision by Superintendent Lewis Claude Way in the spring of 1919 to grant an exclusive transportation franchise for travel within Rocky Mountain National Park which banned from the park entrepreneurial rent-car (or "jitney") drivers who made their summer living taking people on sightseeing tours. These independent drivers, Way and his superiors in Washington believed, not only added to the congestion along the Park's small and inadequate road system but inflicted high prices and poor service upon their hapless customers. Mills, a resort owner with his own touring car service, adamantly disagreed, seeing the decision as the establishment of an "illegal, unnecessary and unjust" "Prussian-like" monopoly controlled by arrogant bureaucrats indifferent to the public's right of free access to the nation's parks.

Mills challenged Superintendent Way by sending one of his cars and drivers into the Park, and, when expelled, sued the federal government for violating his "common rights as a citizen of the State of Colorado in traveling over the Park roads." Compromise proved impossible and gradually the controversy assumed larger dimensions, becoming focused on a suit filed by the State of Colorado challenging the right of the federal government to regulate traffic over roads never formally placed under the jurisdiction of the United States. By the time that the so-called "Cede Jurisdiction" controversy worked its way to a close in February 1929, Enos Mills was dead. That event had come suddenly and without warning nearly seven years earlier, on the evening of September 21, 1922. Enos Mills was 52.

The above summary of Enos Mills' legacy, literary career, and life, supplemented by the chronology that follows, are intended to provide the context for this new volume of Mills' selected essays. As the new century unfolds, and we mark the hundredth anniversary of events leading to the emergence of Enos Mills as a significant force in Western American conservation, culminating with the centennial of the dedication of Rocky Mountain

National Park in September 2015, it seems highly appropriate (even necessary) to have conveniently at hand an annotated collection of his essays to provide a new generation of readers with a sense of the Mills legacy. The intended audiences for this book are several, among them those interested in nature in general and the nature of Colorado in particular, those interested in Western American history and literature, and those interested the history of conservation in America, and in the many faces of environmentalism. It is also, and particularly, intended for the thousands of visitors who come each year to Estes Park, Colorado, Mills' home, where his presence and legacy are celebrated in Rocky Mountain National Park, which owes its existence to his tenacity and vision, Estes Park village where a statue of Mills and his dog "Scotch" has recently been installed in Bond Park, and at his small homestead cabin adjacent to Route 7 in the Tahosa Valley, nine miles to the south.

The essays I have chosen for inclusion in *Enos Mills' Colorado* are intended to be representative of Enos Mills' published writings. Some are stories of his adventures and tight escapes on lonely mountain tops, others display his considerable abilities as a close observer of the natural world. Readers will meet Mills the "Colorado Snow Observer" and Mills who risks death when he becomes "Snow Blinded on the Summit." They will meet his famous collie dog "Scotch," who "saves the day," and the two bear cubs, Jennie and Johnnie, which Mills kept for pets and then gave to the Denver Zoo. They will read about beaver, big-horn sheep, mountain lions, and grizzlies, as well as about a lowly shrub with the poetic name "kinnikinick." Finally, and perhaps most importantly, they will read about the nature guide, that new profession of wilderness interpreter which Mills came to believe was absolutely essential if America's natural resources were to be understood and protected. As editor, I have refrained from intervening. Though I have added a series of annotations which may prove helpful in locating place and identifying Mills' references and allusions, my goal is to allow Enos Mills to speak to a current generation of readers with the same freshness and spontaneity with which he addressed his own.

Enos A. Mills:
A Chronology

1870   April 22, Enos Abijah Mills born in Linn County, Kansas.

1884   Journeys to Estes Park, Colorado, by way of Kansas City and Denver. Works at Elkhorn Lodge.

1885   Works at Elkanah Lamb's Longs Peak House. First ascent of Longs Peak guided by Carlyle Lamb. Begins work on homestead cabin. Spends winter working on a ranch in eastern Colorado.

1886   Works again for the Lambs. Helps Carlyle Lamb construct Longs Peak trail. Completes his own cabin.

1887   Summer in Estes Park. First solo ascent of Longs Peak. Travels to Butte, Montana, to work as a tool boy at the Anaconda copper mine.

1888   Summer in Estes Park. Promoted to miner at Butte.

1889   Guides his first party to the summit of Longs Peak. Fall, fire closes Anaconda mine. December, meets John Muir on beach in San Francisco.

1890   Visits Death Valley, Yosemite, Sequoias, Virginia City and Reno; explores California coast south to San Diego. September, enrolls in Heald's Business College in San Francisco.

1892   Spring, visits Alaska.

1893   Works in Ward, Colorado. Visits Chicago World's Fair and family in Kansas.

1894   Revisits Alaska. Deserted by guides, Mills walks alone more than 200 miles from north of Chilcoot Pass south to Juneau.

1895   Fall, makes his first forestry speech in Kansas City.

1896   February, addresses teachers' convention in Linn County, Kansas, and receives $25. Begins reporting Estes Park resort news for Denver newspapers.

1896–1897   Spends winter working in the mines of Victor and Cripple Creek, Colorado.

1900   June 6, sails for Southampton, England, to visit Paris Exposition with Elkanah Lamb. Visits Switzerland, Venice, Florence, Rome, and England. Sails for home July 14.

1902   Purchases Longs Peak House from Carlyle Lamb. Publishes his first magazine article in *Outdoor Life*. Scotch arrives as a puppy.

1902–1903   December-January, as snow observer, completes six-day, 120-mile trip in inspecting headwaters of South Platte.

1903   February, makes the first winter climb of Longs
Peak, and journeys across Flattop Mountain to
Grand Lake. June, repeats Elkanah Lamb's 1871
descent of the East Face of Longs Peak. October,
visits Mesa Verde.

1904   February, as snow observer, completes 70-mile trip
inspecting the headwaters of the Grand, Big
Thompson, and Michigan rivers.

1905   First book, *The Story of Estes Park and a Guide
Book,* published. Fall-winter, undertakes 80-lec-
ture tour of East, including Kansas City,
Memphis, New Orleans, Columbus, Chicago.

1906   June, main building of Longs Peak Inn burns
while Enos is lecturing in St. Paul, and is quickly
rebuilt. Completes his last season as a Longs Peak
guide. Makes 32 ascents during the month of
August. Lectures extensively. Meets John
Burroughs.

1907   January, accepts Roosevelt's invitation to
become a special government lecturer on forestry.

1908   Builds Timberline House on Longs Peak trail,
halfway to the summit.

1909   May, resigns as government lecturer. *Wild Life
on the Rockies* published. Fall, begins to campaign
actively for a new national park in the Estes Park
region.

1910   June, Scotch is accidentally killed trying to
extinguish the fuse on a charge of dynamite
being used by a road crew near Longs Peak Inn.

1911 *The Spell of the Rockies* published.

1913 *In Beaver World* published.

1914 *The Story of a Thousand-Year Pine* published.

1915 January 16, Rocky Mountain National Park created by act of Congress. September 4, Park dedicated, with Enos Mills as master of ceremonies. *Rocky Mountain Wonderland* published.

1916 Enlarges Longs Peak Inn. *The Story of Scotch* published.

1917 January, attends National Parks Conference in Washington and presides at session discussing "The Recreational Use of National Parks." *Your National Parks* published.

1918 Marries Esther Burnell (1889–1946) on August 12 in ceremony at homestead cabin.

1919 Enda Mills born on April 27. Transportation concession controversy begins. *Being Good to Bears: And Other True Animal Stories* and *The Grizzly: Our Greatest Wild Animal* published.

1920 *The Adventures of a Nature Guide* published.

1921 *Waiting in the Wilderness* published.

1922 January, injured in a New York City subway collision. Enos Mills dies on September 22. *Watched by Wild Animals* published.

1923   *Wild Animal Homesteads* published.

1924   *The Rocky Mountain National Park* published.

1926   *Romance of Geology* published.

1931   *Bird Memories of the Rockies* published.

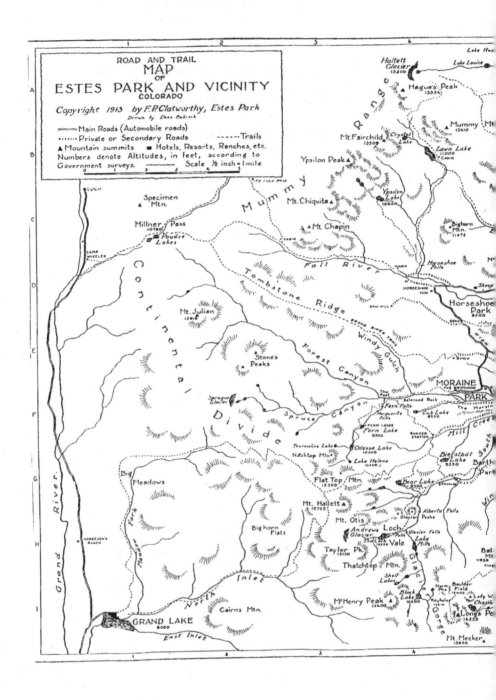

ROAD AND TRAIL
MAP
OF
ESTES PARK AND VICINITY
COLORADO

Copyright 1913 by F.P.Clatworthy, Estes Park
Drawn by Dean Babcock

━━━ Main Roads (Automobile roads)
••••••• Private or Secondary Roads   ------ Trails
▲ Mountain summits   ■ Hotels, Resorts, Ranches, etc.
Numbers denote Altitudes, in feet, according to
Government surveys. ━━━━ Scale ½ inch = 1 mile

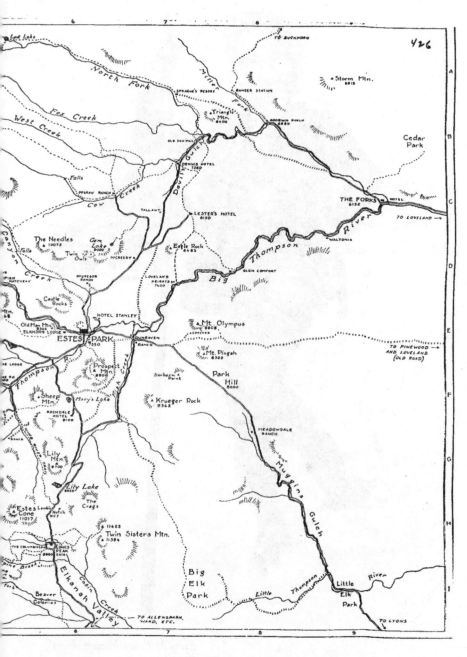

Map of Estes Park in 1913, by Fred Clatworthy.
Courtesy Estes Park Museum.

Enos Mills with snowshoes.
Courtesy Denver Public Library,
Colorado Historical Society, and Denver Art Museum.

Colorado Snow Observer

"Where are you going?" was the question asked me one snowy winter day. After hearing that I was off on a camping-trip, to be gone several days, and that the place where I intended to camp was in deep snow on the upper slopes of the Rockies, the questioners laughed heartily. Knowing me, some questioners realized that I was in earnest, and all that they could say in the nature of argument or appeal was said to cause me to "forego the folly." But I went, and in the romance of a new world—on the Rockies in winter—I lived intensely through ten strong days and nights, and gave to my life new and rare experiences. Afterwards I made other winter excursions, all of which were stirring and satisfactory. The recollection of these winter experiences is as complete and exhilarating as any in the vista of my memory.

Some years after my first winter camping-trip, I found myself holding a strange position,—that of the "State Snow Observer of Colorado." I have never heard of another position like it. Professor L. G. Carpenter, the celebrated irrigation engineer, was making some original investigations concerning forests and the water-supply. He persuaded me to take the position, and under his direction I worked as a government experiment officer. For three successive winters I traversed the upper slopes of the Rockies and explored the crest of the continent, alone. While on this work, I was instructed to make notes on "those things that are likely to be of interest or value to the Department of Agriculture or the Weather Bureau,"—and to be careful not to lose my life.

On these winter trips I carried with me a camera, thermometer, barometer, compass, notebook, and folding axe. The food carried usually was only raisins. I left all bedding behind. Notwithstanding I was alone and in the wilds, I did not carry any kind of a gun.

The work made it necessary for me to ramble the wintry heights in sunshine and storm. Often I was out, or rather up, in a blizzard, and on more than one occasion I was out for two weeks on the snow-drifted crest of the continent, without seeing anyone. I went beyond the trails and visited the silent places alone. I invaded gulches, eagerly walked the splendid forest aisles, wandered in the dazzling glare on dreary alpine moorlands, and scaled the peaks over mantles of ice and snow. I had many experiences,—amusing, dangerous, and exciting. There was abundance of life and fun in the work. On many an evening darkness captured me and compelled me to spend the night in the wilds without bedding, and often without food. During these nights I kept a camp-fire blazing until daylight released me. When the night was mild, I managed to sleep a little—in installments,—rising from time to time to give wood to the eager fire. Sometimes a scarcity of wood kept me busy gathering it all night; and sometimes the night was so cold that I did not risk going to sleep. During these nights I watched my flaming fountain of fire brighten, fade, surge, and change, or shower its spray of sparks upon the surrounding snow-flowers. Strange reveries I have had by these winter camp-fires. On a few occasions mountain lions interrupted my thoughts with their piercing, lonely cries; and more than once a reverie was pleasantly changed by the whisper of a chickadee in some near-by tree as a cold comrade snuggled up to it. Even during the worst of nights, when I thought of my lot at all, I considered it better than that of those who were sick in houses or asleep in the stuffy, deadly air of the slums.

> Believe me, 'tis something to be cast
> Face to face with thine own self at last.

Not all nights were spent outdoors. Many a royal evening was passed in the cabin of a miner or a prospector, or by the fireside of a family who for some reason had left the old home behind and sought seclusion in wild scenes, miles from neighbors. Among Colorado's mountains there are an unusual number of strong characters who are trying again. They are strong because broken plans, lost fortunes, or shattered health elsewhere have not ended their efforts or changed their ideals. Many are trying to restore health, some are trying again to prosper, others are just making a start in life, but there are a few who, far from the madding crowd, are living happily the simple life. Sincerity, hope, and repose enrich the lives of those who live among the crags and pines of mountain fastnesses. Many a happy evening I have had with a family, or an old prospector, who gave me interesting scraps of autobiography along with a lodging for the night.

The snow-fall on the mountains of Colorado is very unevenly distributed, and is scattered through seven months of the year. Two places only a few miles apart, and separated by a mountain-range, may have very different climates, and one of these may have twice as much snow-fall as the other. On the middle of the upper slopes of the mountains the snow sometimes falls during seven months of the year. At an altitude of eleven thousand feet the annual fall amounts to eighteen feet. This is several times the amount that falls at an altitude of six thousand feet. In a locality near Crested Butte the annual fall is thirty feet, and during snowy winters even fifty feet. Most winter days are clear, and the climate less severe than is usually imagined.

One winter I walked on snowshoes on the upper slopes of the "snowy" range of the Rockies, from the Wyoming line on the north to near the New Mexico line on the south. This was a long walk, and it was full of amusement and adventure. I walked most of the way on the crest of the continent. The broken nature of the surface gave me ups and downs. Sometimes I would descend to the level of seven thousand feet, and occasionally I climbed some peak that was fourteen thousand feet above the tides.

I had not been out many days on this trip when I was caught in a storm on the heights above tree-line. I at once started downward for the woods. The way among the crags and precipices was slippery; the wind threatened every moment to hurl me over a cliff; the wind-blown snow filled the air so that I could see only a few feet, and at times not at all. But it was too cold to stop. For two hours I fought my way downward through the storm, and so dark was it during the last half-hour that I literally felt my way with my staff. Once in the woods, I took off a snowshoe, dug a large hole in the snow down to the earth, built a fire, and soon forgot the perilous descent. After eating from my supply of raisins, I dozed a little, and woke to find all calm and the moon shining in glory on a snowy mountain-world of peaks and pines. I put on my snowshoes, climbed upward beneath the moon, and from the summit of Lead Mountain, thirteen thousand feet high, saw the sun rise in splendor on a world of white.

The tracks and records in the snow which I read in passing made something of a daily newspaper for me. They told much of news of the wilds. Sometimes I read of the games that the snowshoe rabbit had played; of a starving time among the brave mountain sheep on the heights; of the quiet content in the ptarmigan neighborhood; of the dinner that the pines had given the grouse; of the amusements and exercises on the deer's stamping-ground; of the cunning of foxes; of the visits of magpies, the excursions of lynxes, and the red records of mountain lions.

The mountain lion is something of a game-hog and an epicure. He prefers warm blood for every meal, and is very wasteful. I have much evidence against him; his worst one-day record that I have shows five tragedies. In this time he killed a mountain sheep, a fawn, a grouse, a rabbit, and a porcupine; and as if this were not enough, he was about to kill another sheep when a dark object on snowshoes shot down the slope near by and disturbed him. The instances where he has attacked human beings are rare, but he will watch and follow one for hours with the utmost caution and curiosity. One morning after a night-journey through the wood, I turned back and doubled my trail. After going a short distance I came to the track of a lion alongside my own. I went back several miles and read the lion's movements. He had watched me closely. At every place where I rested he had crept up close, and at the place where I had sat down against a stump he had crept up to the opposite side of the stump,—and I fear while I dozed!

One night during this expedition I had lodging in an old and isolated prospector's cabin, with two young men who had very long hair. For months they had been in seclusion, "gathering wonderful herbs," hunting out prescriptions for every human ill, and waiting for their hair to grow long. I hope they prepared some helpful or at least harmless prescriptions, for, ere this, they have become picturesque, and I fear prosperous, medicine-men on some populous street-corner. One day I had dinner on the summit of Mt. Lincoln, fourteen thousand feet above the ocean. I ate with some miners who were digging out their fortune; and was "the only caller in five months."

But I was not always a welcome guest. At one of the big mining-camps I stopped for mail and to rest for a day or so. I was all "rags and tags," and had several broken strata of geology and charcoal on my face in addition. Before I had got well into the town, from all quarters came dogs, each of which seemed determined to make it necessary for me to buy some clothes. As I had already determined to do this, I kept the dogs at bay for a time, and then sought refuge in a first-class hotel; from this the porter, stimulated by an excited order from the clerk, promptly and literally kicked me out!

In the robings of winter how different the mountains than when dressed in the bloom of summer! In no place did the change seem more marked than on some terrace over which summer flung the lacy drapery of a white cascade, or where a wild waterfall "leapt in glory." These places in winter were glorified with the fine arts of ice, — "frozen music," as some one has defined architecture, — for here winter had constructed from water a wondrous array of columns, panels, filigree, fretwork, relief-work, arches, giant icicles, and stalagmites as large as, and in ways resembling, a big tree with a fluted full-length mantle of ice.

Along the way were extensive areas covered with the ruins of fire-killed trees. Most of the forest fires which had caused these were the result of carelessness. The timber destroyed by these fires had been needed by thousands of home-builders. The robes of beauty which they had burned from the mountain-sides are a serious loss. These fire ruins preyed upon me, and I resolved to do something to save the remaining forests. The opportunity came shortly after the resolution was made. Two days before reaching the objective point, farthest south, my food gave out, and I fasted. But as soon as I reached the end, I started to descend the heights, and very naturally knocked at the door of the first house I came to, and asked for something to eat. I supposed I was at a pioneer's cabin. A handsome, neatly dressed young lady came to the door, and when her eyes fell upon me she blushed and then turned pale. I was sorry that my appearance had alarmed her, but I repeated my request for something to eat. Just then, through the half-open door behind the young lady, came the laughter of children, and a glance into the room told me that I was before a mountain schoolhouse. By this time the teacher, to whom I was talking, startled me by inviting me in. As I sat eating a luncheon to which the teacher and each one of the six school-children contributed, the teacher explained to me that she was recently from the East, and that I so well fitted her ideas of a Western desperado that she was frightened at first. When I finished eating; I made my first after-dinner speech; it was also my first attempt to make a forestry address. One point I tried to bring out was concerning the destruction wrought by forest fires. Among other things I said: "During the past few years in Colorado, forest fires, which ought never to have been started, have destroyed many million dollars' worth of timber, and the area over which the fires have burned aggregates twenty-five thousand square miles. This area of forest would put on the equator an evergreen-forest belt one mile wide that would reach entirely around the world. Along with this forest have perished many of the animals and thousands of beautiful birds who had homes in it."

I finally bade all good-bye, went on my way rejoicing, and in due course arrived at Denver, where a record of one of my longest winter excursions was written.

In order to give an idea of one of my briefer winter walks, I close this chapter with an account of a round-trip snowshoe journey from Estes Park to Grand Lake, the most thrilling and adventurous that has ever entertained me on the trail.

One February morning I set off alone on snowshoes to cross the "range," for the purpose of making some snow-measurements. The nature of my work for the State required the closest observation of the character and extent of the snow in the mountains. I hoped to get to Grand Lake for the night, but I was on the east side of the range, and Grand Lake was on the west. Along the twenty-five miles of trail there was only wilderness, without a single house. The trail was steep and the snow very soft. Five hours were spent in gaining timber-line, which was only six miles from my starting-place, but four thousand feet above it. Rising in bold grandeur above me was the summit of Long's Peak; and this, with the great hills of drifted snow, out of which here and there a dwarfed and distorted tree thrust its top, made timber-line seem weird and lonely.

From this point the trail wound for six miles across bleak heights before it came down to timber on the other side of the range. I set forward as rapidly as possible, for the northern sky looked stormy. I must not only climb up fifteen hundred feet, but must also skirt the icy edges of several precipices in order to gain the summit. My friends had warned me that the trip was a foolhardy one even on a clear, calm day, but I was fated to receive the fury of a snowstorm while on the most broken portion of the trail.

The tempest came on with deadly cold and almost blinding violence. The wind came with awful surges, and roared and boomed among the crags. The clouds dashed and seethed along the surface, shutting out all landmarks. I was every moment in fear of slipping or being blown over a precipice, but there was no shelter; I was on the roof of the continent, twelve thousand five hundred feet above sea-level, and to stop in the bitter cold meant death.

It was still three miles to timber on the west slope, and I found it impossible to keep the trail. Fearing to perish if I tried to follow even the general course of the trail, I abandoned it altogether, and started for the head of a gorge, down which I thought it would be possible to climb to the nearest timber. Nothing definite could be seen. The clouds on the snowy surface and the light electrified air gave the eye only optical illusions. The outline of every object was topsy-turvy and dim. The large stones that I thought to step on were not there; and, when apparently passing others, I bumped into them. Several times I fell headlong by stepping out for a drift and finding a depression.

In the midst of these illusions I walked out on a snow-cornice that overhung a precipice! Unable to see clearly, I had no realization of my danger until I felt the snow giving way beneath me. I had seen the precipice in summer, and knew it was more than a thousand feet to the bottom! Down I tumbled, carrying a large fragment of the snow-cornice with me. I could see nothing, and I was entirely helpless. Then, just as the full comprehension of the awful thing that was happening swept over me, the snow falling beneath me suddenly stopped. I plunged into it, completely burying myself. Then I, too, no longer moved downward; my mind gradually admitted the knowledge that my body, together with a considerable mass of the snow, had fallen upon a narrow ledge and caught there. More of the snow came tumbling after me, and it was a matter of some minutes before I succeeded in extricating myself.

When I thrust my head out of the snow-mass and looked about me, I was first appalled by a glance outward, which revealed the terrible height of the precipice on the face of which I was hanging. Then I was relieved by a glance upward, which showed me that I was only some twenty feet from the top, and that a return thither would not be very difficult. But if I had walked from the top a few feet farther back, I should have fallen a quarter of a mile.

One of my snowshoes came off as I struggled out, so I took off the other shoe and used it as a scoop to uncover the lost web. But it proved very slow and dangerous work. With both shoes off I sank chest-deep in the snow; if I ventured too near the edge of the ledge, the snow would probably slip off and carry me to the bottom of the precipice. It was only after two hours of effort that the shoe was recovered.

When I first struggled to the surface of the snow on the ledge, I looked at once to find a way back to the top of the precipice. I quickly saw that by following the ledge a few yards beneath the unbroken snow-cornice I could climb to the top over some jagged rocks. As soon as I had recovered the shoe, I started round the ledge. When I had almost reached the jagged rocks, the snow-cornice caved upon me, and not only buried me, but came perilously near knocking me into the depths beneath. But at last I stood upon the top in safety.

A short walk from the top brought me out upon a high hill of snow that sloped steeply down into the woods. The snow was soft, and I sat down in it and slid "a blue streak"—my blue overalls recording the streak—for a quarter of a mile, and then came to a sudden and confusing stop; one of my webs had caught on a spine of one of the dwarfed and almost buried trees at timber-line.

When I had traveled a short distance below timber-line, a fearful crashing caused me to turn; I was in time to see fragments of snow flying in all directions, and snow-dust boiling up in a great geyser column. A snow-slide had swept down and struck a granite cliff. As I stood there, another slide started on the heights above timber, and with a far-off roar swept down in awful magnificence, with a comet-like tail of snow-dust. Just at timber-line it struck a ledge and glanced to one side, and at the same time shot up into the air so high that for an instant I saw the treetops beneath it. But it came back to earth with awful force, and I felt the ground tremble as it crushed a wide way through the woods. It finally brought up at the bottom of a gulch with a wreckage of hundreds of noble spruce trees that it had crushed down and swept before it.

As I had left the trail on the heights, I was now far from it and in a rugged and wholly unfrequented section, so that coming upon the fresh tracks of a mountain lion did not surprise me. But I was not prepared for what occurred soon afterward. Noticing a steamy vapor rising from a hole in the snow by the protruding roots of an overturned tree, I walked to the hole to learn the cause of it. One whiff of the vapor stiffened my hair and limbered my legs. I shot down a steep slope, dodging trees and rocks. The vapor was rank with the odor from a bear.

At the bottom of the slope I found the frozen surface of a stream much easier walking than the soft snow. All went well until I came to some rapids, where, with no warning whatever, the thin ice dropped me into the cold current among the boulders. I scrambled to my feet, with the ice flying like broken glass. The water came only a little above my knees, but as I had gone under the surface, and was completely drenched, I made an enthusiastic move toward the bank. Now snowshoes are not adapted for walking either in swift water or among boulders. I realized this thoroughly after they had several times tripped me, sprawling, into the liquid cold. Finally I sat down in the water, took them off, and came out gracefully.

I gained the bank with chattering teeth and an icy armor. My pocket thermometer showed two degrees above zero. Another storm was bearing down upon me from the range, and the sun was sinking. But the worst of it all was that there were several miles of rough and strange country between me and Grand Lake that would have to be made in the dark. I did not care to take any more chances on the ice, so I spent a hard hour climbing out of the cañon. The climb warmed me and set my clothes steaming.

My watch indicated six o'clock. A fine snow was falling, and it was dark and cold. I had been exercising for twelve hours without rest, and had eaten nothing since the previous day, as I never take breakfast. I made a fire and lay down on a rock by it to relax, and also to dry my clothes. In half an hour I started on again. Rocky and forest-covered ridges lay between me and Grand Lake. In the darkness I certainly took the worst way. I met with too much resistance in the thickets and too little on the slippery places, so that when, at eleven o'clock that night, I entered a Grand Lake Hotel, my appearance was not prepossessing.

The next day, after a few snow-measurements, I set off to recross the range. In order to avoid warm bear-dens and cold streams, I took a different route. It was a much longer way than the one I had come by, so I went to a hunter's deserted cabin for the night. The cabin had no door, and I could see the stars through the roof. The old sheet-iron stove was badly rusted and broken. Most of the night I spent chopping wood, and I did not sleep at all. But I had a good rest by the stove, where I read a little from a musty pamphlet on palmistry that I found between the logs of the cabin. I always carry candles with me. When the wind is blowing, the wood damp, and the fingers numb, they are of inestimable value in kindling a fire. I do not carry firearms, and during the night, when a lion gave a blood-freezing screech, I wished he were somewhere else.

Daylight found me climbing toward the top of the range through the Medicine Bow National Forest, among some of the noblest evergreens in Colorado. When the sun came over the range, the silent forest vistas became magnificent with bright lights and deep shadows. At timber-line the bald rounded summit of the range, like a gigantic white turtle, rose a thousand feet above me. The slope was steep and very icy; a gusty wind whirled me about. Climbing to the top would be like going up a steep ice-covered house-roof. It would be a dangerous and barely possible undertaking. But as I did not have courage enough to retreat, I threw off my snowshoes and started up. I cut a place in the ice for every step. There was nothing to hold to, and a slip meant a fatal slide.

With rushes from every quarter, the wind did its best to freeze or overturn me. My ears froze, and my fingers grew so cold that they could hardly hold the ice-axe. But after an hour of constant peril and ever-increasing exhaustion, I got above the last ice and stood upon the snow. The snow was solidly packed, and, leaving my snowshoes strapped across my shoulders, I went scrambling up. Near the top of the range a ledge of granite cropped out through the snow, and toward this I hurried. Before making a final spurt to the ledge, I paused to breathe. As I stopped, I was startled by sounds like the creaking of wheels on a cold, snowy street. The snow beneath me was slipping! I had started a snowslide.

Almost instantly the slide started down the slope with me on it. The direction in which it was going and the speed it was making would in a few seconds carry it down two thousand feet of slope, where it would leap over a precipice into the woods. I was on the very upper edge of the snow that had started, and this was the tail-end of the slide. I tried to stand up in the rushing snow, but its speed knocked my feet from under me, and in an instant I was rolled beneath the surface. Beneath the snow, I went tumbling on with it for what seemed like a long time, but I know, of course, that it was for only a second or two; then my feet struck against something solid. I was instantly flung to the surface again, where I either was spilled off, or else fell through, the end of the slide, and came to a stop on the scraped and frozen ground, out of the grasp of the terrible snow.

I leaped to my feet and saw the slide sweep on in most impressive magnificence. At the front end of the slide the snow piled higher and higher, while following in its wake were splendid streamers and scrolls of snow-dust. I lost no time in getting to the top, and set off southward, where, after six miles, I should come to the trail that led to my starting-place on the east side of the range. After I had made about three miles, the cold clouds closed in, and everything was fogged. A chilly half-hour's wait and the clouds broke up. I had lost my ten-foot staff in the snow-slide, and feeling for precipices without it would probably bring me out upon another snow-cornice, so I took no chances.

I was twelve thousand five hundred feet above sea-level when the clouds broke up, and from this great height I looked down upon what seemed to be the margin of the polar world. It was intensely cold, but the sun shone with dazzling glare, and the wilderness of snowy peaks came out like a grand and jagged ice-field in the far south. Halos and peculiarly luminous balls floated through the color-tinged and electrical air. The horizon had a touch of cobalt blue, and on the dome above, white flushes appeared and disappeared like faint auroras. After five hours on these silent but imposing heights I struck my first day's trail, and began a wild and merry coast down among the rocks and trees to my starting-place.

I hope to have more winter excursions, but perhaps I have had my share. At the bare thought of those winter experiences I am again on an unsheltered peak struggling in a storm; or I am in a calm and spendid forest upon whose snowy, peaceful aisles fall the purple shadows of crags and pines.

Faithful Scotch

I carried little Scotch all day long in my over-coat pocket as I rode through the mountains on the way to my cabin. His cheerful, cunning face, his good behavior, and the clever way in which he poked his head out of my pocket, licked my hand, and looked at the scenery, completely won my heart before I had ridden an hour. That night he showed so strikingly the strong, faithful characteristics for which collies are noted that I resolved never to part with him. Since then we have had great years together. We have been hungry and happy together, and together we have played by the cabin, faced danger in the wilds, slept peacefully among the flowers, followed the trails by starlight, and cuddled down in winter's drifting snow.

On my way home through the mountains with puppy Scotch, I stopped for a night near a deserted ranch-house and shut him up in a small abandoned cabin. He at once objected and set up a terrible barking and howling, gnawing fiercely at the crack beneath the door and trying to tear his way out. Fearing he would break his little puppy teeth, or possibly die from frantic and persistent efforts to be free, I concluded to release him from the cabin. My fears that he would run away if left free were groundless. He made his way to my saddle, which lay on the ground near by, crawled under it, turned round beneath it, and thrust his little head from beneath the arch of the horn and lay down with a look of contentment, and also with an air which said, "I'll take care of this saddle. I'd like to see anyone touch it."

Longs Peak Inn in 1905, before expansion.
Courtesy National Park Service—Rocky Mountain National Park.

And watch it he did. At midnight a cowboy came to my camp-fire. He had been thrown from his bronco and was making back to his outfit on foot. In approaching the fire his path lay close to my saddle, beneath which Scotch was lying. Tiny Scotch flew at him ferociously; never have I seen such faithful ferociousness in a dog so small and young. I took him in my hands and assured him that the visitor was welcome, and in a moment little Scotch and the cowboy were side by side gazing at the fire. I suppose his bravery and watchful spirit may be instinct inherited from his famous forbears who lived so long and so cheerfully on Scotland's heaths and moors. But, with all due respect for inherited qualities, he also has a brain that does a little thinking and meets emergencies promptly and ably.

He took serious objection to the coyotes which howled, serenaded, and made merry in the edge of the meadow about a quarter of a mile from my cabin. Just back of their howling-ground was a thick forest of pines, in which were scores of broken rocky crags. Into the tangled forest the coyotes always retreated when Scotch gave chase, and into this retreat he dared not pursue them. So long as the coyotes sunned themselves, kept quiet, and played, Scotch simply watched them contentedly from afar; but the instant they began to howl and yelp, he at once raced over and chased them into the woods. They often yelped and taunted him from their safe retreat, but Scotch always took pains to lie down on the edge of the open and remain there until they became quiet or went away.

During the second winter that Scotch was with me and before he was two years of age, one of the wily coyotes showed a tantalizing spirit and some interesting cunning which put Scotch on his mettle. One day when Scotch was busy driving the main pack into the woods, one that trotted lame with the right fore leg emerged from behind a rocky crag at the edge of the open and less than fifty yards from Scotch. Hurrying to a willow clump about fifty yards in Scotch's rear, he set up a broken chorus of yelps and howls, seemingly with delight and to the great annoyance of Scotch, who at once raced back and chased the noisy taunter into the woods.

The very next time that Scotch was chasing the pack away, the crippled coyote again sneaked from behind the crag, took refuge behind the willow clump, and began delivering a perfect shower of broken yelps. Scotch at once turned back and gave chase. Immediately the entire pack wheeled from retreat and took up defiant attitudes in the open, but this did not seem to trouble Scotch; he flung himself upon them with great ferocity, and finally drove them all back into the woods. However, the third time that the cunning coyote had come to his rear, the entire pack stopped in the edge of the open and, for a time, defied him. He came back from this chase panting and tired and carrying every expression of worry. It seemed to prey upon him to such an extent that I became a little anxious about him.

One day, just after this affair, I went for the mail, and allowed Scotch to go with me. I usually left him at the cabin, and he stayed unchained and was faithful, though it was always evident that he was anxious to go with me and also that he was exceedingly lonely when left behind. But on this occasion he showed such eagerness to go that I allowed him the pleasure.

At the post-office he paid but little attention to the dogs which, with their masters, were assembled there, and held himself aloof from them, squatting on the ground with head erect and almost an air of contempt for them, but it was evident that he was watching their every move. When I started homeward, he showed great satisfaction by leaping and barking.

That night was wildly stormy, and I concluded to go out and enjoy the storm on some wind-swept crags. Scotch was missing and I called him, but he did not appear, so I went alone. After being tossed by the wind for more than an hour, I returned to the cabin, but Scotch was still away. This had never occurred before, so I concluded not to go to bed until he returned. He came home after daylight, and was accompanied by another dog,—a collie, which belonged to a rancher who lived about fifteen miles away. I remembered to have seen this dog at the post-office the day before. My first thought was to send the dog home, but I finally concluded to allow him to remain, to see what would come of his presence, for it was apparent that Scotch had gone for him. He appropriated Scotch's bed in the tub, to the evident satisfaction of Scotch. During the morning the two played together in the happiest possible manner for more than an hour. At noon I fed them together.

In the afternoon, while I was writing, I heard the varied voices of the coyote pack, and went out with my glass to watch proceedings, wondering how the visiting collie would play his part.

There went Scotch, as I supposed, racing for the yelping pack, but the visiting collie was not to be seen. The pack beat the usual sullen, scattering retreat, and while the dog, which I supposed to be Scotch, was chasing the last slow tormenter into the woods, from behind the crag came the big limping coyote, hurrying toward the willow clump from behind which he was accustomed to yelp triumphantly in Scotch's rear. I raised the glass for a better look, all the time wondering where the visiting collie was keeping himself. I was unable to see him, yet I recollected he was with Scotch less than an hour before.

The lame coyote came round the willow clump as usual, and threw up his head as though to bay at the moon. Then the unexpected happened. On the instant, Scotch leaped into the air out of the willow clump, and came down upon the coyote's back! They rolled about for some time, when the coyote finally shook himself free and started at a lively limping pace for the woods, only to be grabbed again by the visiting collie, which had been chasing the pack, and which I had mistaken for Scotch. The pack beat a swift retreat. For a time both dogs fought the coyote fiercely, but he at last tore himself free, and escaped into the pines, badly wounded and bleeding. I never saw him again. That night the visiting collie went home. As Scotch was missing that night for a time, I think he may have accompanied him at least a part of the way.

One day a young lady from Michigan came along and wanted to climb Long's Peak all alone, without a guide. I agreed to consent to this if first she would climb one of the lesser peaks unaided, on a stormy day. This the young lady did, and by so doing convinced me that she had a keen sense of direction and an abundance of strength, for the day on which she climbed was a stormy one, and the peak was completely befogged with clouds. After this, there was nothing for me to do but allow her to climb Long's Peak alone.

Just as she was starting, that cool September morning, I thought to provide for an emergency by sending Scotch with her. He knew the trail well and would, of course, lead her the right way, providing she lost the trail. "Scotch," said I, "go with this young lady, take good care of her, and stay with her till she returns. Don't you desert her." He gave a few barks of satisfaction and started with her up the trail, carrying himself in a manner which indicated that he was both honored and pleased. I felt that the strength and alertness of the young lady, when combined with the faithfulness and watchfulness of Scotch, would make the journey a success, so I went about my affairs as usual. When darkness came on that evening, the young lady had not returned.

She climbed swiftly until she reached the rocky alpine moorlands above timber-line. Here she lingered long to enjoy the magnificent scenery and the brilliant flowers. It was late in the afternoon when she arrived at the summit of the peak. After she had spent a little time there resting and absorbing the beauty and grandeur of the scene, she started to return. She had not proceeded far when clouds and darkness came on, and on a slope of slide-rock she lost the trail.

Scotch had minded his own affairs and enjoyed himself in his own way all day long. Most of the time he followed her closely, apparently indifferent to what happened, but when she, in the darkness, left the trail and started off in the wrong direction, he at once came forward, and took the lead with an alert, aggressive air. The way in which he did this should have suggested to the young lady that he knew what he was about, but she did not appreciate this fact. She thought he had become weary and wanted to run away from her, so she called him back. Again she started in the wrong direction; this time Scotch got in front of her and refused to move. She pushed him out of the way. Once more he started off in the right direction, and this time she scolded him and reminded him that his master had told him not to desert her. Scotch dropped his ears and sheepishly fell in behind her and followed meekly along. He had obeyed orders.

After traveling a short distance, the young lady realized that she had lost her way, but it never occurred to her that she had only to trust Scotch and he would lead her directly home. However, she had the good sense to stop where she was and there, among the crags, by the stained remnants of winter's snow, thirteen thousand feet above sea-level, she was to spend the night. The cold wind blew a gale, roaring and booming among the crags, the alpine brooklet turned to ice, while, in the lee of the crag, shivering with cold, hugging shaggy Scotch in her arms, she lay down for the night.

I had given my word not to go in search of her if she failed to return. However, I sent out four guides to look for her. They suffered much from cold as they vainly searched among the crags through the dark hours of the windy night. Just at sunrise one of them found her, almost exhausted, but, with slightly frost-bitten fingers, still hugging Scotch in her arms. He gave her food and drink and additional wraps, and without delay started with her down the trail. As soon as she was taken in charge by the guide, patient Scotch left her and hurried home. He had saved her life.

Scotch's hair is long and silky, black with a touch of tawny about the head and a little bar of white on the nose. He has the most expressive and pleasing dog's face I have ever seen. There is nothing he enjoys so well as to have some one kick the football for him. For an hour at a time he will chase it and try to get hold of it, giving an occasional eager, happy bark. He has good eyes, and these, with his willingness to be of service, have occasionally made him useful to me in finding articles which I, or some one else, had forgotten or lost on the trail. Generally it is difficult to make him understand just what has been lost or where he is to look for it, but when once he understands, he keeps up the search, sometimes for hours if he does not find the article before. He is always faithful in guarding any object that I ask him to take care of. I have but to throw down a coat and point at it, and he will at once lie down near by, there to remain until I come to dismiss him. He will allow no one else to touch it. His attitude never fails to convey the impression that he would die in defense of the thing intrusted to him, but desert it or give it up, never!

One February day I took Scotch and started up Long's Peak, hoping to gain its wintry summit. Scotch easily followed in my snowshoe-tracks. At an altitude of thirteen thousand feet on the wind-swept steeps there was but little snow, and it was necessary to leave snowshoes behind. After climbing a short distance on these icy slopes, I became alarmed for the safety of Scotch. By and by I had to cut steps in the ice. This made the climb too perilous for him, as he could not realize the danger he was in should he miss a step. There were places where slipping from these steps meant death, so I told Scotch to go back. I did not, however, tell him to watch my snowshoes, for so dangerous was the climb that I did not know that I should ever get back to them myself. However, he went to the snowshoes, and with them he remained for eight cold hours until I came back by the light of the stars.

On a few occasions I allowed Scotch to go with me on short winter excursions. He enjoyed these immensely, although he had a hard time of it and but very little to eat. When we camped among the spruces in the snow, he seemed to enjoy sitting by my side and silently watching the evening fire, and he contentedly cuddled with me to keep warm at night.

One cold day we were returning from a four days' excursion when, a little above timber-line, I stopped to take some photographs. To do this it was necessary for me to take off my sheepskin mittens, which I placed in my coat-pocket, but not securely, as it proved. From time to time, as I climbed to the summit of the Continental Divide, I stopped to take photographs, but on the summit the cold pierced my silk gloves and I felt for my mittens, to find that one of them was lost. I stooped, put an arm around Scotch, and told him I had lost a mitten, and that I wanted him to go down for it to save me the trouble. "It won't take you very long, but it will be a hard trip for me. Go and fetch it to me." Instead of starting off hurriedly, willingly, as he had invariably done before in obedience to my commands, he stood still. His alert, eager ears drooped, but no other move did he make. I repeated the command in my most kindly tones. At this, instead of starting down the mountain, for the mitten, he slunk slowly away toward home. It was clear that he did not want to climb down the steep icy slope of a mile to timber-line, more than a thousand feet below. I thought he had misunderstood me, so I called him back, patted him, and then, pointing down the slope, said, "Go for the mitten, Scotch; I will wait here for you." He started for it, but went unwillingly. He had always served me so cheerfully that I could not understand, and it was not until late the next afternoon that I realized that he had not understood me, but that he had loyally, and at the risk of his life, tried to obey me.

The summit of the Continental Divide, where I stood when I sent him back, was a very rough and lonely region. On every hand were broken snowy peaks and rugged cañons. My cabin, eighteen miles away, was the nearest house to it, and the region was utterly wild. I waited a reasonable time for Scotch to return, but he did not come back. Thinking he might have gone by without my seeing him, I walked some distance along the summit, first in one direction and then in the other, but, seeing neither him nor his tracks, I knew that he had not yet come back. As it was late in the afternoon, and growing colder, I decided to go slowly on toward my cabin. I started along a route that I felt sure he would follow, and I reasoned that he would overtake me. Darkness came on and still no Scotch, but I kept going forward. For the remainder of the way I told myself that he might have got by me in the darkness.

When, at midnight, I arrived at the cabin, I expected to be greeted by him, but he was not there. I felt that something was wrong and feared that he had met with an accident. I slept two hours and rose, but still he was missing, so I concluded to tie on my snowshoes and go to meet him. The thermometer showed fourteen below zero.

I started at three o'clock in the morning, feeling that I should meet him without going far. I kept going on and on, and when, at noon, I arrived at the place on the summit from which I had sent him back, Scotch was not there to cheer the wintry, silent scene.

I slowly made my way down the slope, and at two in the afternoon, twenty-four hours after I had sent Scotch back, I paused on a crag and looked below. There in the snowy world of white he lay by the mitten in the snow. He had misunderstood me, and had gone back to guard the mitten instead of to get it. He could hardly contain himself for joy when he saw me. He leaped into the air, barked, jumped, rolled over, licked my hand, whined, grabbed the mitten, raced round, and round me, and did everything that an alert, affectionate, faithful dog could do to show that he appreciated my appreciation of his supremely faithful services.

After waiting for him to eat a luncheon, we started merrily towards home, where we arrived at one o'clock in the morning. Had I not returned, I suppose Scotch would have died beside the mitten. In a region cold, cheerless, oppressive, without food, and perhaps to die, he lay down by the mitten because he understood that I had told him to. In the annals of dog heroism, I know of no greater deed.

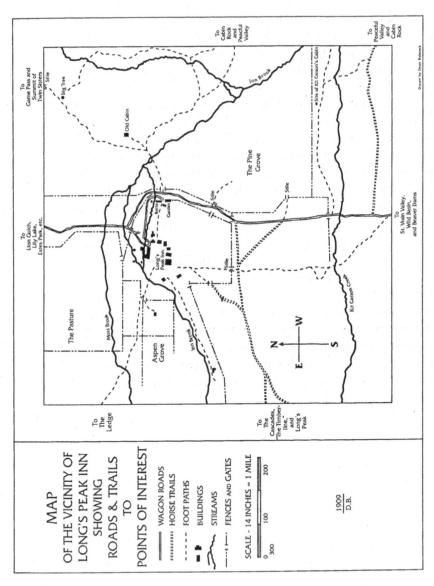

Map of Longs-Peak Inn and Vicinity. Drawn by Dean Babcock.
Courtesy Estes Park Public Library.

Kinnikinick

The kinnikinick is a plant pioneer. Often it is the first plant to make a settlement or establish a colony on a barren or burned-over area. It is hardy, and is able to make a start and thrive in places so inhospitable as to afford most plants not the slightest foothold. In such places the kinnikinick's activities make changes which alter conditions so beneficially that in a little while plants less hardy come to join the first settler. The pioneer work done by the kinnikinick on a barren and rocky realm has often resulted in the establishment of a flourishing forest there.

The kinnikinick, or *Arctostaphylos Uva-Ursi,* as the botanists name it, may be called a ground-loving vine. Though always attractive, it is in winter that it is at its best. Then its bright green leaves and red berries shine among the snow-flowers in a quiet way that is strikingly beautiful.

Since it is beautiful as well as useful, I had long admired this ever-cheerful, ever-spreading vine before I appreciated the good though humble work it is constantly doing. I had often stopped to greet it—the only green thing upon a rock ledge or a sandy stretch,—had walked over it in forest avenues beneath tall and stately pines, and had slept comfortably upon its spicy, elastic rugs, liking it from the first. But on one of my winter tramps I fell in love with this beautiful evergreen.

The day was a cold one, and the high, gusty wind was tossing and playing with the last snowfall. I had been snowshoeing through the forest, and had come out upon an unsheltered ridge that was a part of a barren area which repeated fires had changed from a forested condition to desert. The snow lay several feet deep in the woods, but as the gravelly distance before me was bare, I took off my snowshoes. I went walking, and at times blowing, along the bleak ridge, scarcely able to see through the snow-filled air. But during a lull the air cleared of snow-dust and I paused to look about me. The wind still roared in the distance, and against the blue eastern sky it had a column of snow whirling that was dazzling white in the afternoon sun. On my left a mountain rose with easy slope to crag-crowned heights, and for miles swept away before me with seared side barren and dull. A few cloudlets of snowdrifts and a scattering of mere tufts of snow stood out distinctly on this big, bare slope.

I wondered what could be holding these few spots of snow on this wind-swept slope. I finally went up to examine one of them. Thrust out and lifted just above the snow of the tuft before me was the jeweled hand of a kinnikinick; and every snow-deposit on the slope was held in place by the green arms of this plant. Here was this beautiful vine-like shrub gladly growing on a slope that had been forsaken by all other plants.

To state the situation fairly, all had been burned off by fire and Kinnikinick was the first to come back, and so completely had fires consumed the plant-food that many plants would be unable to live here until better conditions prevailed and the struggle for existence was made less severe. Kinnikinick was making the needed changes; in time it would prepare the way, and other plants, and the pines too, would come back to carpet and plume the slope and prevent wind and water from tearing and scarring the earth.

The seeds of Kinnikinick are scattered by birds, chipmunks, wind, and water. I do not know by what agency the seeds had come to this slope, but here were the plants, and on this dry, fire-ruined, sun-scorched, wind-beaten slope they must have endured many hardships. Many must have perished before these living ones had made a secure start in life.

Once Kinnikinick has made a start, it is constantly assisted to succeed by its own growing success. Its arms catch and hold snow, and this gives a supply of much-needed water. This water is snugly stored beneath the plant, where but little can be reached or taken by the sun or the thirsty winds. The winds, too, which were so unfriendly while it was trying to make a start, now become helpful to the brave, persistent plant. Every wind that blows brings something to it, — dust, powdered earth, trash, the remains of dead insects; some of this material is carried for miles. All goes to form new soil, or to fertilize or mulch the old. This supplies Kinnikinick's great needs. The plant grows rich from the constant tribute of the winds. The soil-bed grows deeper and richer and is also constantly outbuilding and enlarging, and Kinnikinick steadily increases its size.

In a few years a small oasis is formed in, or rather on, the barren. This becomes a place of refuge for seed wanderers, — in fact, a nursery. Up the slope I saw a young pine standing in a kinnikinick snow-cover. In the edge of the snow-tuft by me, covered with a robe of snow, I found a tiny tree, a mere baby pine. Where did this pine come from? There were no seed-bearing pines within miles. How did a pine seed find its way to this cosy nursery? Perhaps the following is its story: The seed of this little pine, together with a score or more of others, grew in a cone out near the end of the pine-tree limb. This pine was on a mountain several miles from the fire-ruined slope, when one windy autumn day some time after the seeds were ripe, the cone began to open its fingers and the seeds came dropping out. The seed of this baby tree was one of these, and when it tumbled out of the cone the wind caught it, and away it went over trees, rocks, and gulches, whirling and dancing in the autumn sunlight. After tumbling a few miles in this wild flight, it came down among some boulders. Here it lay until, one very windy day, it was caught up and whirled away again. Before long it was dashed against a granite cliff and fell to the ground; but in a moment, the wind found it and drove it, with a shower of trash and dust, bounding and leaping across a barren slope, plump into this kinnikinick nest. From this shelter the wind could not drive it. Here the little seed might have said, "This is just the place I was looking for; here is shelter from the wind and sun; the soil is rich and damp; I am so tired, I think I'll take a sleep." When the little seed awoke, it wore the green dress of the pine family. The kinnikinick's nursery had given it a start in life.

Under favorable conditions Kinnikinick is a comparatively rapid grower. Its numerous vine-like limbs — little arms — spread or reach outward from the central root, take a new hold upon the earth and prepare to reach again. The ground beneath it in a little while is completely hidden by its closely crowding leafy arms. In places these soft, pliable rugs unite and form extensive carpets. Strip off these carpets and often all that remains is a barren exposure of sand or gravel on bald or broken rocks, whose surfaces and edges have been draped or buried by its green leaves and red berries.

In May kinnikinick rugs become flower-beds. Each flower is a narrow-throated, pink-lipped, creamy-white jug, and is filled with a drop of exquisitely flavored honey. The jugs in a short time change to smooth purple berries, and in autumn they take on their winter dress of scarlet. When ripe the berries taste like mealy crab-apples. I have often seen chipmunks eating the berries, or apples, sitting up with the fruit in both their deft little hands, and eating it with such evident relish that I frequently found myself thinking of these berries as chipmunk's apples.

Kinnikinick is widely distributed over the earth, and is most often found on gravelly slopes or sandy stretches. Frequently you will find it among scattered pines, trying to carpet their cathedral floor. Many a summer day I have lain down and rested on these flat and fluffy forest rugs, while between the tangled tops of the pines I looked at the blue of the sky or watched the white clouds so serenely floating there. Many a summer night upon these elastic spreads I have lain and gazed at the thick sown stars, or watched the ebbing, fading camp-fire, at last to fall asleep and to rest as sweetly and serenely as ever did the Scotchman upon his heathered Highlands. Many a morning I have awakened late after a sleep so long that I had settled into the yielding mass and Kinnikinick had put up an arm, either to shield my face with its hand, or to show me, when I should awaken, its pretty red berries and bright green leaves.

One morning, while visiting in a Blackfoot Indian camp, I saw the men smoking kinnikinick leaves, and I asked if they had any legend concerning the shrub. I felt sure they must have a fascinating story of it which told of the Great Spirit's love for Kinnikinick, but they had none. One of them said he had heard the Piute Indians tell why the Great Spirit had made it, but he could not remember the account. I inquired among many

Indians, feeling that I should at last learn a happy legend concerning it, but in vain. One night, however, by my camp-fire; I dreamed that some Alaska Indians told me this legend: —

Long, long ago, Kinnikinick was a small tree with brown berries and broad leaves which dropped to the ground in autumn. One year a great snow came while the leaves were still on, and all trees were flattened upon the ground by the weight of the clinging snow. All broad-leaved trees except Kinnikinick died. When the snow melted, Kinnikinick was still alive, but pressed out upon the ground, crushed so that it could not rise. It started to grow, however, and spread out its limbs on the surface very like a root growth. The Great Spirit was so pleased with Kinnikinick's efforts that he decided to let it live on in its new form, and also that he would send it to colonize many places where it had never been. He changed its berries from brown to red, so that the birds could see its fruit and scatter its seeds far and wide. Its leaves were reduced in size and made permanently green, so that Kinnikinick, like the pines it loves and helps, could wear green all the time.

Whenever I see a place that has been made barren and ugly by the thoughtlessness of man, I like to think of Kinnikinick, for I know it will beautify these places if given a chance to do so. There are on earth millions of acres now almost desert that may some time be changed and beautified by this cheerful, modest plant. Some time many bald and barren places in the Rockies will be plumed with pines, bannered with flowers, have brooks, butterflies, and singing birds,—all of these, and homes, too, around which children will play,—because of the reclaiming work which will be done by charming Kinnikinick.

Besieged by Bears

Two old prospectors, Sullivan and Jason, once took me in for the night, and after supper they related a number of interesting experiences. Among these tales was one of the best bear-stories I have ever heard. The story was told in the graphic, earnest, realistic style so often possessed by those who have lived strong, stirring lives among crags and pines. Although twenty years had gone by, these prospectors still had a vivid recollection of that lively night when they were besieged by three bears, and in recounting the experience they mingled many good word-pictures of bear behavior with their exciting and amusing story. "This happened to us," said Sullivan, "in spite of the fact that we were minding our own business and had never hunted bears."

The siege occurred at their log cabin during the spring of 1884. They were prospecting in Geneva Park, where they had been all winter, driving a tunnel. They were so nearly out of supplies that they could not wait for snowdrifts to melt out of the trail. Provisions must be had, and Sullivan thought that, by allowing twice the usual time, he could make his way down through the drifts and get back to the cabin with them. So one morning, after telling Jason that he would be back the next evening, he took their burro and set off down the mountain. On the way home next day Sullivan had much difficulty in getting the loaded burro through the snowdrifts, and when within a mile of the cabin, they stuck fast. Sullivan unpacked and rolled the burro out of the snow, and was busily repacking, when the animal's uneasiness made him look round.

In the edge of the woods, only a short distance away, were three bears, apparently a mother and her two well-grown children. They were sniffing the air eagerly and appeared somewhat excited. The old bear would rise on her hind paws, sniff the air, then drop back to the ground. She kept her nose pointed toward Sullivan, but did not appear to look at him. The smaller bears moved restlessly about; they would walk a few steps in advance, stand erect, draw their fore paws close to their breasts, and sniff, sniff, sniff the air, upward and in all directions before them. Then they would slowly back up to the old bear. They all seemed very good-natured.

When Sullivan was unpacking the burro, the wrapping had come off two hams which were among the supplies, and the wind had carried the delicious aroma to the bears, who were just out of their winter dens after weeks of fasting. Of course, sugar-cured hams smelled good to them. Sullivan repacked the burro and went on. The bears quietly eyed him for some distance. At a turn in the trail he looked back and saw the bears clawing and smelling the snow on which the provisions had lain while he was getting the burro out of the snowdrift. He went on to the cabin, had supper, and forgot the bears.

The log cabin in which he and Jason lived was a small one; it had a door in the side and a small window in one end. The roof was made of a layer of poles thickly covered with earth. A large shepherd-dog often shared the cabin with the prospectors. He was a playful fellow, and Sullivan often romped with him. Near their cabin were some vacant cabins of other prospectors, who had "gone out for the winter" and were not yet back for summer prospecting.

The evening was mild, and as soon as supper was over Sullivan filled his pipe, opened the door, and sat down on the edge of the bed for a smoke, while Jason washed the dishes. He had taken only a few pulls at his pipe when there was a rattling at the window. Thinking the dog was outside, Sullivan called, "Why don't you go round to the door?" This invitation was followed by a momentary silence, then smash! a piece of sash and fragments of window-glass flew past Sullivan and rattled on the floor. He jumped to his feet. In the dim candle-light he saw a bear's head coming in through the window. He threw his pipe of burning tobacco into the bear's face and eyes, and then grabbed for some steel drills which lay in the corner on the floor. The earth roof had leaked, and the drills were ice-covered and frozen fast to the floor.

While Sullivan was dislodging the drills, Jason began to bombard the bear vigorously with plates from the table. The bear backed out; she was looking for food, not clean plates. However, the instant she was outside, she accepted Sullivan's invitation and went round to the door! And she came for it with a rush! Both Sullivan and Jason jumped to close the door. They were not quick enough, and instead of one bear there were three! The entire family had accepted the invitation, and all were trying to come in at once!

When Sullivan and Jason threw their weight against the door it slammed against the big bear's nose,—a very sensitive spot. She gave a savage growl. Apparently she blamed the two other bears either for hurting her nose or for being in the way. At any rate, a row started; halfway in the door the bears began to fight; for a few seconds it seemed as if all the bears would roll inside. Sullivan and Jason pushed against the door with all their might, trying to close it. During the struggle the bears rolled outside and the door went shut with a bang. The heavy securing crossbar was quickly put into place; but not a moment too soon, for an instant later the old bear gave a furious growl and flung herself against the door, making it fairly crack; it seemed as if the door would be broken in. Sullivan and Jason hurriedly knocked their slab bed to pieces and used the slats and heavy sides to prop and strengthen the door. The bears kept surging and clawing at the door, and while the prospectors were spiking the braces against it and giving their entire attention to it, they suddenly felt the cabin shake and heard the logs strain and give. They started back, to see the big bear struggling in the window. Only the smallness of the window had prevented the bear from getting in unnoticed, and surprising them while they were bracing the door. The window was so small that the bear in trying to get in had almost wedged fast. With hind paws on the ground, fore paws on the window-sill, and shoulders against the log over the window, the big bear was in a position to exert all her enormous strength. Her efforts to get in sprung the logs and gave the cabin the shake which warned.

Sullivan grabbed one of the steel drills and dealt the bear a terrible blow on the head. She gave a growl of mingled pain and fury as she freed herself from the window. Outside she backed off growling.

For a little while things were calmer. Sullivan and Jason, drills in hand, stood guard at the window. After some snarling in front of the window the bears went round to the door. They clawed the door a few times and then began to dig under it. "They are tunneling in for us," said Sullivan. "They want those hams; but they won't get them."

After a time the bears quit digging and started away, occasionally stopping to look hesitatingly back. It was almost eleven o'clock, and the full moon shone splendidly through the pines. The prospectors hoped that the bears were gone for good. There was an old rifle in the cabin, but there were no cartridges, for Sullivan and Jason never hunted and rarely had occasion to fire a gun. But, fearing that the animals might return, Sullivan concluded to go to one of the vacant cabins for a loaded Winchester which he knew to be there.

As soon as the bears disappeared, he crawled out of the window and looked cautiously around; then he made a run for the vacant cabin. The bears heard him running, and when he had nearly reached the cabin, they came round the corner of it to see what was the matter. He was up a pine tree in an instant. After a few growls the bears moved off and disappeared behind a vacant cabin. As they had gone behind the cabin which contained the loaded gun, Sullivan thought it would be dangerous to try to make the cabin, for if the door should be swelled fast, the bears would surely get him. Waiting until he thought it safe to return, he dropped to the ground and made a dash for his own cabin. The bears heard him and again gave chase, with the evident intention of getting even for all their annoyances. It was only a short distance to his cabin, but the bears were at his heels when he dived in through the broken window.

A bundle of old newspapers was then set on fire and thrown among the bears, to scare them away. There was some snarling, until one of the young bears with a stroke of a fore paw scattered the blazing papers in all directions; then the bears walked round the cabin-corner out of sight and remained quiet for several minutes.

Just as Jason was saying, "I hope they are gone for good," there came a thump on the roof which told the prospectors that the bears were still intent on the hams. The bears began to claw the earth off the roof. If they were allowed to continue, they would soon clear off the earth and would then have a chance to tear out the poles. With a few poles torn out, the bears would tumble into the cabin, or perhaps their combined weight might cause the roof to give way and drop them into the cabin. Something had to be done to stop their clawing and if possible get them off the roof. Bundles of hay were taken out of the bed mattress. From time to time Sullivan would set fire to one of these bundles, lean far out through the window, and throw the blazing hay upon the roof among the bears. So long as he kept these fireworks going, the bears did not dig; but they stayed on the roof and became furiously angry. The supply of hay did not last long, and as soon as the annoyance from the bundles of fire ceased, the bears attacked the roof again with renewed vigor.

Then it was decided to prod the bears with red-hot drills thrust up between the poles of the roof. As there was no firewood in the cabin, and as fuel was necessary in order to heat the drills, a part of the floor was torn up for that purpose.

The young bears soon found hot drills too warm for them and scrambled or fell off the roof. But the old one persisted. In a little while she had clawed off a large patch of earth and was tearing the poles with her teeth.

The hams had been hung up on the wall in the end of the cabin; the old bear was tearing just above them. Jason threw the hams on the floor and wanted to throw them out of the window. He thought that the bears would leave contented if they had them. Sullivan thought differently; he said that it would take six hams apiece to satisfy the bears, and that two hams would be only a taste which would make the bears more reckless than ever. The hams stayed in the cabin.

The old bear had torn some of the poles in two and was madly tearing and biting at others. Sullivan was short and so were the drills. To get within easier reach, he placed the table almost under the gnawing bear, sprang upon it, and called to Jason for a red-hot drill. Jason was about to hand him one when he noticed a small bear climbing in at the window, and, taking the drill with him, he sprang over to beat the bear back. Sullivan jumped down to the fire for a drill, and in climbing back on the table he looked up at the gnawed hole and received a shower of dirt in his face and eyes. This made him flinch and he lost his balance and upset the table. He quickly straightened the table and sprang upon it, drill in hand. The old bear had a paw and arm thrust down through the hole between the poles. With a blind stroke she struck the drill and flung it and Sullivan from the table. He shouted to Jason for help, but Jason, with both young bears trying to get in at the window at once, was striking right and left. He had bears and troubles of his own and did not heed Sullivan's call. The old bear thrust her head down through the hole and seemed about to fall in, when Sullivan in desperation grabbed both hams and threw them out of the window.

The young bears at once set up a row over the hams, and the old bear, hearing the fight, jumped off the roof and soon had a ham in her mouth.

While the bears were fighting and eating, Sullivan and Jason tore up the remainder of the floor and barricaded the window. With both door and window closed, they could give their attention to the roof. All the drills were heated, and both stood ready to make it hot for the bears when they should again climb on the roof. But the bears did not return to the roof. After eating the last morsel of the hams they walked round to the cabin door, scratched it gently, and then became quiet. They had lain down by the door.

It was two o'clock in the morning. The inside of the cabin was in utter confusion. The floor was strewn with wreckage; bedding, drills, broken boards, broken plates, and hay were scattered about. Sullivan gazed at the chaos and remarked that it looked like poor housekeeping. But he was tired, and, asking Jason to keep watch for a while, he lay down on the blankets and was soon asleep.

Toward daylight the bears got up and walked a few times round the cabin. On each round they clawed at the door, as though to tell Sullivan that they were there, ready for his hospitality. They whined a little, half good-naturedly, but no one admitted them, and finally, just before sunrise, they took their departure and went leisurely smelling their way down the trail.

The Forest Fire

Forest fires led me to abandon the most nearly ideal journey through the wilds I had ever embarked upon, but the conflagrations that took me aside filled a series of my days and nights with wild, fiery exhibitions and stirring experiences. It was early September and I had started southward along the crest of the continental divide of the Rocky Mountains in northern Colorado. All autumn was to be mine and upon this alpine skyline I was to saunter southward, possibly to the land of cactus and mirage. Not being commanded by either the calendar or the compass, no day was to be marred by hurrying. I was just to linger and read all the nature stories in the heights that I could comprehend or enjoy. From my starting-place, twelve thousand feet above the tides, miles of continental slopes could be seen that sent their streams east and west to the two far-off seas. With many a loitering advance, with many a glad going back, intense days were lived. After two great weeks I climbed off the treeless heights and went down into the woods to watch and learn the deadly and dramatic ways of forest fires.

This revolution in plans was brought about by the view from amid the broken granite on the summit of Long's Peak. Far below and far away the magnificent mountain distances reposed in the autumn sunshine. The dark crags, snowy summits, light-tipped peaks, bright lakes, purple forests traced with silver streams and groves of aspen,—all fused and faded away in the golden haze. But these splendid scenes were being blurred and blotted out by the smoke of a dozen or more forest fires.

Little realizing that for six weeks I was to hesitate on fire-threatened heights and hurry through smoke-filled forests, I

Longs Peak Inn in 1906, before completion of new main building.
Courtesy National Park Service—Rocky Mountain National Park.

took a good look at the destruction from afar and then hastened toward the nearest fire-front. This was a smoke-clouded blaze on the Rabbit-Ear Range that was storming its way eastward. In a few hours it would travel to the Grand River, which flowed southward through a straight, mountain-walled valley that was about half a mile wide. Along the river, occupying about half the width of the valley, was a picturesque grassy avenue that stretched for miles between ragged forest-edges.

There was but little wind and, hoping to see the big game that the flames might drive into the open, I innocently took my stand in the centre of the grassy stretch directly before the fire. This great smoky fire-billow, as I viewed it from the heights while I was descending, was advancing with a formidable crooked front about three miles across. The left wing was more than a mile in advance of the active though lagging right one. As I afterward learned, the difference in speed of the two wings was caused chiefly by topography; the forest conditions were similar, but the left wing had for some time been burning up a slope while the right had traveled down one. Fire burns swiftly up a slope, but slowly down it. Set fire simultaneously to the top and the bottom of a forest on a steep slope and the blaze at the bottom will overrun at least nine-tenths of the area. Flame and the drafts that it creates sweep upward.

Upon a huge lava boulder in the grassy stretch I commanded a view of more than a mile of the forest-edge and was close to where a game trail came into it out of the fiery woods. On this burning forest-border a picturesque, unplanned wild-animal parade passed before me.

Scattered flakes of ashes were falling when a herd of elk led the exodus of wild folk from the fire-doomed forest. They came stringing out of the woods into the open, with both old and young going forward without confusion and as though headed for a definite place or pasture. They splashed through a beaver pond without stopping and continued their way up the river. There was no show of fear, no suggestion of retreat. They never looked back. Deer straggled out singly and in groups. It was plain that all were fleeing from danger, all were excitedly trying to get out of the way of something; and they did not appear to know where they were going. Apparently they gave more troubled attention to the roaring, the breath, and the movements of that fiery, mysterious monster than to the seeking of a place of permanent safety. In the grassy open, into which the smoke was beginning to drift and hang, the deer scattered and lingered. At each roar of the fire they turned hither and thither excitedly to look and listen. A flock of mountain sheep, in a long, narrow, closely pressed rank and led by an alert, aggressive bighorn, presented a fine appearance as it raced into the open. The admirable directness of these wild animals put them out of the category occupied by tame, "silly sheep." Without slackening pace they swept across the grassy valley in a straight line and vanished in the wooden slope beyond. Now and then a coyote appeared from somewhere and stopped for a time in the open among the deer; all these wise little wolves were a trifle nervous, but each had himself well in hand. Glimpses were had of two stealthy mountain lions, now leaping, now creeping, now swiftly fleeing.

Bears were the most matter-of-fact fellows in the exodus. Each loitered in the grass and occasionally looked toward the oncoming danger. Their actions showed curiosity and anger, but not alarm. Each duly took notice of the surrounding animals, and one old grizzly even struck viciously at a snarling coyote. Two black bear cubs, true to their nature, had a merry romp. Even these serious conditions could not make them solemn. Each tried to prevent the other from climbing a tree that stood alone in the open; around this tree they clinched, cuffed, and rolled about so merrily that the frightened wild folks were attracted and momentarily forgot their fears. The only birds seen were some grouse that whirred and sailed by on swift, definite wings; they were going somewhere.

With subdued and ever-varying roar the fire steadily advanced. It constantly threw off an upcurling, unbroken cloud of heavy smoke that hid the flames from view. Now and then a whirl of wind brought a shower of sparks together with bits of burning bark out over the open valley.

Just as the flames were reaching the margin of the forest a great bank of black smoke curled forward and then appeared to fall into the grassy open. I had just a glimpse of a few fleeing animals, then all became hot, fiery, and dark. Red flames darted through swirling black smoke. It was stifling. Leaping into a beaver pond, I lowered my own sizzling temperature and that of my smoking clothes. The air was too hot and black for breathing; so I fled, floundering through the water, down Grand River.

A quarter of a mile took me beyond danger-line and gave me fresh air. Here the smoke ceased to settle to the earth, but extended in a light upcurling stratum a few yards above it. Through this smoke the sunlight came so changed that everything around was magically covered with a canvas of sepia or rich golden brown. I touched the burned spots on hands and face with real, though raw, balsam and then plunged into the burned-over district to explore the extensive ruins of the fire.

A prairie fire commonly consumes everything to the earth-line and leaves behind it only a black field. Rarely does a forest fire make so clean a sweep; generally it burns away the smaller limbs and the foliage, leaving the tree standing all blackened and bristling. This fire, like thousands of others, consumed the litter carpet on the forest floor and the mossy covering of the rocks; it ate the underbrush, devoured the foliage, charred and burned the limbs, and blackened the trunks. Behind was a dead forest in a desolate field, a territory with millions of bristling, mutilated trees, a forest ruin impressively picturesque and pathetic. From a commanding ridge I surveyed this ashen desert and its multitude of upright figures all blurred and lifeless; these stood every-where,—in the gulches, on the slopes, on the ridges against the sky,—and they bristled in every vanishing distance. Over the entire area only a few trees escaped with their lives; these were isolated in soggy glacier meadows or among rock fields and probably were defended by friendly air-currents when the fiery billow rolled over them.

When I entered the burn that afternoon the fallen trees that the fire had found were in ashes, the trees just killed were smoking, while the standing dead trees were just beginning to burn freely. That night these scattered beacons strangely burned among the multitudinous dead. Close to my camp all through that night several of these fire columns showered sparks like a fountain, glowed and occasionally lighted up the scene with flaming torches. Weird and strange in the night were the groups of silhouetted figures in a shadow-dance between me and the flickering, heroic torches.

The greater part of the area burned over consisted of mountain-slopes and ridges that lay between the altitudes of nine thousand and eleven thousand feet. The forest was made up almost entirely of Engelmann and Douglas spruces, alpine fir, and flexilis pine. A majority of these trees were from fifteen to twenty-four inches in diameter, and those examined were two hundred and fourteen years of age. Over the greater extent of the burn the trees were tall and crowded, about two thousand to the acre. As the fire swept over about eighteen thousand acres, the number of trees that perished must have approximated thirty-six million.

Fires make the Rocky Mountains still more rocky. This bald fact stuck out all through this burn and in dozens of others afterward visited. Most Rocky Mountain fires not only skin off the humus but so cut up the fleshy soil and so completely destroy the fibrous bindings that the elements quickly drag much of it from the bones and fling it down into the stream-channels. Down many summit slopes in these mountains, where the fires went to bed-rock, the snows and waters still scoot and scour. The fire damage to some of these steep slopes cannot be repaired for generations and even centuries. Meantime these disfigured places will support only a scattered growth of trees and sustain only a sparse population of animals.

In wandering about I found that the average thickness of humus—decayed vegetable matter—consumed by this fire was about five inches. The removal of even these few inches of covering had in many places exposed boulders and bed-rock. On many shallow-covered steeps the soil-anchoring roots were consumed and the productive heritage of ages was left to be the early victim of eager running water and insatiable gravity.

Probably the part of this burn that was most completely devastated was a tract of four or five hundred acres in a zone a little below timberline. Here stood a heavy forest on solid rock in thirty-two inches of humus. The tree-roots burned with the humus, and down crashed the trees into the flames. The work of a thousand years was undone in a day!

The loss of animal life in this fire probably was not heavy; in five or six days of exploring I came upon fewer than three dozen fire victims of all kinds. Among the dead were groundhogs, bobcats, snowshoe rabbits, and a few grouse. Flying about the waste were crested jays, gray jays ("camp birds"), and magpies. Coyotes came early to search for the feast prepared by the fire.

During the second day's exploration on the burn, a grizzly bear and I came upon two roasted deer in the end of a gulch. I was first to arrive, so Mr. Grizzly remained at what may have been a respectful distance, restlessly watching me. With his nearness and impolite stare I found it very embarrassing to eat alone. However, two days of fasting had prepared me for this primitive feast; and, knowing that bears were better than their reputation,

I kept him waiting until I was served. On arising to go, I said, "Come, you may have the remainder; there is plenty of it."

The fire was followed by clear weather, and for days the light ash lay deep and undisturbed over the burn. One morning conditions changed and after a few preliminary whirlwinds a gusty gale set in. In a few minutes I felt and appeared as though just from an ash-barrel. The ashen dust-storm was blinding and choking, and I fled for the unburned heights. So blinding was the flying ash that I was unable to see; and, to make matters worse, the trees with fire-weakened foundations and limbs almost severed by flames commenced falling. The limbs were flung about in a perfectly reckless manner, while the falling trees took a fiendish delight in crashing down alongside me at the very moment that the storm was most blinding. Being without nerves and incidentally almost choked, I ignored the falling bodies and kept going.

Several times I rushed blindly against limb-points and was rudely thrust aside; and finally I came near walking off into space from the edge of a crag. After this I sought temporary refuge to the leeward of a boulder, with the hope that the weakened trees would speedily fall and end the danger from that source. The ash flew thicker than ever did gale-blown desert dust; it was impossible to see and so nearly impossible to breathe that I was quickly driven forth. I have been in many dangers, but this is the only instance in which I was ever irritated by Nature's blind forces. At last I made my escape from them.

From clear though wind-swept heights I long watched the burned area surrender its slowly accumulated, rich store of plant-food to the insatiable and all-sweeping wind. By morning, when the wind abated, the garnered fertility and phosphates of generations were gone, and the sun cast the shadows of millions of leafless trees upon rock bones and barren earth. And the waters were still to take their toll.

Of course Nature would at once commence to repair and would again upbuild upon the foundations left by the fire; such, however, were the climatic and geological conditions that improving changes would come but slowly. In a century only a good beginning could be made. For years the greater portion of the burn would be uninhabitable by bird or beast; those driven forth by this fire would seek home and food in the neighboring territory, where this influx of population would compel interesting readjustments and create bitter strife between the old wild-folk population and the new.

This fire originated from a camp-fire which a hunting-party had left burning; it lived three weeks and extended eastward from the starting place. Along most of its course it burned to the timber-line on the left, while rocky ridges, glacier meadows, and rock fields stopped its extension and determined the side line on the right; it ran out of the forest and stopped in the grassy Grand River Valley. Across its course were a number of rocky ridges and grassy gorges where the fire could have been easily stopped by removing the scattered trees,—by burning the frail bridges that enabled the fire to travel from one dense forest to abundant fuel beyond. In a city it is common to smother a fire with water or acid, but with a forest fire usually it is best to break its inflammable line of communication by removing from before it a width of fibrous material. The axe, rake, hoe, and shovel are the usual fire-fighting tools.

A few yards away from the spot where the fire started I found, freshly cut in the bark of an aspen, the inscription:—

J S M
YALE 18

A bullet had obliterated the two right-hand figures.

For days I wandered over the mountains, going from fire to smoke and studying burns new and old. One comparatively level tract had been fire-swept in 1791. On this the soil was good. Lodge-pole pine had promptly restocked the burn, but these trees were now being smothered out by a promising growth of Engelmann spruce.

Fifty-seven years before my visit a fire had burned over about four thousand acres and was brought to a stand by a lake, a rocky ridge, and a wide fire-line that a snow-slide had cleared through the woods. The surface of the burn was coarse, disintegrated granite and sloped toward the west, where it was exposed to prevailing high westerly winds. A few kinnikinnick rugs apparently were the only green things upon the surface, and only a close examination revealed a few stunted trees starting. It was almost barren. Erosion was still active; there were no roots to bind the finer particles together or to anchor them in place. One of the most striking features of the entire burn was that the trees killed by the fire fifty-seven years ago were standing where they died. They had excellent root-anchorage in the shattered surface, and many of them probably would remain erect for years. The fire that killed them had been a hot one, and it had burned away most of the limbs, and had so thoroughly boiled the pitch through the exterior of the trunk that the wood was in an excellent state of preservation.

Another old burn visited was a small one in an Engelmann spruce forest on a moderate northern slope. It had been stopped while burning in very inflammable timber. It is probable that on this occasion either a rain or snow had saved the surrounding forest. The re-growth had slowly extended from the margin of the forest to the centre of the burn until it was restocked.

One morning I noticed two small fires a few miles down the mountain and went to examine them. Both were two days old, and both had started from unextinguished camp-fires. One had burned over about an acre and the other about four times that area. If the smaller had not been built against an old snag it probably would have gone out within a few hours after the congressman who built it moved camp. It was wind-sheltered and the blaze had traveled slowly in all directions and burned a ragged circle that was about sixty feet across.

The outline of the other blaze was that of a flattened ellipse, like the orbit of many a wandering comet in the sky. This had gone before the wind, and the windward end of its orbit closely encircled the place of origin. The camp-fire nucleus of this blaze had also been built in the wrong place,—against a fallen log which lay in a deep bed of decaying needles.

Of course each departing camper should put out his camp-fire. However, a camp-fire built on a humus-covered forest floor, or by a log, or against a dead tree, is one that is very difficult to extinguish. With the best of intentions one may deluge such a fire with water without destroying its potency. A fire thus secreted appears, like a lie, to have a spark of immortality in it.

A fire should not be built in contact with substances that will burn, for such fuel will prolong the fire's life and may lead it far into the forest. There is but little danger to the forest from a fire that is built upon rock, earth, sand, or gravel. A fire so built is isolated and it usually dies an early natural death. Such a fire— one built in a safe and sane place—is easily extinguished.

The larger of these two incipient fires was burning quietly, and that night I camped within its orbit. Toward morning the wind began to blow, this slow-burning surface fire began to leap, and before long it was a crown fire, traveling rapidly among the tree-tops. It swiftly expanded into an enormous delta of flame. At noon I looked back and down upon it from a mountain-top, and it had advanced about three miles into a primeval forest sea, giving off more smoke than a volcano.

I went a day's journey and met a big fire that was coming aggressively forward against the wind. It was burning a crowded, stunted growth of forest that stood in a deep litter carpet. The smoke, which flowed freely from it, was distinctly ashen green; this expanded and maintained in the sky a smoky sheet that was several miles in length.

Before the fire lay a square mile or so of old burn which was covered with a crowded growth of lodge-pole pine that stood in a deep, crisscrossed entanglement of fallen fire-killed timber. A thousand or more of these long, broken dead trees covered each acre with wreckage, and in this stood upward of five thousand live young ones. This would make an intensely hot and flame-writhing fire. It appears that a veteran spruce forest had occupied this burn prior to the fire. The fire had occurred fifty-seven years before. Trees old and young testified to the date. In the margin of the living forest on the edge of the burn were numerous trees that were fire-scarred fifty-seven years before; the regrowth on the burn was an even-aged fifty-six-year growth.

That night, as the fire neared the young tree growth, I scaled a rock ledge to watch it. Before me, and between the fire and the rocks, stood several veteran lodge-pole pines in a mass of dead-and-down timber. Each of these trees had an outline like that of a plump Lombardy poplar. They perished in the most spectacular manner. Blazing, wind-blown bark set fire to the fallen timber around their feet; this fire, together with the close, oncoming fire-front, so heated the needles on the lodge-poles that they gave off a smoky gas; this was issuing from every top when a rippling rill of purplish flame ran up one of the trunks. Instantly there was a flash and white flames flared upward more than one hundred feet, stood gushing for a few seconds, and then went out completely. The other trees in close succession followed and flashed up like giant geysers discharging flame. This discharge was brief, but it was followed by every needle on the trees glowing and changing to white incandescence, then vanishing. In a minute these leafless lodge-poles were black and dead.

The fire-front struck and crossed the lodge-pole thicket in a flash; each tree flared up like a fountain of gas and in a moment a deep, ragged-edged lake of flame heaved high into the dark, indifferent night. A general fire of the dead-and-down timber followed, and the smelter heat of this cut the green trees down, the flames widely, splendidly illuminating the surrounding mountains and changing a cloud-filled sky to convulsed, burning lava.

Not a tree was left standing, and every log went to ashes. The burn was as completely cleared as a fire-swept prairie; in places there were holes in the earth where tree-roots had burned out. This burn was an ideal place for another lodge-pole growth, and three years later these pines were growing thereon as thick as wheat in a field. In a boggy area within the burn an acre or two of aspen sprang up; this area, however, was much smaller than the one that the fire removed from the bog. Aspens commonly hold territory and extend their holdings by sprouting from roots; but over the greater portion of the bog the fire had either baked or burned the roots, and this small aspen area marked the wetter part of the bog, that in which the roots had survived.

After destroying the lodge-pole growth the fire passed on, and the following day it burned away as a quiet surface fire through a forest of scattered trees. It crept slowly forward, with a yellow blaze only a few inches high. Here and there this reddened over a pile of cone-scales that had been left by a squirrel, or blazed up in a pile of broken limbs or a fallen tree-top; it consumed the litter mulch and fertility of the forest floor, but seriously burned only a few trees.

Advancing along the blaze, I came upon a veteran yellow pine that had received a large pot-hole burn in its instep. As the

Western yellow pine is the best fire-fighter in the conifer family, it was puzzling to account for this deep burn. On the Rocky Mountains are to be found many picturesque yellow pines that have a dozen times triumphed over the greatest enemy of the forest. Once past youth, these trees possess a thick, corky, asbestos-like bark that defies the average fire. Close to this injured old fellow was a rock ledge that formed an influential part of its environment; its sloping surface shed water and fertility upon its feet; cones, twigs, and trash had also slid down this and formed an inflammable pile which, in burning, had bored into its ankle. An examination of its annual rings in the burned hole revealed the fact that it too had been slightly burned fifty-seven years before. How long would it be until it was again injured by fire or until some one again read its records?

Until recently a forest fire continued until stopped by rain or snow, or until it came to the edge of the forest. I have notes on a forest fire that lived a fluctuating life of four months. Once a fire invades an old forest, it is impossible speedily to get rid of it. "It never goes out," declared an old trapper. The fire will crawl into a slow-burning log, burrow down into a root or eat its way beneath a bed of needles, and give off no sign of its presence. In places such as these it will hibernate for weeks, despite rain or snow, and finally some day come forth as ferocious as ever.

About twenty-four hours after the lodge-pole blaze a snowstorm came to extinguish the surface fire. Two feet of snow—more than three inches of water—fell. During the storm I was comfortable beneath a shelving rock, with a fire in front; here I had a meal of wild raspberries and pine-nuts and reflected concerning the uses of forests, and wished that every one might better understand and feel the injustice and the enormous loss caused by forest fires.

During the last fifty years the majority of the Western forest fires have been set by unextinguished camp-fires, while the majority of the others were the result of some human carelessness. The number of preventable forest fires is but little less than the total number. True, lightning does occasionally set a forest on fire; I have personal knowledge of a number of such fires, but I have never known lightning to set fire to a green tree. Remove the tall dead trees from forests, and the lightning will lose the greater part of its kindling.

In forest protection, the rivers, ridge-tops, rocky gulches, rock-fields, lake-shores, meadows, and other natural fire-resisting boundary lines between forests are beginning to be used and can be more fully utilized for fire-lines, firefighting, and fire-defying places. These natural fire-barriers may be connected by barren cleared lanes through the forest, so that a fire-break will isolate or run entirely around any natural division of forest. With such a barrier a fire could be kept within a given section or shut out of it.

In order to fight fire in a forest it must be made accessible by means of roads and trails; these should run on or alongside the fire-barrier so as to facilitate the movements of fire patrols or fire-fighters. There should be with every forest an organized force of men who are eternally vigilant to prevent or to fight forest fires. Fires should be fought while young and small, before they are beyond control.

There should be crows'-nests on commanding crags and in each of these should be a lookout to watch constantly for starting fires or suspicious smoke in the surrounding sea of forest. The lookout should have telephonic connection with rangers down the slopes. In our national forests incidents like the following are beginning to occur: Upon a summit is stationed a ranger who has two hundred thousand acres of forest to patrol with his eyes. One morning a smudgy spot appears upon the purple forest sea about fifteen miles to the northwest. The lookout gazes for a moment through his glass and, although not certain as to what it is, decides to get the distance with the range-finder. At that instant, however, the wind acts upon the smudge and shows that a fire exists and reveals its position. A ranger, through a telephone at the forks of the trail below, hears from the heights, "Small fire one mile south of Mirror Lake, between Spruce Fork and Bear Pass Trail, close to O'Brien's Spring." In less than an hour a ranger leaps from his panting pony and with shovel and axe hastily digs a narrow trench through the vegetable mould in a circle around the fire. Then a few shovelfuls of sand go upon the liveliest blaze and the fire is under control. As soon as there lives a good, sympathetic public sentiment concerning the forest, it will be comparatively easy to prevent most forest fires from starting and to extinguish those that do start.

With the snow over, I started for the scene of the first fire, and on the way noticed how much more rapidly the snow melted in the open than in a forest. The autumn sun was warm, and at the end of the first day most of the snow in open or fireswept places was gone, though on the forest floor the slushy, compacted snow still retained the greater portion of its original moisture. On the flame-cleared slopes there was heavy erosion; the fire had destroyed the root-anchorage of the surface and consumed the trash that would ordinarily have absorbed and delayed the water running off; but this, unchecked, had carried off with it tons of earthy material. One slope on the first burn suffered heavily; a part of this day's "wash" was deposited in a beaver pond, of half an acre, which was filled to the depth of three feet. The beavers, finding their subterranean exits filled with wash, had escaped by tearing a hole in the top of their house.

Leaving this place, I walked across the range to look at a fire that was burning beyond the bounds of the snowfall. It was in a heavily forested cove and was rapidly undoing the constructive work of centuries. This cove was a horseshoe-shaped one and apparently would hold the fire within its rocky ridges. While following along one of these ridges, I came to a narrow, tree-dotted pass, the only break in the confining rocky barrier. As I looked at the fire down in the cove, it was plain that with a high wind the fire would storm this pass and break into a heavily forested alpine realm beyond. In one day two men with axes could have made this pass impregnable to the assaults of any fire, no matter how swift the wind ally; but men were not then defending our forests and an ill wind was blowing.

Many factors help to determine the speed of these fires, and a number of observations showed that under average conditions a fire burned down a slope at about one mile an hour; on the level it traveled from two to eight miles an hour, while up a slope it made from eight to twelve. For short distances fires occasionally roared along at a speed of fifty or sixty miles an hour. and made a terrible gale of flames.

I hurried up into the alpine realm and after half an hour scaled a promontory and looked back to the pass. A great cloud of smoke was streaming up just beyond and after a minute tattered sheets of flame were shooting high above it. Presently a tornado of smoke and flame surged into the pass and for some seconds nothing could be seen. As this cleared, a succession of tongues and sheets of flame tried to reach over into the forest on the other side of the pass, but finally gave it up. Just as I was beginning to feel that the forest around me was safe, a smoke-column arose among the trees by the pass. Probably during the first assault of the flames a fiery dart had been hurled across the pass.

Up the shallow forested valley below me came the flames, an inverted Niagara of red and yellow, with flying spray of black. It sent forward a succession of short-lived whirlwinds that went to pieces explosively, hurling sparks and blazing bark far and high. During one of its wilder displays the fire rolled forward, an enormous horizontal whirl of flame, and then, with thunder and roar, the molten flames swept upward into a wall of fire; this tore to pieces, collapsed, and fell forward in fiery disappearing clouds. With amazing quickness the splendid hanging garden on the terraced heights was crushed and blackened. By my promontory went this magnificent zigzag surging front of flame, blowing the heavens full of sparks and smoke and flinging enormous fiery rockets. Swift and slow, loud and low, swelling and vanishing, it sang its eloquent death song.

A heavy stratum of tarlike smoke formed above the fire as it toned down. Presently this black stratum was uplifted near the centre and then pierced with a stupendous geyser of yellow flame, which reddened as it fused and tore through the tarry smoke and then gushed astonishingly high above.

A year or two prior to the fire a snow slide from the heights had smashed down into the forest. More than ten thousand trees were mowed, raked, and piled in one mountainous mass of wreckage upon some crags and in a narrow-throated gulch between them. This woodpile made the geyser flames and a bonfire to startle even the giants. While I was trying to account for this extraordinary display, there came a series of explosions in rapid succession, ending in a violent crashing one. An ominous, elemental silence followed. All alone I had enjoyed the surprises, the threatening uncertainties, and the dangerous experiences that swiftly came with the fire-line battles of this long, smoky war; but when those awful explosions came I for a time wished that some one were with me. Had there been, I should have turned and asked, while getting a better grip on my nerves, "What on earth is that?" While the startled mountain-walls were still shuddering with the shock, an enormous agitated column of steam shot several hundred feet upward where the fiery geyser had flamed. Unable to account for these strange demonstrations, I early made my way through heat and smoke to the big bonfire. In the bottom of the gulch, beneath the bonfire, flowed a small stream; just above the bonfire this stream had been temporarily dammed by fire wreckage. On being released, the accumulated waters thus gathered had rushed down upon the red-hot rocks and cliffs and produced these explosions.

In the morning light this hanging terraced garden of yesterday's forest glory was a stupendous charcoal drawing of desolation.

Little Boy Grizzly

One day, while wandering in the pine woods on the slope of Mt. Meeker, I came upon two young grizzly bears. Though they dodged about as lively as chickens, I at last cornered them in a penlike pocket of fallen trees.

Getting them into a sack was one of the liveliest experiences I ever had. Though small and almost starved, these little orphans proceeded to "chew me up" after the manner of big grizzlies, as is told of them in books. After an exciting chase and tussle, I would catch one and thrust him into the sack. In resisting, he would insert his claws into my clothes, or thrust them through the side of the sack; then, while I was trying to tear him loose, or to thrust him forcibly in, he would lay hold of a finger, or take a bite in my leg. Whenever he bit, I at once dropped him, and then all began over again.

Their mother had been killed a few days before I found them; so, of course, they were famished and in need of a home; but so bitterly did they resist my efforts that I barely succeeded in taking them. Though hardly so large as a collie when he is at his prettiest, they were nimble athletes.

At last I started home, the sack over my shoulder, with these lively Ursus horribilis in the bottom of it. Their final demonstration was not needed to convince me of the extraordinary power of their jaws. Nevertheless, while going down a steep slope, one managed to bite into my back through sack and clothes, so effectively that I responded with a yell. Then I fastened the sack at the end of a long pole, which I carried across my shoulder, and I was able to travel the remainder of the distance to my cabin without another attack in the rear.

Johnny and Jenny.
Courtesy National Park Service—Rocky Mountain National Park.

Of course the youngsters did not need to be taught to eat. I simply pushed their noses down into a basin of milk, and the little red tongues at once began to ply; then raw eggs and bread were dropped into the basin. There was no hesitation between courses; they simply gobbled the food as long as I kept it before them.

Jenny and Johnny were pets before sundown. Though both were alert, Johnny was the wiser and the more cheerful of the two. He took training as readily as a collie or shepherd-dog, and I have never seen any dog more playful. All bears are keen of wit, but he was the brightest one of the wild folk that I have ever known. He grew rapidly, and ate me almost out of supplies. We were intimate friends in less than a month, and I spent much time playing and talking with him. One of the first things I taught him was, when hungry, to stand erect with arms extended almost horizontally, with palms forward. I also taught him to greet me in this manner.

One day, after two weeks with me, he climbed to the top of a pole fence to which he was chained. Up there he had a great time; he perched, gazed here and there, pranced back and forth, and finally fell off. His chain tangled and caught. For a few seconds he dangled in the air by the neck, then slipped through his collar and galloped off up the mountainside and quickly disappeared in the woods. I supposed he was gone for good. Although I followed for several hours, I did not even catch sight of him.

This little boy had three days of runaway life, and then concluded to return. Hunger drove him back. I saw him coming and went to meet him; but kept out of sight until he was within twenty feet, then stepped into view. Apparently a confused or entangled mental condition followed my appearance. His first impulse was to let me know that he was hungry by standing erect and outstretching his arms; this he started hastily to do.

In the midst of this performance, it occurred to him that if he wanted anything to eat he must hurry to me; so he interrupted his first action, and started to carry his second into instant effect. These incomplete proceedings interrupted and tripped one another three or four times in rapid succession. Though he tumbled about in comic confusion while trying to do two things at once, it was apparent through all that his central idea was to get something to eat.

And this, as with all boys, was his central idea much of the time. I did not find anything that he would not eat. He simply gobbled scraps from the table,—mountain sage, rhubarb, dandelion, and apples. Of course, being a boy, he liked apples best of all.

If I approached him with meat and honey upon a plate and with an apple in my pocket, he would smell the apple and begin to dance before me, ignoring the eatables in sight. Instantly, on permission, he would clasp me with both fore paws and thrust his nose into the apple pocket. Often, standing between him and Jenny, I alternately fed each a bit. A few times I broke the regular order and gave Jenny two bits in succession. At this Johnny raged, and usually ended by striking desperately at me; I never flinched, and the wise little rogue made it a point each time to miss me by an inch or two. A few other people tried this irritating experiment with him, but he hit them every time. However,

I early tried to prevent anything being done that teased or irritated him. Visitors did occasionally tease him, and frequently they fed the two on bad-temper-producing knickknacks.

Occasionally the two quarreled, but not more frequently than two ordinary children; and these quarrels were largely traceable to fight-producing food mixtures. Anyway, bears will maintain a better disposition with a diet of putrid meat, snakes, mice, and weeds than upon desserts of human concoction.

Naturally bears are fun-loving and cheerful; they like to romp and play. Johnny played by the hour. Most of the time he was chained to a low, small shed that was built for his accommodation. Scores of times each day he covered all the territory that could be traversed while he was fastened with a twelve-foot chain. Often he skipped back and forth in a straight line for an hour or more. These were not the restless, aimless movements of the caged tiger, but those of playful, happy activity. It was a pleasure to watch this eager play; in it he would gallop to the outer limit of his chain, then, reversing his legs without turning his body, go backward with a queer, lively hippety-hop to the other end, then gallop forward again. He knew the length of his chain to an inch. No matter how wildly he rushed after some bone-stealing dog, he was never jerked off his feet by forgetting his limitations.

He and Scotch, my collie, were good friends and jolly playmates. In their favorite play Scotch tried to take a bone which Johnny guarded; this brought out from both a lively lot of feinting, dodging, grabbing, and striking. Occasionally they clinched, and when this ended, Johnny usually tried for a good bite or two on Scotch's shaggy tail. Scotch appeared always to have in mind that the end of Johnny's nose was sensitive, and he landed many a good slap on this spot.

Apparently, Johnny early appreciated the fact that I would not tease him, and also that I was a master who must be obeyed. One day, however, he met with a little mishap, misjudged things, and endeavored to make it lively for me. I had just got him to the point where he enjoyed a rocking-chair. In this chair he sat up like a little man. Sometimes his fore paws lay awkwardly in his lap, but more often each rested on an arm of the big chair. He found rocking such a delight that it was not long until he learned to rock himself. This brought on the mishap. He had grown over-confident, and one day was rocking with great enthusiasm. Suddenly, the big rocker, little man and all, went over backward. Though standing by, I was unable to save him, and did not move. Seeing his angry look when he struck the floor, and guessing his next move, I leaped upon the table. Up he sprang, and delivered a vicious blow that barely missed, but which knocked a piece out of my trousers.

Apparently no other large animal has such intense curiosity as the grizzly. An object in the distance, a scent, a sound, or a trail, may arouse this, and for a time overcome his intense and wary vigilance. In satisfying this curiosity he will do unexpected and apparently bold things. But the instant the mystery is solved he is himself again, and may run for dear life from some situation into which his curiosity has unwittingly drawn him. An unusual noise behind Johnny's shed would bring him out with a rush, to determine what it was. If not at once satisfied as to the cause, he would put his fore paws on the top of the shed and peer over in the most eager and inquiring manner imaginable.

Enos Mills' brother, Joe, posing with the propped-up grizzly—the mother of Johnny and Jenny.
Courtesy National Park Service—Rocky Mountain National Park.

Like a scout, he spied mysterious and dim objects afar. If a man, a dog, or a horse, appeared in the distance, he quickly discovered the object, and at once stood erect, with fore paws drawn up, until he had a good look at it. The instant he made out what it was, he lost interest in it. At all times he was vigilant to know what was going on about him.

He was like a boy in his fondness for water. Usually, when unchained and given the freedom of the place, he would spend much of the time in the brook, rolling, playing, and wading. He and I had a few foot-races, and usually, in order to give me a better chance, we ran down hill. In a two-hundred-yard dash he usually paused three or four times and waited for me to catch up; and I was not a slow biped, either.

The grizzly, though apparently awkward and lumbering, is really one of the most agile of beasts. I constantly marveled at Johnny's lightness of touch, or the deftness of movement of his fore paws. With but one claw touching it, he could slide a coin back and forth on the floor more rapidly and lightly than I could. He would slide an eggshell swiftly along without breaking it. Yet by using but one paw, he could, without apparent effort, overturn rocks that were heavier than himself.

One day, while he slept in the yard, outstretched in the sun, I opened a large umbrella and put it over him, and waited near for him to wake up. By and by the sleepy eyes half opened, but without a move he closed them and slept again. Presently he was wide awake, making a quiet study of the strange thing over him, but except to roll his eyes, not a move did he make. Then a puff of wind gave sudden movement to the umbrella, rolling it over a point or two. At this he leaped to his feet, terribly frightened, and made a dash to escape this mysterious monster. But, as he jumped, the wind whirled the umbrella, and plump into it he landed. An instant of desperate clawing, and he shook off the wrecked umbrella and fled in terror. A minute or two later I found him standing behind the house, still frightened and trembling. When I came up and spoke to him, he made three or four lively attempts to bite my ankles. Plainly, he felt that I had played a mean and uncalled for trick upon him. I talked to him for some time and endeavored to explain the matter to him.

A sudden movement of a new or mysterious object will usually frighten any animal. On more than one occasion people have taken advantage of this characteristic of wild beasts, and prevented an attack upon themselves. In one instance I unconsciously used it to my advantage. In the woods, one day, as I have related elsewhere, two wolves and myself unexpectedly met. With bared teeth they stood ready to leap upon me. Needing something to keep up my courage and divert my thoughts, it occurred to me to snap a picture of them. This effectively broke the spell, for when the kodak door flew open they wheeled and fled.

Autumn came, and I was to leave for a forestry tour. The only man that I could persuade to stay at my place for the winter was one who neither understood nor sympathized with my wide-awake and aggressive young grizzly. Realizing that the man and the bear would surely clash, and perhaps to the man's disadvantage, I settled things once and for all by sending Johnny to the Denver Zoo.

He was seven months old when we parted and apparently as much attached to me as any dog to master. I frequently had news of him, but let two years go by before I allowed myself the pleasure of visiting him. He was lying on the ground asleep when I called, while around him a number of other bears were walking about. He was no longer a boy bear, but a big fellow. In my eagerness to see him I forgot to be cautious and, climbing to the top of the picket fence, leaped into the pen, calling, "Hello, Johnny!" as I leaped, and repeating this greeting as I landed on the ground beside him. He jumped up, fully awake, and at once recognized me. Instantly, he stood erect, with both arms extended, and gave a few happy grunts of joy and by way of greeting.

I talked to him for a little while and patted him as I talked. Then I caught a fore paw in my hand and we hopped and pranced about as in old times. A yell from the outside brought me to my senses. Instinctively I glanced about for a way of escape, though I really did not feel that I was in danger. We were, however, the observed of all observers, and I do not know which throng was staring with greater interest and astonishment,—the bears in the pen or the spectators on the outside.

In a Mountain Blizzard

At the close of one of our winter trips, my collie Scotch and I started across the continental divide of the Rocky Mountains in face of weather conditions that indicated a snowstorm or a blizzard before we could gain the other side. We had eaten the last of our food twenty-four hours before and could no longer wait for fair weather. So off we started to scale the snowy steeps of the cold, gray heights a thousand feet above. The mountains already were deeply snow-covered and it would have been a hard trip even without the discomforts and dangers of a storm.

I was on snowshoes and for a week we had been camping and tramping through the snowy forests and glacier meadows at the source of Grand River, two miles above the sea. The primeval Rocky Mountain forests are just as near to Nature's heart in winter as in summer. I had found so much to study and enjoy that the long distance from a food-supply, even when the last mouthful was eaten, had not aroused me to the seriousness of the situation. Scotch had not complained, and appeared to have the keenest collie interest in the tracks and trails, the scenes and silences away from the haunts of man. The snow lay seven feet deep, but by keeping in my snowshoe tracks Scotch easily followed me about. Our last camp was in the depths of an alpine forest at an altitude of ten thousand feet. Here, though zero weather prevailed, we were easily comfortable beside a fire under the protection of an overhanging cliff.

After a walk through woods the sun came blazing in our faces past the snow-piled crags on Long's Peak, and threw slender blue shadows of the spiry spruces far out in a white glacier meadow to meet us. Reentering the tall but open woods, we saw, down the long aisles and limb-arched avenues, a forest of tree columns, entangled in sunlight and shadow, standing on a snowy marble floor.

We were on the Pacific slope, and our plan was to cross the summit by the shortest way between timber-line and timber-line on the Atlantic side. This meant ascending a thousand feet, descending an equal distance, traveling five miles amid bleak, rugged environment. Along the treeless, gradual ascent we started, realizing that the last steep icy climb would be dangerous and defiant. Most of the snow had slid from the steeper places, and much of the remainder had blown away. Over the unsheltered whole the wind was howling. For a time the sun shone dimly through the wind-driven snow-dust that rolled from the top of the range, but it disappeared early behind wild, windswept clouds.

After gaining a thousand feet of altitude through the friendly forest, we climbed out and up above the trees on a steep slope at timberline. This place, the farthest up for trees, was a picturesque, desolate place. The dwarfed, gnarled, storm-shaped trees amid enormous snow-drifts told of endless, and at times deadly, struggles of the trees with the elements. Most of the trees were buried, but here and there a leaning or a storm-distorted one bent bravely above the snows.

At last we were safely on a ridge and started merrily off, hoping to cover speedily the three miles of comparatively level plateau.

How the wind did blow! Up more than eleven thousand feet above the sea, with not a tree to steady or break, it had a royal sweep. The wind appeared to be putting forth its wildest efforts to blow us off the ridge. There being a broad way, I kept well from the edges. The wind came with a dash and heavy rush, first from one quarter, then from another. I was watchful and faced each rush firmly braced. Generally, this preparedness saved me; but several times the wind apparently expanded or exploded beneath me, and, with an upward toss, I was flung among the icy rocks and crusted snows. Finally I took to dropping and lying flat whenever a violent gust came ripping among the crags.

There was an arctic barrenness to this alpine ridge,—not a house within miles, no trail, and here no tree could live to soften the sternness of the landscape or to cheer the traveler. The way was amid snowy piles, icy spaces, and windswept crags.

The wind slackened and snow began to fall just as we were leaving the smooth plateau for the broken part of the divide. The next mile of way was badly cut to pieces with deep gorges from both sides of the ridge. The inner ends of several of these broke through the centre of the ridge and extended beyond the ends of the gorges from the opposite side. This made the course a series of sharp, short zigzags.

We went forward in the flying snow. I could scarcely see, but felt that I could keep the way on the broken ridge between the numerous rents and cañons. On snowy, icy ledges the wind took reckless liberties. I wanted to stop but dared not, for the cold was intense enough to freeze one in a few minutes.

Fearing that a snow-whirl might separate us, I fastened one end of my light, strong rope to Scotch's collar and the other end to my belt. This proved to be fortunate for both, for while we were crossing an icy, though moderate, slope, a gust of wind swept me off my feet and started us sliding. It was not steep, but was so slippery I could not stop, nor see where the slope ended, and I grabbed in vain at the few icy projections. Scotch also lost his footing and was sliding and rolling about, and the wind was hurrying us along, when I threw myself flat and dug at the ice with fingers and toes. In the midst of my unsuccessful efforts we were brought to a sudden stop by the rope between us catching over a small rock-point that was thrust up through the ice. Around this in every direction was smooth, sloping ice; this, with the high wind, made me wonder for a moment how we were to get safely off the slope. The belt axe proved the means, for with it I reached out as far as I could and chopped a hole in the ice, while with the other hand I clung to the rock-point. Then, returning the axe to my belt, I caught hold in the chopped place and pulled myself forward, repeating this until on safe footing.

In oncoming darkness and whirling snow I had safely rounded the ends of two gorges and was hurrying forward over a comparatively level stretch, with the wind at my back boosting along. Scotch was running by my side and evidently was trusting me to guard against all dangers. This I tried to do. Suddenly, however, there came a fierce dash of wind and whirl of snow that hid everything. Instantly I flung myself flat, trying to stop quickly. Just as I did this I caught the strange, weird sound made by high wind as it sweeps across a cañon, and at once realized that we were close to a storm-hidden gorge. I stopped against a rock, while Scotch slid in and was hauled back with the rope.

The gorge had been encountered between two out-thrusting side gorges, and between these in the darkness I had a cold time feeling my way out. At last I came to a cairn of stones which I recognized. The way had been missed by only a few yards, but this miss had been nearly fatal.

Not daring to hurry in the darkness in order to get warm, I was becoming colder every moment. I still had a stiff climb between me and the summit, with timber-line three rough miles beyond. To attempt to make it would probably result in freezing or tumbling into a gorge. At last I realized that I must stop and spend the night in a snow-drift. Quickly kicking and trampling a trench in a loose drift, I placed my elk-skin sleeping-bag therein, thrust Scotch into the bag, and then squeezed into it myself.

I was almost congealed with cold. My first thought after warming up was to wonder why I had not earlier remembered the bag. Two in a bag would guarantee warmth, and with warmth a snow-drift on the crest of the continent would not be a bad place in which to lodge for the night.

The sounds of wind and snow beating upon the bag grew fainter and fainter as we were drifted and piled over with the latter. At the same time our temperature rose, and before long it was necessary to open the flap of the bag slightly for ventilation.

At last the sounds of the storm could barely be heard. Was the storm quieting down, or was its roar muffled and lost in the deepening cover of snow, was the unimportant question occupying my thoughts when I fell asleep.

Scotch awakened me in trying to get out of the bag. It was morning. Out we crawled, and, standing with only my head above the drift, I found the air still and saw a snowy mountain world all serene in the morning sun. I hastily adjusted sleeping-bag and snowshoes, and we set off for the final climb to the summit.

The final one hundred feet or so rose steep, jagged, and ice-covered before me. There was nothing to lay hold of; every point of vantage was plated and coated with non-prehensile ice. There appeared only one way to surmount this icy barrier and that was to chop toe and hand holes from the bottom to the top of this icy wall, which in places was close to vertical. Such a climb would not be especially difficult or dangerous for me, but could Scotch do it? He could hardly know how to place his feet in the holes or on the steps properly; nor could he realize that a slip or a misstep would mean a slide and a roll to death.

Leaving sleeping-bag and snowshoes with Scotch, I grasped my axe and chopped my way to the top and then went down and carried bag and snowshoes up. Returning for Scotch, I started him climbing just ahead of me, so that I could boost and encourage him. We had gained only a few feet when it became plain that sooner or later he would slip and bring disaster to both. We stopped and descended to the bottom for a new start.

Though the wind was again blowing a gale, I determined to carry him. His weight was forty pounds, and he would make a top-heavy load and give the wind a good chance to upset my balance and tip me off the wall. But, as there appeared no other way, I threw him over my shoulder and started up.

Many times Scotch and I had been in ticklish places together, and more than once I had pulled him up rocky cliffs on which he could not find footing. Several times I had carried him over gulches on fallen logs that were too slippery for him. He was so trusting and so trained that he relaxed and never moved while in my arms or on my shoulder.

Arriving at the place least steep, I stopped to transfer Scotch from one shoulder to the other. The wind was at its worst; its direction frequently changed and it alternately calmed and then came on like an explosion. For several seconds it had been roaring down the slope; bracing myself to withstand its force from this direction, I was about moving Scotch, when it suddenly shifted to one side and came with the force of a breaker. It threw me off my balance and tumbled me heavily against the icy slope.

Though my head struck solidly, Scotch came down beneath me and took most of the shock. Instantly we glanced off and began to slide swiftly. Fortunately I managed to get two fingers into one of the chopped holes and held fast. I clung to Scotch with one arm; we came to a stop, both saved. Scotch gave a yelp of pain when he fell beneath me, but he did not move. Had he made a jump or attempted to help himself, it is likely that both of us would have gone to the bottom of the slope.

Gripping Scotch with one hand and clinging to the icy hold with the other, I shuffled about until I got my feet into two holes in the icy wall. Standing in these and leaning against the ice, with the wind butting and dashing, I attempted the ticklish task of lifting Scotch again to my shoulder—and succeeded. A minute later we paused to breathe on the summit's icy ridge, between two oceans and amid seas of snowy peaks.

Working Like a Beaver

One September day I saw a number of beaver at work upon a half-finished house. One part of the house had been carried up about two feet above the water, and against this were leaned numerous sticks, which stood upon the top of the foundation just above water-level. After these sticks were arranged, they were covered with turf and mud which the beaver scooped from the bottom of the pond. In bringing this earth covering up, the beaver invariably came out of the water at a given point, and over a short slide worn on the side of the house climbed up to the height where they were to deposit their load, which was carried in the fore paws. Then they edged round and put the mudball upon the house. From this point they descended directly to the water, but when they emerged with the next handful, they came out at the bottom of the slide, and again climbed up it.

The beaver often does a large amount of work in a short time. A small dam may be built up in a few nights, or a number of trees felled, or possibly a long burrow or tunnel clawed in the earth during a brief period. In most cases, however, beaver works of magnitude are monuments of old days, and have required a long time to construct, being probably the work of more than one generation. It is rare for a large dam or canal to be constructed in one season. A thousand feet of dam is the accumulated work of years. An aged beaver may have lived all his life in one locality, born in the house in which his parents were born, and he might rise upon the thousand-foot dam which held his pond and say, "My grandparents half a dozen centuries ago commenced this dam, and I do not know which one of my ancestors completed it."

Although the beaver is a tireless and an effective worker, he does not work unless there is need to do so. Usually his summer is a rambling vacation spent away from home. His longest period of labor is during September and October, when the harvest is gathered and general preparations made for the long winter. Baby beavers take part in the harvest-getting, though probably without accomplishing very much. During most winters he has weeks of routine in the house and ponds with nothing urgent to do except sleep and eat.

He works not only tooth and nail, but tooth and tail. The tail is one of the most conspicuous organs of the beaver. Volumes have been written concerning it. It is nearly flat, is black in color, and is a convenient and much-used appendage. It serves for a rudder, a stool, a prop, a scull, and a signal club. It may be used for a trowel, but I have never seen it so used. It serves one purpose that apparently has not been discussed in print; on a few occasions I have seen a beaver carry a small daub of mud or some sticks clasped between the tail and the belly. It gives this awkward animal increased awkwardness and even an uncouth appearance to see him humped up, with tail tucked between his legs, in order to clasp something between it and his belly.

He is accomplished in the use of arms and hands. With hands he is able to hold sticks and handle them with great dexterity. Like any clawing animal he uses his hands or fore paws, to dig holes or tunnels and to excavate burrows and water-basins. His hind feet are the chief propelling power in swimming, although the tail, which may be tuned almost on edge and is capable of diagonal movement, is sometimes brought into play as a scull when the beaver is at his swiftest. In the water beaver move about freely and apparently with the greatest enjoyment. They are delightfully swift and agile swimmers, in decided contrast with their awkward slowness upon the ground. They can swim two hundred yards under water without once coming to the surface, and have the ability to remain under water from five to ten minutes. On one occasion a beaver remained under water longer than eleven minutes, and came to the top none the worse, apparently, for this long period of suspended breathing.

It is in standing erect that the beaver is at his best. In this attitude the awkwardness and the dull appearance of all-fours are absent, and he is a statue of alertness. With feet parallel and in line, tail at right angles to the body and resting horizontally on the ground, and hands held against the breast, he has the happy and childish eagerness of a standing chipmunk, and the alert and capable attitude of an erect and listening grizzly bear.

The beaver is larger than most people imagine. Mature male specimens are about thirty-eight inches in length and weigh about thirty-eight pounds, but occasionally one is found that weighs seventy or more pounds. Ten mature males which I measured in the Rocky Mountains showed an average length of forty inches, with an average weight of forty-seven pounds. The tails of these ten averaged ten inches in length, four and a half inches in width across the centre, and one inch in thickness. Behind the shoulders the average circumference was twenty-one inches, and around the abdomen twenty-eight. Ten mature females which I measured were only a trifle smaller.

There are twenty teeth; in each jaw there are eight molars and two incisors. The four front teeth of the beaver are large, orange-colored, strong, and have a self-sharpening edge of enamel. The ears are very short and rounded. The sense of smell appears to be the most highly developed of the beaver's senses. Next to this, that of hearing appears to be the most informational. The eyes are weak. The hind feet are large and webbed, and resemble those of a goose. The second claw of each hind foot is double, and is used in combing the fur and in dislodging the parasites from the skin. The fore paws of the beaver are hand-like, and have long, strong claws. They are used very much after the fashion in which monkeys use their hands, and serve a number of purposes.

The color of the beaver is a reddish brown, sometimes shading into a very dark brown. Occasional specimens are white or black. The beaver is not a handsome animal, and when in action on the land he is awkward. The black skin which covers his tail appears to be covered with scales; the skin merely has this form and appearance, the scales do not exist. The tail somewhat resembles the end of an oar.

The all-important tools of this workman are his four orange-colored front teeth. These are edge tools that are adaptable and self-sharpening. They are set in strong jaws and operated by powerful muscles. Thus equipped, he can easily cut wood. These teeth grow with surprising rapidity. If accident befalls them, so that the upper and the lower fail to bear and wear, they will grow by each other and in a short time become of an uncanny length. I have found several dead beaver who had apparently died of starvation; their teeth overlapped with jaws wide open and thus prevented their procuring food. For a time I possessed an overgrown tooth that was crescent shaped and a trifle more than six inches long.

Pounds considered, the beaver is a powerful animal, and over a rough trail will drag objects of twice his own weight or roll a log-section of gigantic size. Up a strong current he will tow an eighty or one-hundred-pound sapling without apparent effort. Three or four have rolled a one-hundred-and-twenty-pound boulder into place in the dam. Commonly he does things at opportune times and in the easiest way. His energy is not wasted in building a dam where one is not needed nor in constructive work in times of high water. He accepts deep water as a matter of fact and constructs dams to make shallow places deep.

Beaver food is largely inner bark of deciduous or broad-leaved trees. Foremost among these trees which they use for food is the aspen, although the cottonwood and willow are eaten almost as freely. The bark of the birch, alder, maple, box-elder, and a number of other trees is also used. Except in times of dire emergency the beaver will not eat the bark of the pine, spruce, or fir tree. It is fortunate that the trees which the beaver fell and use for food or building purposes are water-loving trees, which not only sprout from both stump and root, but grow with exceeding rapidity. Among other lesser foods used are berries, mushrooms, sedge, grass, and the leaves and stalks of a number of plants. In winter dried grass and leaves are sometimes used, and in this season the rootstocks of the pond-lily and the roots of the willow, alder, birch, and other water-loving trees that may be got from the bottom of the pond. Beaver are vegetarians; they do not eat fish or flesh.

Apparently beaver prefer to cut trees that are less than six inches in diameter, and where slender poles abound it is rare for anything to be cut of more than four inches. But it is not uncommon to see trees felled that are from twelve to fifteen inches in diameter. In my possession are three beaver-cut stumps each of which has a greater diameter than eighteen inches, the largest being thirty-four inches. The largest beaver-cut stump that I have ever measured was on the Jefferson River in Montana, near the mouth of Pipestone Creek. This was three feet six inches in diameter.

The beaver sits upright with fore paws against the tree, or clasping it; half squatting on his hind legs, with tail either extending behind as a prop or folded beneath him as a seat, he tilts his head from side to side and makes deep bites into the tree about sixteen inches above the ground. In the overwhelming majority of beaver-cut trees that I have seen, most of the cutting was done from one side,—from one seat as it were. Though the notch taken out was rudely done, it was after the fashion of the axe-man. The beaver bites above and below, then, driving his teeth behind the piece thus cut off, will wedge, pry, or pull out the chip. Ofttimes in doing this he appears to use his jaw as a lever. With the aspen, or with other trees equally soft, about one hour is required to gnaw down a four-inch sapling. With one bite he will snip off a limb from half to three quarters of an inch in diameter.

After a tree is felled on land, the limbs are cut off and the trunk is gnawed into sections. The length of these sections appears to depend upon the size of the tree-trunk and also the distance to the water, the number of beaver to assist in its transportation, and the character of the trail. Commonly a six- or eight-inch tree is cut into lengths of about four to six feet. If the tree falls into the water of the pond or the canal, it is, if the limbs are not too long, transported butt foremost to the desired spot in its uncut, untrimmed entirety. Ofttimes with a large tree the trunk is left and only the limbs taken.

The green wood which the beaver uses for his winter's food-supply is stored on the bottom of the pond. How does he sink it to the bottom? There is an old and oft-repeated tale which says that the beaver sucks the air from the green wood so as to sink it promptly. Another tale has it that the beaver dives to the bottom carrying with him a green stick which he thrusts into the mud and it is thus anchored. Apparently the method is a simple one. The green wood stored is almost as heavy as water, and once in the pond it becomes water-logged and sinks in a short time; however, the first pieces stored are commonly large, heavy chunks, which are forced to the bottom by piling others on top of them. Frequently the first few pieces of the food-pile consist of entire trees, limbs and all. These usually are placed in a rude circle with butts inward and tops outward. This forms an entangling foundation which holds in place the smaller stuff piled thereon.

Most willows by beaver colonies are small and comparatively light. These do not sink readily, are not easily managed, and are rarely used in the bottom of the pile. Commonly, when these light cuttings are gathered into the food-pile, they are laid on top, where numerous up-thrusting limbs entangle and hold them. The foundation and larger portion of the food-pile are formed of heavy pieces of aspen, alder, or some other streamside tree, which cannot be moved out of place by an ordinary wind or water-current and which quickly sink to the bottom.

Among enemies of this fur-clad fellow are the wolverine, the otter, the lion, the lynx, the coyote, the wolf, and the bear. Hawks and owls occasionany capture a young beaver. Beaver spend much time dressing their fur and bathing, as they are harassed by lice and other parasites. At rare intervals they are afflicted with disease. They live from twelve to fifteen years and sometimes longer. Man is the worst enemy of the beaver.

A thousand trappers unite to tell the same pitiable tale of a trapped beaver's last moments. If the animal has not succeeded in drowning himself or tearing off a foot and escaping, the trapper smashes the beaver's head with his hatchet. The beaver, instead of trying to rend the man with sharp cutting teeth, raises himself and with upraised hand tries to ward off the death-blow. Instead of one blow, a young trapper frequently has to give two or three, but the beaver receives them without a struggle or a sound, and dies while vainly trying to shield his head with both hands.

Justly renowned for his industry, the beaver is a master of the fine art of rest. He has many a vacation and conserves his energies. He keeps his fur clean and his house in a sanitary condition. Ever in good condition, he is ready at all times for hard work and is capable of efficient work over long periods. He is ready for emergencies.

As animal life goes, that of the beaver stands among the best. His life is full of industry and is rich in repose. He is home-loving and avoids fighting. His lot is cast in poetic places.

The beaver has a rich birthright, though born in a windowless hut of mud. Close to the primeval place of his birth the wild folk of both woods and water meet and often mingle. Around are the ever-changing and never-ending scenes and silences of the water or the shore. Beaver grow up with the many-sided wild, playing amid the brilliant flowers and great boulders, in the piles of driftwood and among the fallen logs on the forest's mysterious edge. They learn to swim and slide, to dive quickly and deeply from sight, to sleep, and to rest moveless in the sunshine; ever listening to the strong, harmonious stir of wind and water, living with the stars in the sky and the stars in the pond; beginning serious life when brilliant clouds of color enrich autumn's hills; helping to harvest the trees that wear the robes of gold, while the birds go by for the southland in the reflective autumn days. If Mother Nature should ever call me to live upon another planet, I could wish that I might be born a beaver, to inhabit a house in the water.

Transportation
Facilities

Two successive dry years had greatly reduced the water-level of Lily Lake, and the consequent shallowness of the water made a serious situation for its beaver inhabitants. This lake covered about ten acres, and was four feet deep in the deepest part, while over nine tenths of the area the water was two feet or less in depth. It was supplied by springs. Early in the autumn of 1911 the water completely disappeared from about one half of the area, and most of the remainder became so shallow that beaver could no longer swim beneath the surface. This condition exposed them to the attack of enemies and made the transportation of supplies to the house slow and difficult.

In the lake the beaver had dug an extensive system of deep canals,—the work of years. By means of these deep canals the beaver were able to use the place until the last, for these were full of water even after the lake-bed was completely exposed. One day in October while passing the lake, I noticed a coyote on the farther shore stop suddenly, prick up his ears, and give alert attention to an agitated forward movement in the shallow water of a canal. Then he plunged into the water and endeavored to seize a beaver that was struggling forward through water that was too shallow for his heavy body. Although this beaver made his escape, other members of the colony may not have been so fortunate.

The drouth continued and by mid-October the lake went entirely dry except in the canals. Off in one corner stood the beaver house, a tiny rounded and solitary hill in the miniature

black plain of lake-bed. With one exception the beaver abandoned the site and moved on to other scenes, I know not where.
One old beaver remained. Whether he did this through the fear
of not being equal to the overland journey across the dry rocky
ridge and down into Wind River, or whether from deep love of
the old home associations, no one can say. But he remained and
endeavored to make provision for the oncoming winter. Close
to the house he dug or enlarged a well that was about six feet in
diameter and four feet in depth. Seepage filled this hole, and into
it he piled a number of green aspen chunks and cuttings, a mea-
gre food-supply for the long, cold winter that followed.
Extreme cold began in early November, and not until April was
there a thaw.

Before the lake-bed was snow-covered, all the numerous
canals and basins which the beaver had excavated could be
plainly seen and examined. The magnitude of the work which
the beaver had performed in making these is beyond comprehension. I took a series of photographs of these excavations and
made numerous measurements. To the north of the house a pool
had been dug that was three feet deep, thirty feet long, and
about twenty wide. There extended from this a canal that was
one hundred and fifty feet long. The food basin was thirty feet
wide and four feet deep. This had a canal connection with the
house. In the bottom of the basin was one of the feeble springs
which supply the lake. Another canal, which extended three
hundred and fifty feet in a northerly direction from the house,
was from three to four feet wide and three feet deep. The largest
ditch or canal was seven hundred and fifty feet long and three
feet deep throughout. This extended eastward, then northeast-
erly, and for one hundred feet was five feet wide. In the remaining six hundred and fifty feet it was three to four feet wide.
There were a number of minor ditches and canals connecting the
larger ones, and altogether the extent of all made an impressive
show in the empty lake-basin.

Meantime the old beaver had a hard winter. The cold weather
persisted, and finally the well in which he had deposited winter
food froze to the bottom. Even the entrance-holes into the
house were frozen shut. This sealed him in. The old fellow,
whose teeth were worn and whose claws were bad, apparently

tried in vain to break out. On returning from three months' absence, two friends and I investigated the old beaver's condition. We broke through the frozen walls of the house and crawled in. The old fellow was still alive, though greatly emaciated. For some time—I know not how long—he had subsisted on the wood and the bark of some green sticks which had been built into an addition of the house during the autumn. We cut several green aspens into short lengths and threw them into the house. The broken hole was then closed. The old fellow accepted these cheerfully. For six weeks aspens were occasionally thrown to him, and at the end of this time the spring warmth had melted the deep snow. The water rose and filled the pond and unsealed the entrance to the house, and again the old fellow emerged into the water. The following summer he was joined, or rejoined, by a number of other beaver.

In many localities the canals or ditches dug and used by the beaver form their most necessary and extensive works. These canals require enormous labor and much skill. In point of interest they even excel the house and the dam. It is remarkable that of the thousands of stories concerning the beaver only a few have mentioned the beaver canals. These are labor-saving improvements, and not only enable the beaver to live easily and safely in places where he otherwise could not live at all, but apparently they allow him to live happily. The excavations made in taking material for house or dam commonly are turned to useful purpose. The beaver not only builds his mound-like house, but uses the basin thus formed in excavating earthy material for the house for a winter food depository. Ofttimes, too, in building the dam he does it by piling up the material dug from a ditch which runs parallel and close to the dam, and which is useful to him as a deep waterway after the dam is completed.

In transporting trees for food-supply, water transportation is so much easier and safer than land, that wherever the immediate surroundings of the pond are comparatively level the beaver endeavors to lead water out to tree groves by digging a canal from the edge of the pond to these groves. The felled trees are by this means easily floated into the pond. One of the simplest forms of beaver canal is a narrow, outward extension of the pond. This varies in length from a few yards to one hundred feet or more.

Another and fairly common form of canal is one that is built across low narrow necks of land which thrust out into large beaver ponds, or on narrow stretches of land around which crooked streams wander.

The majority of beaver ponds are comparatively shallow over the greater portion of their area. In many cases it is not easy, or even possible, to deepen them. They may be so shallow that the pond freezes to the bottom in winter except in its small deeper portion. The shallow ponds are made more usable by a number of canals in the bottom. These canals assure deep-water stretches under all conditions. Most beaver ponds have a canal that closely parallels the dam. In some instances this is extended around the pond a few yards inside the shore-line. Two canals usually extend from the house. One of these connects with the canal by the dam, the other runs to the place on the shore (commonly at the end of a trail or slide) most visited by the beaver.

In Jefferson Valley, Montana, not far from Three Forks, I enjoyed the examination of numerous beaver workings, and made measurements of the most interesting system of beaver canals that I have ever seen. The beaver house for which these canals did service was situated on the south bank of the river, about three feet above the summer level of the water and about two hundred feet north of the hilly edge of the valley. From the river a crescent-shaped canal, about thirty-five feet in length, had been dug halfway around the base of the house. Connected with this was a basin for winter food; this was five feet deep and thirty-five feet in diameter. From this a canal extended southward two hundred and seven feet. One hundred and ten feet distant from the house was a boulder that was about ten feet in diameter. This was imbedded in about two feet of soil. Around this boulder the canal made a detour, and then resumed its comparatively straight line southward.

Over the greater portion of its length this canal was four feet wide, and at no point was it narrower than three feet. Its average depth was twenty-eight inches. For one hundred and forty-seven feet it ran through an approximately level stretch of the valley, and seepage filled it with water. A low, semi-circular dam, about fifty feet in length, crossed it at the one-hundred-and forty-seven-foot mark, and served to catch and run seepage water into it, and also to act as a wall across the canal to hold the water. The most southerly sixty feet of this canal on the edge of the foothills ran uphill, and was about four feet deep at the upper end, four feet higher than the end by the house. The dam across it was supplemented by a wall forty-eight feet further on. This wall was simply a short dam across the canal, in a part that was inclined, and plainly for the purpose of retaining water in the canal. The upper part of the canal was filled with water by a streamlet from off the slope. Apparently this canal was old, for there was growing on its banks near the house, a spruce tree, four inches in diameter, that had grown since the canal was made.

The wall or small dam which beaver build across canals that are inclined represents an interesting phase of beaver development. That these walls are built for the purpose of retaining water in the canal appears certain. They are most numerous in canals of steepest incline, though rarely less than twenty feet apart. I have not seen a wall in an almost dead-level canal, except it was there for the purpose of raising the height of the water. This wall or buttress is after all but a dam, and like most dams it is built for the purpose of raising and maintaining the level of water.

Extending at right angles westward from the end of the old canal was a newer one of two hundred and twenty-one feet. A wall separated and united the two. One hundred and sixty feet of this new canal ran along the contour of a hill, approximately at a dead level. Then came a wall, and from this the last sixty-one feet extended southward up a shallow ravine. In this part there were two walls. The upper end of the sixty-one-foot extension was nine feet higher than the house, and four hundred and twenty-eight feet distant from it. The two-hundred-and-twenty-one-foot extension was from twenty-six to thirty-four inches wide, and averaged twenty-two inches deep. The entire new part was supplied with spring water, which the beaver had diverted from a ravine to the west and led by a seventy-foot ditch into the upper end of their canal. Thirty feet from the end of the canal were two burrows, evidently safe places into which the beaver could retreat in case of sudden attack from wolves or other foe. There were two other of these burrows, one at the outer end of the old canal and the other alongside the boulder one hundred and ten feet from the house.

At the time I saw these canals, the only trees near were those of an aspen grove which surrounded the extreme end. It was autumn, and on both tributary slopes by the end of the canal, aspens were being cut, dragged, and rolled down these slopes into the upper end of the canal, then floated through its waters, dragged over and across the walls, and at last piled up for winter food in the basin by the house. In all probability this long, large canal had been built a few yards at a time, being extended as the trees near-by were cut down and used.

Where beaver long inhabit a locality it is not uncommon for them to have two or three distinct and well-used trails from points on the water's edge which lead into neighboring groves or tree-clumps. These are the beaten tracks traveled by the beaver as they go forth from the water for food, and over which they drag their trees and saplings into the water. On steep slopes by the water these are called slides. This name is also given to places in the dam over which beaver frequently pass in their outgoings and incomings. Commonly these trails avoid ridges and ground swells by keeping in the bottom of a ravine; logs are cut through and rolled out of the way, or a tunnel driven beneath; obstructions are removed, or a good way made round them. Their log roads compare favorably with the log roads of woodsmen who cut with steel instead of enamel.

In most old beaver colonies, where the character of the bottom of the pond permits it, there are two or more tunnels or subways beneath the floor of the principal pond. The main tunnel begins close to the foundation of the house, and penetrates the earth a foot or more beneath the water to a point on land a few feet beyond the shore-line. If there are a number of small ponds in a colony that are separated by fingers of land, it is not uncommon for these bits of land to be penetrated by a thoroughfare tunnel. These tunnels through the separating bits of land enable the beaver to go from one pond to another without exposing themselves to dangers on land, and also offer an easy means of intercommunication between ponds when these are ice-covered. Pond subways also afford a place of refuge or a means of escape in case the house is destroyed, the dam broken, or the pond drained, or in case the pond should freeze to the bottom. Commonly these are full of water, but some are empty. On the Missouri and other rivers, where there are several feet of cut banks above the water, beaver commonly dug a steeply inclined tunnel from the river's edge to the top of a bank a few feet back.

Most of this tunnel work is hidden and remains unknown. A striking example was in the Spruce Tree Colony, elsewhere described. These colonists, apparently disgusted by having their ponds completely filled with sediment which came down as the result of a cloudburst, abandoned the old colony-site. A new site was selected on a moraine, only a short distance from the old one. Here in the sod a basin was scooped out, and a dam made with the excavated material. The waters from a spring which burst forth in the moraine, about two hundred yards up the slope and perhaps one hundred feet above, trickled down and in due time formed a pond. The following year this pond was enlarged, and another one built upon a terrace about one hundred feet up the slope. From year to year there were enlargements of the old pond and the building of new pondlets, until there were seven on the terraces of this moraine. These, together with the connecting slides and canals, required more water than the spring supplied, especially in the autumn when the beaver were floating their winter supplies from pond to pond. Within the colony area, too, were many water-filled underground passages or subway tunnels. One of these penetrated the turf beneath the willows for more than two hundred feet.

While watching the autumnal activities of this colony, as described in another chapter, I broke through the surface and plunged my leg into an underground channel or subway that was half filled with water. Taking pains to trace this stream downward, I found that it emptied into the uppermost of the ponds along with the waters from a small spring. Then, tracing the channel upwards, I found that, about one hundred and forty feet distant from the uppermost pond, it connected with the waters of the brook on which the old colony formerly had a place. This tunnel over most of its course was about two feet beneath the surface, was fourteen inches in diameter, and ran beneath the roots of spruce trees. The water which the tunnel led from the brook plainly was being used to increase the supply needed in the canals, ponds, and pools of the Spruce Tree Colony. The intake of this was in a tiny pond which the beaver had formed by a damlet across the brook. That this increased supply of water was of great advantage to the busy and populous Spruce Tree Colony, there can be no doubt. Was this tunnel planned and made for this especial purpose, or was the increased water-supply of the colony the result of accident by the brook's breaking into this subway tunnel?

The canals which beaver dig, the slides which they use, the trails which they clear and establish, conclusively show that these animals appreciate the importance of good waterways and good roads,—in other words, good transportation facilities.

The Ruined Colony

Twenty-six years ago, while studying glaciation on the slope of Long's Peak, I came upon a cluster of eight beaver houses. These crude conical mud huts were in a forest pond far up on the mountainside. In this colony of our first engineers were so many things of interest that the fascinating study of the dead Ice King's ruins and records was indefinitely given up in order to observe Citizen Beaver's works and ways.

A pile of granite boulders on the edge of the pond stood several feet above the water-level, and from the top of these the entire colony and its operations could be seen. On these I spent days observing and enjoying the autumnal activities of Beaverdom.

It was the busiest time of the year for these industrious folk. General and extensive preparations were now being made for the long winter amid the mountain snows. A harvest of scores of trees was being gathered and work on a new house was in progress, while the old houses were receiving repairs. It was a serene autumn day when I came into the picturesque village of these primitive people. The aspens were golden, the willows rusty, the grass tanned, and the pines were purring in the easy air.

The colony-site was in a small basin amid morainal débris at an altitude of nine thousand feet above the sea-level. I at once christened it the Moraine Colony. The scene was utterly wild. Peaks of crags and snow rose steep and high above all; all around crowded a dense evergreen forest of pine and spruce. A few small swamps reposed in this forest, while here and there in it bristled several gigantic windrows of boulders. A ragged belt of aspens surrounded the several ponds and separated the pines

Longs Peak Inn, May 1920 (Enos Mills standing in doorway).
Courtesy National Park Service—Rocky Mountain National Park.

and spruces from the fringe of water-loving willows along the shores. There were three large ponds in succession and below these a number of smaller ones. The dams that formed the large ponds were willow-grown, earthy structures about four feet in height, and all sagged downstream. The houses were grouped in the middle pond, the largest one, the dam of which was more than three hundred feet long. Three of these lake dwellings stood near the upper margin, close to where the brook poured in. The other five were clustered by the outlet, just below which a small willow-grown, boulder-dotted island lay between the divided waters of the stream.

A number of beavers were busy gnawing down aspens, while others cut the felled ones into sections, pushed and rolled the sections into the water, and then floated them to the harvest piles, one of which was being made beside each house. Some were quietly at work spreading a coat of mud on the outside of each house. This would freeze and defy the tooth and claw of the hungriest or the strongest predaceous enemy. Four beavers were leisurely lengthening and repairing a dam. A few worked singly, but most of them were in groups. All worked quietly and with apparent deliberation, but all were in motion, so that it was a busy scene. "To work like a beaver!" What a stirring exhibition of beaver industry and forethought I viewed from my boulder-pile!

At times upward of forty of them were in sight. Though there was a general coöperation, yet each one appeared to do his part without orders or direction. Time and again a group of workers completed a task, and without pause silently moved off, and began another. Everything appeared to go on mechanically. It produced a strange feeling to see so many workers doing so many kinds of work effectively and automatically. Again and again I listened for the superintendent's voice; constantly I watched to see the overseer move among them; but I listened and watched in vain. Yet I feel that some of the patriarchal fellows must have carried a general plan of the work, and that during its progress orders and directions that I could not comprehend were given from time to time.

The work was at its height a little before mid-day. Nowadays it is rare for a beaver to work in daylight. Men and guns have prevented daylight workers from leaving descendants. These not only worked but played by day. One morning for more than an hour there was a general frolic, in which the entire population appeared to take part. They raced, dived, crowded in general mix-ups, whacked the water with their tails, wrestled, and dived again. There were two or three play-centres, but the play went on without intermission, and as their position constantly changed, the merrymakers splashed water all over the main pond before they calmed down and in silence returned to work. I gave most attention to the harvesters, who felled the aspens and moved them, bodily or in sections, by land and water to the harvest piles. One tree on the shore of the pond, which was felled into the water, was eight inches in diameter and fifteen feet high. Without having even a limb cut off, it was floated to the nearest harvest pile. Another, about the same size, which was procured some fifty feet from the water, was cut into four sections and its branches removed; then a single beaver would take a branch in his teeth, drag it to the water, and swim with it to a harvest pile. But four beavers united to transport the largest section to the water. They pushed with fore paws, with breasts, and with hips. Plainly it was too heavy for them. They paused. "Now they will go for help," I said to myself, "and I shall find out who the boss is." But to my astonishment one of them began to gnaw the piece in two, and two more began to clear a narrow way to the water, while the fourth set himself to cutting down another aspen. Good roads and open waterways are the rule, and perhaps the necessary rule, of beaver colonies.

I became deeply interested in this colony, which was situated within two miles of my cabin, and its nearness enabled me to be a frequent visitor and to follow closely its fortunes and misfortunes. About the hut-filled pond I lingered when it covered with winter's white, when fringed with the gentian's blue, and while decked with the pond-lily's yellow glory.

Fire ruined it during an autumn of drouth. One morning, while watching from the boulder-pile, I noticed an occasional flake of ash dropping into the pond. Soon smoke scented the air, then came the awful and subdued roar of a forest fire. I fled, and from above the timber-line watched the storm-cloud of black smoke sweep furiously forward, bursting and closing to the terrible leaps of red and tattered flames. Before noon several thousand acres of forest were dead, all leaves and twigs were in ashes, all tree-trunks blistered and blackened.

The Moraine Colony was closely embowered in a pitchy forest. For a time the houses in the water must have been wrapped in flames of smelter heat. Could these mud houses stand this? The beavers themselves I knew would escape by sinking under the water. Next morning I went through the hot, smoky area and found every house cracked and crumbling; not one was inhabitable. Most serious of all was the total loss of the uncut food-supply, when harvesting for winter had only begun.

Would these energetic people starve at home or would they try to find refuge in some other colony? Would they endeavor to find a grove that the fire had missed and there start anew? The intense heat had consumed almost every fibrous thing above the surface. The piles of garnered green aspen were charred to the waterline; all that remained of willow thickets and aspen groves were thousands of blackened pickets and points, acres of coarse charcoal stubble. It was a dreary, starving outlook for my furred friends.

I left the scene to explore the entire burned area. After wandering for hours amid ashes and charcoal, seeing here and there the seared carcass of a deer or some other wild animal, I came upon a beaver colony that had escaped the fire. It was in the midst of several acres of swampy ground that was covered with fire-resisting willows and aspens. The surrounding pine forest was not dense, and the heat it produced in burning did no damage to the scattered beaver houses.

From the top of a granite crag I surveyed the green scene of life and the surrounding sweep of desolation. Here and there a sodden log smouldered in the ashen distance and supported a tower of smoke in the still air. A few miles to the east, among the scattered trees of a rocky summit, the fire was burning itself out; to the west the sun was sinking behind crags and snow; near by, on a blackened limb, a south-bound robin chattered volubly but hopelessly.

While I was listening, thinking, and watching, a mountain lion appeared and leaped lightly upon a block of granite. He was on my right, about one hundred feet away and about an equal distance from the shore of the nearest pond. He was interested in the approach of something. With a nervous switching of his tail he peered eagerly forward over the crown of the ridge just before him, and then crouched tensely and expectantly upon his rock.

A pine tree that had escaped the fire screened the place toward which the lion looked and where something evidently was approaching. While I was trying to discover what it could be, a coyote trotted into view. Without catching sight of the near-by lion, he suddenly stopped and fixed his gaze upon the point that so interested the crouching beast. The mystery was solved when thirty or forty beavers came hurrying into view. They had come from the ruined Moraine Colony.

I thought to myself that the coyote, stuffed as he must be with the seared flesh of fire-roasted victims, would not attack them; but a lion wants a fresh kill for every meal, and so I watched the movements of the latter. He adjusted his feet a trifle and made ready to spring. The beavers were getting close; but just as I was about to shout to frighten him, the coyote leaped among them and began killing.

In the excitement of getting off the crag I narrowly escaped breaking my neck. Once on the ground, I ran for the coyote, shouting wildly to frighten him off; but he was so intent upon killing that a violent kick in the ribs first made him aware of my presence. In anger and excitement he leaped at me with ugly teeth as he fled. The lion had disappeared, and by this time the beavers in the front ranks were jumping into the pond, while the others were awkwardly speeding down the slope. The coyote had killed three. If beavers have a language, surely that night the refugees related to their hospitable neighbors some thrilling experiences.

The next morning I returned to the Moraine Colony over the route followed by the refugees. Leaving their fire-ruined homes, they had followed the stream that issued from their ponds. In places the channel was so clogged with fire wreckage that they had followed alongside the water rather than in it, as is their wont. At one place they had hurriedly taken refuge in the stream. Coyote tracks in the scattered ashes explained this. But after going a short distance they had climbed from the water and again traveled the ashy earth.

Beavers commonly follow water routes, but in times of emergency or in moments of audacity they will journey overland. To have followed this stream down to its first tributary, then up this to where the colony in which they found refuge was situated, would have required four miles of travel. Overland it was less than a mile. After following the stream for some distance, at just the right place they turned off, left the stream, and dared the overland dangers. How did they know the situation of the colony in the willows, or that it had escaped fire, and how could they have known the shortest, best way to it?

The morning after the arrival of the refugees, work was begun on two new houses and a dam, which was about sixty feet in length and built across a grassy open. Green cuttings of willow, aspen, and alder were used in its construction. Not a single stone or handful of mud was used. When completed it appeared like a windrow of freshly raked shrubs. It was almost straight, but sagged a trifle downstream. Though the water filtered freely through, it flooded the flat above. As the two new houses could not shelter all the refugees, it is probable that some of them were sheltered in bank tunnels, while room for others may have been found in the old houses.

That winter the colony was raided by some trappers; more than one hundred pelts were secured, and the colony was left in ruins and almost depopulated.

The Moraine Colony site was deserted for a long time. Eight years after the fire I returned to examine it. The willow growth about the ruins was almost as thrifty as when the fire came. A growth of aspen taller than one's head clung to the old shore-lines, while a close seedling growth of lodge-pole pine throve in the ashes of the old forest. One low mound, merry with bloom-ing columbine, was the only house ruin to be seen.

The ponds were empty and every dam was broken. The stream, in rushing unobstructed through the ruins, had eroded deeply. This erosion revealed the records of ages, and showed that the old main dam had been built on the top of an older dam and a sediment-filled pond. The second dam was on top of an older one still. In the sediment of the oldest—the bottom pond—I found a spearhead, two charred logs, and the skull of a buffalo. Colonies of beaver, as well as those of men, are often found upon sites that have a tragic history. Beavers, with Omar, might say,—

When you and I behind the veil are past,
Oh but the long long while the world shall last.

The next summer, 1893, the Moraine site was resettled. During the first season the colonists spent their time repairing dams and were content to live in holes. In autumn they gathered no harvest, and no trace of them could be found after the snow; so it is likely that they had returned to winter in the colony whence they had come. But early in the next spring there were reinforced numbers of them at work establishing a permanent settlement. Three dams were repaired, and in the autumn many of the golden leaves that fell found lodgment in the fresh plaster of two new houses.

In the new Moraine Colony one of the houses was torn to pieces by some animal, probably a bear. This was before Thanksgiving. About mid-winter a prospector left his tunnel a few miles away, came to the colony and dynamited a house, and "got seven of them." Next year two houses were built on the ruins of the two just fallen. That year's harvest-home was broken by deadly attacks of enemies. In gathering the harvest the beavers showed a preference for some aspens that were growing in a moist place about one hundred feet from the water. Whether it was the size of these or their peculiar flavor that determined their election in preference to nearer ones, I could not determine. One day, while several beavers were cutting here, they were surprised by a mountain lion which leaped upon and killed one of the harvesters. The next day the lion surprised and killed another. Two or three days later a coyote killed one on the same blood-stained spot, and then overtook and killed two others as they fled for the water. I could not see these deadly attacks from the boulder-pile, but in each case the sight of flying beavers sent me rushing upon the scene, where I beheld the cause of their desperate retreat. But despite dangers they persisted until the last of these aspens was harvested. During the winter the bark was eaten from these, and the next season their clean wood was used in the walls of a new house.

One autumn I had the pleasure of seeing some immigrants pass me *en route* for a new home in the Moraine Colony. Of course they may have been only visitors, or have come temporarily to assist in the harvesting; but I like to think of them as immigrants, and a number of things testified that immigrants they were. One evening I had been lying on a boulder by the stream below the colony, waiting for a gift from the gods. It came. Out of the water within ten feet of me scrambled the most patriarchal, as well as the largest, beaver that I have ever seen. I wanted to take off my hat to him, I wanted to ask him to tell me the story of his life, but from long habit I simply lay still and watched and thought in silence. He was making a portage round a cascade. As he scrambled up over the rocks, I noticed that he had but two fingers on his right hand. He was followed, in single file, by four others; one of these was minus a finger on the left hand. The next morning I read that five immigrants had arrived in the Moraine Colony. They had registered their footprints in the muddy margin of the lower pond. Had an agent been sent to invite these colonists, or had they come out of their own adventurous spirit? The day following their arrival I trailed them backward in the hope of learning whence they came and why they had moved. They had traveled in the water most of the time; but in places they had come out on the bank to go round a waterfall or to avoid an obstruction. Here and there I saw their tracks in the mud and traced them to a beaver settlement in which the houses and dams had been recently wrecked. A nearby rancher told me that he had been "making it hot" for all beavers in his meadow. During the next two years I occasionally saw this patriarchal beaver or his tracks thereabout.

It is the custom among old male beavers to idle away two or three months of each summer in exploring the neighboring brooks and streams, but they never fail to return in time for autumn activities. It thus becomes plain how, when an old colony needs to move, some one in it knows where to go and the route to follow.

The Moraine colonists gathered an unusually large harvest during the autumn of 1909. Seven hundred and thirty-two sapling aspens and several hundred willows were massed in the main pond by the largest house. This pile, which was mostly below the water-line, was three feet deep and one hundred and twenty-four feet in circumference. Would a new house be built this fall? This unusually large harvest plainly told that either children or immigrants had increased the population of the colony. Of course, a hard winter may also have been expected.

No; they were not to build a new house, but the old house by the harvest pile was to be enlarged. One day, just as the evening shadow of Long's Peak had covered the pond, I peeped over a log on top of the dam to watch the work. The house was only forty feet distant. Not a ripple stirred among the inverted peaks and pines in the clear, shadow-enameled pond. A lone beaver rose quietly in the scene from the water near the house.

Swimming noiselessly, he made a circuit of the pond. Then for a time, and without any apparent purpose, he swam back and forth over a short, straight course; he moved leisurely, and occasionally made a shallow, quiet dive. He did not appear to be watching anything in particular or to have anything special on his mind. Yet his eyes may have been scouting for enemies and his mind may have been full of house plans. Finally he dived deeply, and the next I saw of him he was climbing up the side of the house addition with a pawful of mud.

By this time a number of beavers were swimming in the pond after the manner of the first one. Presently all began to work. The addition already stood more than two feet above the waterline. The top of this was crescent-shaped and was about seven feet long and half as wide. It was made mostly of mud, which was plentifully reinforced with willow cuttings and aspen sticks. For a time all the workers busied themselves in carrying mud and roots from the bottom of the pond and placing these on the slowly rising addition. Eleven were working at one time. By and by three swam ashore, each in a different direction and each a few seconds apart. After a minute or two they returned from the shore, each carrying or trailing a long willow. These were dragged to the top of the addition, laid down, and trampled in the mud. Meantime the mud-carriers kept steadily at their work; again willows were brought, but this time four beavers went, and, as before, each was independent of the others. I did not see how this work could go on without some one bossing the thing, but I failed to detect any beaver acting as overseer. While there was general coöperation, each acted independently most of the time and sometimes was apparently oblivious of the others. These beavers simply worked, slowly, silently, and steadily; and they were still working away methodically and with dignified deliberation when darkness hid them.

Beaver Pioneers

I often wish that an old beaver neighbor of mine would write the story of his life. Most of the time for eighteen years his mud hut was among the lilies of Lily Lake, Estes Park, Colorado. He lived through many wilderness dangers, escaped the strategy of trappers, and survived the dangerous changes that come in with the home-builder. His life was long, stirring, and adventurous. If, in the first chapter of his life-story, he could record some of the strong, thrilling experiences which his ancestors must have related to him, his book would be all the better.

"Flat-top," my beaver neighbor, was a pioneer and a colony-founder. It is probable that he was born in a beaver house on Wind River, and it is likely that he spent the first six years of his life along this crag and aspen bordered mountain stream. The first time I saw him he was leading an emigrant party out of this stream's steep-walled upper course. He and his party settled, or rather resettled, Lily Lake.

Flat-top was the name I gave him because of his straight back. In most beaver the shoulders swell plumply above the back line after the outline of the grizzly bear. Along with this peculiarity, which enabled me to be certain of his presence, was another. This was his habit of gnawing trees off close to the earth when he felled them. The finding of an occasional low-cut stump assured me of his presence during the periods I failed to see him.

The first beaver settlement in the lake appears to have been made in the early seventies, long before Flat-top was born, by a pair of beaver who were full of the pioneer spirit. These settlers apparently were the sole survivors of a large party of emigrants who tried to climb the rugged mountains to the lake, having been driven from their homes by encroaching human settlers. After a long, tedious journey, full of hardships and dangers, they climbed into the lake that was to them, for years, a real promised land.

Driven from Willow Creek, they set off up-stream in search of a new home, probably without knowing of Lily Lake, which was five miles distant and two thousand feet up a steep, rocky mountain. These pilgrims had traveled only a little way up-stream when they found themselves the greater portion of the time out of water. This was only a brook at its best and in most places it was such a shallow, tiny streamlet that in it they could not dive beyond the reach of enemies or even completely cool themselves. In stretches the water spread thinly over a grassy flat or a smooth granite slope; again it was lost in the gravel; or, murmuring faintly, pursued its way out of sight beneath piles of boulder,—marbles shaped by the Ice King. Much of the time they were compelled to travel upon land exposed to their enemies. Water-holes in which they could escape and rest were long distances apart.

This plodding, perilous five-mile journey which the beaver made up the mountain to the lake would be easy and care-free for an animal with the physical make-up of a bear or a wolf, but with the beaver it is not surprising that only two of the emigrants survived this supreme trial and escaped the numerous dangers of the pilgrimage.

Lily Lake is a shallow, rounded lily garden that reposes in a glacier meadow at an altitude of nine thousand feet; its golden pond-lilies often dance among reflected snowy peaks, while over it the granite crags of Lily Mountain rise several hundred feet. A few low, sedgy, grassy acres border half the shore, while along the remainder are crags, aspen groves, willow-clumps, and scattered pines. Its waters come from springs in its western margin and overflow across a low grassy bar on its curving eastern shore.

It was autumn when these beaver pioneers came to Lily Lake's primitive and poetic border. The large green leaves of the pond-lily rested upon the water, while from the long green stems had fallen the sculptured petals of gold; the willows were wearing leaves of brown and bronze, and the yellow tremulous robes of the aspens glowed in the golden sunlight.

These fur-clad pioneers made a dugout—a hole in the bank—and busily gathered winter food until stopped by frost and snow; then, almost care-free, they dozed away the windy winter days while the lake was held in waveless ice beneath the drifting snow.

The next summer a house was built in the lily pads near the shore. Here a number of children were born during the few tranquil years that followed. These times came to an end one bright midsummer day. Lord Dunraven had a ditch cut in the outlet rim of the lake with the intention of draining it that his fish ponds, several miles below in his Estes Park game-preserve, might have water. A drouth had prevailed for several months, and a new water-supply must be had or the fish ponds would go dry. The water poured forth through the ditch, and the days of the colony appeared to be numbered.

A beaver must have water for safety and for the ease of movement of himself and his supplies. He is skillful in maintaining a dam and in regulating the water-supply; these two things require much of his time. In Lily Lake the dam and the water question had been so nicely controlled by nature that with these the colonists had had nothing to do. However, they still knew how to build dams, and water-control had not become a lost art. The morning after the completion of the drainage ditch, a man was sent up to the Lake to find out why the water was not coming down. A short time after the ditch-diggers had departed, the lowering water had aroused the beaver, who had promptly placed a dam in the mouth of the ditch. The man removed this dam and went down to report. The beaver speedily replaced it. Thrice did the man return and destroy their dam, but thrice did the beaver promptly restore it.

The dam-material used in obstructing the ditch consisted chiefly of the peeled sticks from which the beaver had eaten the bark in winter; along with these were mud and grass. The fourth time that the ditch guard returned, he threw away all the material in the dam and then set some steel traps in the water by the mouth of the ditch. The first two beaver who came to reblockade the ditch were caught in these traps and drowned while struggling to free themselves. Other beaver heroically continued the work that these had begun. The cutting down of saplings and the procuring of new material made their work slow, very slow, in the face of the swiftly escaping water; when the ditch was at last obstructed, a part of the material which formed this new dam consisted of the traps and the dead bodies of the two beaver who had bravely perished while trying to save the colony.

The ditch guard returned with a rifle, and came to stay. The first beaver to come within range was shot. The guard again removed the dam, made a fire about twenty feet from the ditch, and planned to spend the night on guard, rifle in hand. Toward morning he became drowsy, sat down by the fire, heard the air in the pines at his back, watched the star-sown water, and finally fell asleep. While he thus slept, with his rifle across his lap, the beaver placed another—their last—obstruction before the out-rushing water.

On awakening, the sleeper tore out the dam and stood guard over the ditch. All that afternoon a number of beaver hovered about, watching for an opportunity to stop the water again. Their opportunity never came, and three who ventured too near the rifleman gave up their lives,—reddening the clear water with their lifeblood in vain.

The lake was drained, and the colonists abandoned their homes. One night, a few days after the final attempt to block-ade the ditch, an unwilling beaver emigrant party climbed silently out of the uncovered entrance of their house and made their way quietly, slowly, beneath the stars, across the mountain, descending thence to Wind River, where they founded a new colony.

Winter came to the old lake-bed, and the lily roots froze and died. The beaver houses rapidly crumbled, and for a few years the picturesque ruins of the beaver settlement, like many a settlement abandoned by man, stood pathetically in the midst of wilderness desolation. Slowly the water rose to its old level in the lake, as the outlet ditch gradually filled with swelling turf and drifting sticks and trash. Then the lilies came back with rafts of green and boats of gold to enliven this lakelet of repose.

One autumn morning, while returning to my cabin after a night near the stars on Lily Mountain, I paused on a crag to watch the changing morning light down Wind River Cañon. While thus engaged, Flat-top and a party of colonists came along a game trail within a few yards of me, evidently bound for the lake, which was only a short distance away. I silently followed them. This was my introduction to Flat-top.

On the shore these seven adventurers paused for a moment to behold the scene, or, possibly, to dream of empire; then they waddled out into the water and made a circuit of the lake. Probably Flat-top had been here before as an explorer. Within two hours after their arrival these colonists began building for a permanent settlement.

It was late to begin winter preparation. The clean, white aspens had shed their golden leaves and stood waiting to welcome the snows. This lateness may account for the makeshift of a hut which the colonists constructed. This was built against the bank with only one edge in the water; the entrance to it was a twelve-foot tunnel that ended in the lake-bottom where the water was two feet deep.

The beaver were collecting green aspen and willow cuttings in the water by the tunnel-entrance when the lake froze over. Fortunately for the colonists, with their scanty supply of food, the winter was a short one, and by the first of April they were able to dig the roots of water plants along the shallow shore where the ice had melted. One settler succumbed during the winter, but by summer the others had commenced work on a permanent house, which was completed before harvest time.

I had a few glimpses of the harvest-gathering and occasionally saw Flat-top. One evening, while watching the harvesters, I saw three new workers. Three emigrants—from somewhere—had joined the colonists. A total of fifteen, five of whom were youngsters, went into winter quarters,—a large, comfortable house, a goodly supply of food, and a location off the track of trappers. The cold, white days promised only peace. But an unpreventable catastrophe came before the winter was half over.

One night a high wind began to bombard the ice-bound lake with heavy blasts. The force of these intermittent gales suggested that the wind was trying to dislodge the entire ice covering of the lake; and indeed that very nearly happened.

Before the crisis came, I went to the lake, believing it to be the best place to witness the full effects of this most enthusiastic wind. Across the ice the gale boomed, roaring in the restraining forest beyond. These broken rushes set the ice vibrating and the water rolling and swelling beneath. During one of these blasts the swelling water burst the ice explosively upward in a fractured ridge entirely across the lake. In the next few minutes the entire surface broke up, and the wind began to drive the cakes upon the windward shore.

A large flatboat cake was swept against the beaver house, sheared it off on the water-line, and overturned the conelike top into the lake. The beaver took refuge in the tunnel which ran beneath the lake-bottom. This proved a deathtrap, for its shore end above the water-line was clogged with ice. As the lake had swelled and surged beneath the beating of the wind, the water had gushed out and streamed back into the tunnel again and again, until ice formed in and closed the outer entrance. Against this ice four beaver were smothered or drowned. I surmised the tragedy but was helpless to prevent it. Meanwhile the others doubled back and took refuge upon the ruined stump of their home. From a clump of near-by pines I watched this wild drama.

Less than half an hour after the house was wrecked, these indomitable animals began to rebuild it. Lashed by icy waves, beaten by the wind, half-coated with ice, these home-loving people strove to rebuild their home. Mud was brought from the bottom of the pond and piled upon the shattered foundation. This mud set—froze—almost instantly on being placed. They worked desperately, and from time to time I caught sight of Flat-top. Toward evening it appeared possible that the house might be restored, but, just as darkness was falling, a roaring gust struck the lake and a great swell threw the new part into the water.

The colonists gave up the hopeless task and that night fled down the mountain. Two were killed before they had gone a quarter of a mile. Along the trail were three other red smears upon the crusted snow; each told of a death and a feast upon the wintry mountain-side among the solemn pines. Flat-top with five others finally gained the Wind River Colony, from which he had led his emigrants two years before.

One day the following June, while examining the lilies in the lake, I came upon a low, freshly cut stump;—Flat-top had returned. A number of colonists were with him and all had come to stay.

All sizable aspen that were within a few yards of the water had been cut away, but at the southwest corner of the lake, about sixty feet from the shore, was an aspen thicket. Flat-top and his fellow workers cut a canal from the lake through a low, sedgy flat into this aspen thicket. The canal was straight, about fourteen inches deep and twenty-six inches wide. Its walls were smoothly cut and most of the excavated material was piled evenly on one side of the canal and about eight inches from it. It had an angular, mechanical appearance, and suggested the work not of a beaver, but of man, and that of a very careful man too.

Down this canal the colonists floated the timbers used in building their two houses. On the completion of the houses, the home-builders returned to the grove and procured winter supplies. In most cases the small aspen were floated to the pile between the houses with an adept skill, without severing the trunk or cutting off a single limb.

The colonists had a few years of ideal beaver life. One summer I came upon Flat-top and a few other beaver by the brook that drains the lake, and at a point about half a mile below its outlet. It was along this brook that Flat-top's intrepid ancestors had painfully climbed to establish the first settlement in the lake. Commonly each summer several beaver descended the mountain and spent a few weeks of vacation along Wind River. Invariably they returned before the end of August; and harvest-gathering usually began shortly after their return.

Year after year the regularly equipped trappers passed the lake without stopping. The houses did not show distinctly from the trail, and the trappers did not know that there were beaver in this place. But this peaceful, populous lake was not forever to remain immune from the wiles of man, and one day it was planted with that barbaric, cruel torture-machine, the steel trap.

A cultured consumptive, who had returned temporarily to nature, was boarding at a ranch house several miles away. While out riding he discovered the colony and at once resolved to depopulate it. The beaver ignored his array of traps until he enlisted the services of an old trapper, whose skill sent most of the beaver to their death before the sepia-colored catkins appeared upon the aspens. Flat-top escaped.

The ruinous raid of the trappers was followed by a dry season, and during the drouth a rancher down the mountain came up prospecting for water. He cut a ditch in the outlet ridge of the lake, and out gushed the water. He started home in a cheerful mood, but long before he arrived, the "first engineers" had blocked his ditch. During the next few days and nights the rancher made many trips from his house to the lake, and when he was not in the ditch, swearing, and opening it, the beaver were in it shutting off the water.

From time to time I dropped around to see the struggle, one day coming upon the scene while the beaver were completing a blockade. For a time the beaver hesitated; then they partly resumed operations and carried material to the spot, but without first showing themselves entirely above water. When it appeared that they must have enough to complete the blockade, I advanced a trifle nearer so as to have a good view while they placed the accumulated material. For a time not a beaver showed himself. By and by an aged one climbed out of the water, pretending not to notice me, and deliberately piled things right and left until he had completed the ditch-damming to his satisfaction. This act was audacious and truly heroic. The hero was Flat-top.

In this contest with the rancher, the beaver persisted and worked so effectively that they at last won and saved their homes, in the face of what appeared to be an unconquerable opposition.

A little while after this incident, a home-seeker came along, and, liking the place, built a cabin in a clump of pines close to the southern shore. Though he was a gray old man without a family, I imagined he would exterminate the beaver and looked upon him with a lack of neighborly feeling.

Several months went by, and I had failed to call upon him, but one day while passing I heard him order a trapper off the place.

This order was accompanied by so strong a declaration of principles—together with a humane plea for the life of every wild animal—that I made haste to call that evening.

One afternoon in a pine thicket, close to the lake-shore, I came upon two gray wolves, both devouring beaver, which had met their death while harvesting aspens for winter. The following spring I had a more delightful glimpse of life in the wilds. Within fifty feet of the lakeshore stood a large pine stump that rose about ten feet from the ground. Feeling that I should escape notice if I sat still on the top, I climbed up. Though it was mid-forenoon, the beaver came out of the lake and wandered about nibbling here and there at the few green plants of early spring. They did not detect me. They actually appeared to enjoy themselves. This is the only time that I ever saw a beaver fully at ease and apparently happy on land. In the midst of their pleasures, a flock of mountain sheep came along and mingled with them. The beaver paused and stared; now and then a sheep would momentarily stare at a beaver, or sniff the air as though he did not quite like beaver odor. In less than a minute the flock moved on, but just as they started, a beaver passed in front of the lead ram, who made a playful pretense of a butt at him; to this the beaver paid not the slightest heed.

During the homesteader's second summer he concluded to raise the outlet ridge, deepen the water, and make a fish pond of the lake. Being poor, he worked alone with wheelbarrow and shovel. The beaver evidently watched the progress of the work, and each morning their fresh footprints showed in the newly piled earth. Shortly before the dam was completed, the homesteader was called away for a few days, and on his return he was astonished to find that the beaver had completed his dam! The part made by the beaver suited him as to height and length, so he covered it over with earth and allowed it to remain. His work in turn was inspected and apparently approved by the beaver.

How long does a beaver live? Trappers say from fifteen to fifty years. I had glimpses of Flat-top through eighteen years, and he must have been not less than four years of age when I first met him. This would make his age twenty-two years; but he may have been six years of age—he looked it—the morning he first led emigrants into Lily Lake; and he may have lived a few years after I saw him last. But only the chosen few among the beaver can succeed in living as long as Flat-top. The last time I saw him was the day he dared me and blockaded the drain ditch and stopped the outrushing water.

Flat-top has vanished, and the kind old homesteader has gone to his last long sleep; but the lake still remains, and still there stands a beaver house among the pond-lilies.

Going to the Top

The seven football-players who engaged me to guide them to the top of Long's Peak did not reveal their identity until we were on the way. Long's Peak, high, massive, and wildly rugged, is the king of the Rocky Mountains, and there were five thousand feet of altitude and seven steeply inclined miles between our starting-point and the granite-piled summit.

We set out on foot. The climbers yelled, threw stones, and wrestled. They were so occupied with themselves during the first mile that I managed to keep them from running over me. Presently they discovered me and gave a cheer, and then proceeded energetically with the evident intention of killing me off.

It was fortunate for me that the experience of more than a hundred guiding trips to the summit was a part of my equipment. In addition to the valuable lessons that had been dearly learned in guiding, I had made dozens of trips to the summit before offering my services as guide. I had made climbs in every kind of weather to familiarize myself thoroughly with the way to the top. These trips—always alone—were first made on clear days, then on stormy ones, and finally at night. When I was satisfied that I could find the trail under the worst conditions, endurance tests were made. One of these consisted in making a quick round trip, then, after only a few minutes' rest, shouldering thirty or forty pounds of supplies and hastening to the rescue of an imaginary climber ill on the summit.

Enos Mills, Longs Peak Guide.
Courtesy Estes Park Museum.

Besides two seasons of this preliminary experience, the rocks, glacial records, birds, trees, and flowers along the trail were studied, other peaks climbed, and books concerning mountain-climbing diligently read. But long before my two hundred and fifty-seven guiding trips were completed, I found myself ignorant of one of the most important factors in guiding, and perhaps, too, in life,—and that is human nature.

Several climbs had been made simply to learn the swiftest pace I could maintain from bottom to summit without a rest. Thus ably coached by experience, I steadied to the work when my noisy football-players started to run away from me. Each player in turn briefly set a hot pace, and in a short time they were ahead of me. Even though they guyed me unmercifully, I refused to be hurried and held to the swiftest pace that I knew could be maintained. Two hours raised us through thirty-five hundred feet of altitude and advanced us five miles. We were above the timber-line, and, though some distance behind the boys, I could tell they were tiring. Presently the guide was again in the lead!

By-and-by one of the boys began to pale, and presently he turned green around the mouth. He tried desperately to bluff it off, but ill he was. In a few minutes he had to quit, overcome with nausea. A moment later another long-haired brave tumbled down. On the others went, but three more were dropped along the trail, and only two of those husky, well-trained athletes reached the summit! That evening, when those sad fellows saw me start off to guide another party up by moonlight, they concluded that I must be a wonder; but as a matter of fact, being an invalid, I had learned something of conservation. This experience fixed in my mind the importance of climbing slowly.

Hurriedly climbing a rugged peak is a dangerous pastime. Trail hurry frequently produces sickness. A brief dash may keep a climber agitated for an hour. During this time he will waste his strength doing things the wrong way,—often, too, annoying or endangering the others.

Finding a way to get climbers to go slowly was a problem that took me time to solve. Early in the guiding game the solution was made impossible by trying to guide large parties and by not knowing human nature. Once accomplished, slow going on the trail noticeably decreased the cases of mountain-sickness, greatly reduced the number of quarrels, and enabled almost all starters to gain the height desired. Slow climbing added pleasure to the trip and enabled every one to return in good form and with splendid pictures in his mind.

To keep the party together,—for the tendency of climbers is to scatter, some traveling rapidly and others slowly,—it became my practice to stop occasionally and tell a story, comment on a bit of scenery, or relate an incident that had occurred near by. As I spoke in a low tone, the climbers ahead shouting "Hurry up!" and the ones behind calling "Wait!" could not hear me. This method kept down friction and usually held the party together. With a large party, however, confusion sometimes arose despite my efforts to anticipate it.

Hoping to get valuable climbing suggestions, I told my experiences one day to a gentleman who I thought might help me; but he simply repeated the remark of Trampas that in every party of six there is a fool! It is almost impossible for a numerous party, even though every one of them may be well-meaning, to travel along a steep trail without friction.

My most unpleasant climb was with a fateful six,—three loving young couples. Two college professors about to be married formed one of the couples. He, the son of wealthy parents, had been sent West to mend his health and manners; he met a young school-ma'am who reformed him. They attended the same college and became professors in a State school. They were to be married at the end of this outing; but on this climb they quarreled. Each married another! Sweethearts for years was the story of the second couple. They, too, quarreled on the trail, but made up again. The story of the third couple is interestingly complicated. He was rich, young, and impetuous; she, handsome and musical. For years she had received his ardent attentions indifferently. As we approached the top of the peak, he became extremely impatient with her. As though to make confusion worse confounded, after years of indifference the young lady became infatuated with her escort. He tried to avoid her, but she feigned a sprained ankle to insure his comforting closeness. They are both single to this day. Meantime the six had a general row among themselves, and at the close of it united to "roast" me!

Whether imp or altitude was to blame for this deviltry matters not; the guide had to suffer for it.

Early in guiding I conceived it to be my duty to start for the top with anyone who cared to try it, and I felt bound also to get the climber to the top if possible. This was poor theory and bad practice. After a few exasperating and exhausting experiences I learned the folly of dragging people to the top who were likely to be too weak to come back. One day a party of four went up. Not one of them was accustomed to walking, and all had apparently lived to eat. After eight hard hours we reached the summit, where all four collapsed. A storm came on, and we were just leaving the top when daylight faded. It rained at intervals all night long, with the temperature a trifle below freezing. We would climb down a short distance, then huddle shivering together for a while. At times everyone was suffering from nausea. We got down to timber-line at one o'clock in the morning. Here a rest by a rousing camp-fire enabled all to go on down. We arrived at the starting place just twenty-four hours after we had left it!

Mountain-climbing is not a good line of activity for an invalid or for one who shies at the edge of a precipice, or for anyone, either, who worries over the possible fate of his family while he is on a narrow ledge. Altitude, the great bugbear to many, is the scapegoat for a multitude of sins. "Feeling the altitude" would often be more correctly expressed as feeling the effects of high living! The ill effects of altitude are mostly imaginary. True, climbing high into a brighter, finer atmosphere diminishes the elastic clasp—the pressure of the air—and causes physiological changes. These usually are beneficial. Climbers who become ill through mountain-climbing would also become ill in hill-climbing. In the overwhelming number of cases the lowland visitor is permanently benefited by a visit to the mountains and especially by a climb in the heights.

Mountain-sickness, with its nausea, first comes to those who are bilious, or to those who are hurrying or exerting themselves more than usual. A slight stomach disorder invites this nausea, and on the heights those who have not been careful of diet, or those who celebrated the climb the evening before it was made, are pretty certain to find out just how mountain-sickness afflicts. Altitude has, I think, but little to do with bringing on so-called mountain-sickness. It is almost identical with sea-sickness, and just as quickly forces the conclusion that life is not worth living! Usually a hot drink, rest, and warmth will cure it in a short time.

Clarence King in his "Mountaineering in the Sierra Nevada" says concerning the effects of altitude, "All the while I made my instrumental observations the fascination of the view so held me that I felt no surprise at seeing water boiling over our little fag-got blaze at a temperature of one hundred and ninety-two de-grees F., nor in observing the barometrical column stand at 17.99 inches; and it was not till a week or so after that I realized we had felt none of the conventional sensations of nausea, headache, and I don't know what all, that people are supposed to suffer at extreme altitudes; but these things go with guides and porters, I believe."

Altitude commonly stimulates the slow tongue, and in the heights many reserved people become talkative and even confid-ing. This, along with the natural sociability of such a trip, the scenery, and the many excitements, usually ripens acquaintances with amazing rapidity. Lifelong friendships have commenced on the trail, and many a lovely romance, too. One day two young people met for the first time in one of my climbing parties. Thirty days afterward they were married, and they have lived happily to date.

In one climb a chaperon gave out and promptly demanded that two young sweethearts turn back. As we moved on without the chaperon, she called down upon my head the curses of all the gods at once! In order to save the day it is sometimes neces-sary for the guide to become an autocrat. Occasionally a climber is not susceptible to suggestion and will obey only the impera-tive mood. A guide is sometimes compelled to stop rock-rolling, or to say "No!" to a plucky but sick climber who is eager to go on. A terrible tongue-lashing came to me one day from a young lady because of my refusal to go farther after she had fainted. She went forward alone for half an hour while I sat watching from a commanding crag. Presently she came to a narrow un-banistered ledge that overhung eternity. She at once retreated and came back with a smile, saying that the spot where she had turned back would enable any one to comprehend the laws of falling bodies.

Occasionally a climber became hysterical and I had my hands full keeping the afflicted within bounds. Mountain ledges are not good places for hysterical performances. One day, when a reverend gentleman and his two daughters were nearing the top, the young ladies and myself came out upon the Narrows a few lengths ahead of their father. The ladies were almost exhausted and were climbing on sheer nerve. The stupendous view revealed from the Narrows overwhelmed them, and both became hysterical at once. It was no place for ceremony; and as it was rather cramped for two performances at once, I pushed the feet from beneath one young lady, tripped the other on top of her, — and sat down on both! They struggled, laughed, and cried, and had just calmed down when the father came round the rocks upon us. His face vividly and swiftly expressed three or four kinds of anger before he grasped the situation. Fearing that he might jump on me in turn, or that he might "get them" too, I watched him without a word. Finally he took in the entire situation, and said with a smile, "Well, I don't know whether it's my move or not!"

Twice, while guiding, I broke my lifelong rule never to take a tip. One tip had with it a surprise to redeem the taking. It came from the gentleman who had organized the party. On the way up he begged leave to set the pace and to lead the party to the top. He appeared sensible, but I made a blunder by consenting to the arrangement, for his pace was too rapid, and at Keyhole he was attacked by nausea. He pluckily insisted that we go on to the summit and leave him behind. It was five hours before we returned to him. For two hours he had lain helpless in a cold rain and was badly chilled. He was so limp and loose-jointed that it was difficult to carry him across the moraine called Boulderfield. At the Inn the following morning he was completely restored. I was still so exhausted from getting him down that when he insisted that he be allowed to give me a tip in addition to the guiding fee I agreed to accept it. The instant I had consented it occurred to me that a tip from a millionaire for the saving of his life would be worth while. I was startled when, with a satisfied expression, he handed me twenty-five cents!

No. 2540. FIRST NARROWS BEYOND KEYHOLE.   F.P. BAKER Photo
                                                    GREELEY
                                                      Col.

Climbers on Longs Peak, ca. 1900.
Courtesy Estes Park Museum.

Early one season, before the ice had melted, one of my five climbers met with an accident in one of the most dangerous places along the way. We were descending, and I was in front, watching each one closely as he crossed a narrow and extremely steep tongue of ice. The gentleman who brought up the rear was a good climber when not talking; but this time he was chattering away and failed to notice me when I signaled him for silence while each climber, in turn, carefully crossed the steep ice in the footholds chopped for that purpose. Still talking, he stepped out on the ice without looking and missed the foothold! Both feet shot from beneath him, and down the smooth, deadly steep he plunged.

Early in guiding I had considered the dangerous places and planned just where to stand while the climbers passed them and just what to do in case of accident. When an accident actually occurred, it was a simple matter to go through a ticklish grandstand performance that had been practiced dozens of times, and which for years I have been ready to put into effect. The instant he slipped, I made a quick leap for a point of rock that barely pierced the steep ice-tongue. This ice was steeper than half pitch. He shot down, clawing desperately and helplessly, with momentum sufficient to knock over half a dozen men. There was just time to grab him by the coat as he shot by the rock. Bracing with all my might to hold him for a fraction of a second so as to divert him and point him at an angle off the ice, I jumped upward as the violent jerk came. We went off as it were on a tangent, and landed in a heap upon the stones, several yards below the spot from which I had leaped to the rescue. His life was saved.

The last season of my guiding career was a full one. Thirty-two ascents were made during the thirty-one days of August. Half a dozen of these were by moonlight. In addition to these climbs a daily round trip was made to Estes Park, eight miles distant and fifteen hundred feet down the mountain. These Estes Park trips commonly were made on horseback, though a few were by wagon. My busiest day was crowded with two wagon trips and one horseback trip to Estes Park, then a moonlight climb to the summit. In a sixty-hour stretch I did not have any sleep or take any food. Being in condition for the work and doing it easily, I was in excellent shape when the guiding ended.

The happiest one of my two hundred and fifty-seven guiding experiences on the rugged granite trail of this peak was with Harriet Peters, a little eight-year-old girl, the youngest child who has made the climb. She was alert and obedient, enjoyed the experience, and reached the top without a slip or a stumble, and with but little assistance from me. It was pleasant to be with her on the summit, listening to her comments and hearing her childlike questions. I have told the whole story of this climb in "Wild Life on the Rockies."

Thoughtfulness and deliberation are essentials of mountain-climbing. Climb slowly. Look before stepping. Ease down off boulders; a jump may jar or sprain. Enjoy the scenery and do most of your talking while at rest. Think of the fellow lower down. A careful diet and training beforehand will make the climb easier and far more enjoyable.

Tyndall has said that a few days of mountain-climbing will burn all the effete matter out of the system. In climbing, the stagnant blood is circulated and refined, the lungs are exercised, every cell is cleansed, and all parts are disinfected by the pure air. Climbing a high peak occasionally will not only postpone death but will give continuous intensity to the joy of living. Every one might well climb at least one high peak, and for those leaving high school or college, the post-graduate work of climbing a rugged peak might be a more informative experience or a more helpful test for living than any examination or the writing of a thesis.

Scenery, like music, is thought-compelling and gives one a rare combination of practical and poetical inspiration. Along with mountain-climbing, scenery shakes us free from ourselves and the world. From new grand heights one often has the strange feeling that he has looked upon these wondrous scenes before; and on the crest one realizes the full meaning of John Muir's exhortation to "climb the mountains and get their good tidings!"

The Grizzly Bear

One day in North Park, Colorado, I came on the carcass of a cow that wolves had recently killed. Knowing that bears were about, I climbed into the substantial top of a stocky pine near by, hoping that one would come to feast. A grizzly came at sundown.

The carcass lay in a grassy opening surrounded by willow-clumps, grassy spaces, and a sprinkling of low-growing, round-topped pines. When about one hundred feet from the carcass, the bear stopped. Standing erect, with his fore paws hanging loosely, he looked, listened, and carefully examined the air with his nose. As the air was not stirring, I felt that he had not, and probably would not, scent me in the treetop perch.

After scouting for a minute or two with all his keen senses, he dropped on all fours and slowly, without a sound, advanced toward the carcass. He circled as he advanced; and, when within thirty feet of the waiting feast, he redoubled his precautions against surprise and ambush. My scent by the carcass probably had nothing to do with these precautions. A grizzly is ever on guard and in places of possible ambush is extremely cautious. He is not a coward; but he does not propose to blunder into trouble.

Slipping cautiously to the edge of a thick willow-clump, he suddenly flung himself into it with a fearful roar, then instantly leaped out on the other side. Evidently he planned to start something if there was anything to start.

Standing fully erect, tense at every point, he waited a moment in ferocious attitude, ready to charge anything that might plunge from the willows; but nothing started. After a brief pause he charged, roaring, through another willow-clump. It was a satisfaction to know that the tree-limb on which I sat was substantial. That a grizzly bear cannot climb a tree is a fact in natural history which gave me immense satisfaction. Every willow-clump near the carcass was charged, with a roar.

Not finding an enemy, he at last went to the carcass. After feasting for a few minutes he rose and snarled. Then, sniffing along my trail a few yards, he stopped to mutter a few growling threats and returned to the feast.

After eating contentedly and to his satisfaction, he moved round the carcass, raking and scraping grass and trash on it. Then, pausing for a minute or two in apparently peaceful contemplation, he doubled back on the trail over which he had come and faded into the twilight.

Alertness and brain-power are characteristics of the grizzly bear. He is eternally vigilant. He has the genius for taking pains. He is watchful even in seclusion; and when he is traveling his amazingly developed senses appear never to rest, but are constantly on scout and sentinel duty,—except on rare occasions when he is temporarily hypnotized by curiosity. I believe his intelligence to be greater than that of the dog, the horse, or the elephant. Apparently he assumes that some one is ever stealthily in pursuit.

In repeatedly following the grizzly with photographic intentions I was almost invariably outwitted. On one occasion I followed one almost constantly for eight days and nights; and though many times I almost had him, yet I never succeeded. Now and then he climbed a rocky crag to look about or he doubled back a short distance on his trail to some point of vantage, where he rose on his hind legs, sniffed the air, looked and listened. At other times he turned at right angles to his general course, went a short distance to a point favorable for seeing, hearing, or smelling his possible pursuer, and there remained for a few minutes. If all seemed well, he commonly returned to his trail and again went forward.

Usually he traveled in the face of the wind; commonly he promptly changed his course if the wind changed. In crossing a grassy opening in the woods he sometimes went boldly across; but on the farther side, concealed by the trees, he waited to see whether a pursuer appeared across the opening. Sometimes he went round an opening to the right or to the left. Apparently there lay a plan behind his every move.

The third day he was well started diagonally down the wall of a cañon. I naturally concluded that he would on this course descend to the bottom and there continue down-stream. Instead of doing this, he stopped at a point about midway down for a long stay. Then from this place he pointed his nose up-stream and descended diagonally to the bottom of the cañon. At the bottom he again made an acute angle to ascend to the top of the opposite wall.

The last three days of this pursuit he knew that I was following him, but there seemed to be no change in his tactics. He simply moved a little more rapidly. Though well acquainted with grizzly habits, I was unable to anticipate his next important move, and he defeated every plan I put into operation.

For several years an outlaw or cattle-killing grizzly terrorized an extensive cattle-grazing section in the mountains of Utah. For months at a stretch he killed a cow or steer at least every other day. He would make a kill one day and on the next would appear across the mountains, forty or more miles away.

Organized expeditions, made up of from thirty to fifty men, with packs of dogs, pursued him day and night for a week or longer; but each time he escaped. Large rewards were offered for his capture. Old trappers and hunters came from afar, but after weeks of trial gave up the pursuit.

The grizzly has a well-developed bump of curiosity. This sometimes betrays him into forgetfulness. On a few occasions I have come on one—and twice one unwittingly came close to me—while he was intent on solving something that had awakened that curiosity.

Once, while watching a forest fire, I climbed a mountain to a point above the tree-line in order to reach a safe and commanding spot from which to view the flames on a near-by slope. At the summit I came upon a grizzly within a few yards of me. He was squatting on his haunches like a dog, and was intently watching the fire-fount below. A deep roar at one place, high-leaping flames at another, a vast smoke-cloud at another, each in turn caught his attention. None of his keen senses warned him of my presence, though I stood near him for two or three minutes. When I yelled at him he slowly turned his head and stared at me in a half-dazed manner. Then he angrily showed his teeth for a second or two, and finally—much to my relief—fled like a frightened rabbit.

On another occasion I saw a grizzly on the opposite side of a narrow cañon, with his fore paws on a boulder, watching with the greatest interest the actions of a fisherman on the bank of the stream below. Every cast of the fly was followed by the head of the bear. The pulling up of a trout caused him almost excited interest. For some minutes he concentrated all his faculties on the fisherman; but suddenly, with no apparent reason that I could discern, he came to his senses and broke away in a most frightened manner, apparently condemning himself for briefly relapsing into dullness.

Two pet grizzlies that I raised always showed marked curiosity. An unusual sound near by or a glimpse of some distant object brought them to tiptoe height, roused their complete attention, and held it until the mystery was solved.

The grizzly is not ferocious. On the contrary, he uses his wits to keep far away from man. He will not make a wanton attack. He will fight in self-defense; or if surprised, and thinking himself cornered, he at once becomes the aggressor. If a mother grizzly feels that her cubs are in danger, she will face any danger for their defense; but the grizzly does not fight unless he thinks a fight cannot be avoided.

He is a masterful fighter. He has strength, endurance, powerful jaws, deadly claws, courage, and brains. Before the white man and the repeating rifle came, he boldly wandered over his domain as absolute master; there was nothing to fear,—not a single aggressive foe existed. I doubt whether toward man the grizzly was ever ferociously aggressive.

That he has changed on account of contact with the white man and the repeating rifle there can be no doubt. Formerly the rightful monarch of the wilds through capability, he roamed freely about, indifferent as to where he went or whether he was seen. He feared no foe and knew no master. The bow and arrow, and the spear, he held in contempt; for the powerful repeating rifle he has a profound respect. He has been wise to adjust himself to this influential factor of environment or evolutionary force. He has thus become less inquisitive and aggressive, and more retiring and wary. He has learned to keep out of sight and out of man's way.

A grizzly acts so promptly in emergencies that he has often been misunderstood. He fights because he thinks he has to, not because he wants to.

On one occasion in Wyoming I was running down a mountain-side, leaping fallen fire-killed timber. In the midst of this I surprised a grizzly by landing within a few feet of him. He leaped to his feet and struck at me with sufficient force to have almost cut me in two had the blow landed. Then he instantly fled.

On other occasions I have seen grizzlies surprised, when, though not cornered, they thought they were and instantly commenced a fierce and effective fight. Dogs, horses, and men were charged in rapid succession and either knocked down or put to flight; yet in these fights he was not the aggressor. He does not belong to the criminal class.

Almost every one is interested in bears; children, the tenderfeet, and Westerners are always glad to have a good bear story. Countless thousands of bear stories have been written,—and generally written by people unacquainted with the character of grizzly bears. Most of these stories are founded on one or another of three fundamental errors. One of these is that the grizzly has a bad temper,—"as cross as a bear" is an exceedingly common expression; another is that bears are ferocious, watchful, and aggressive, always ready to make an attack or to do wanton killing; and the third is that it is almost impossible to kill him. After a desperate fight—in the story—the grizzly at last succumbs, but not, as a rule, until his body is numerously perforated or changed into a lead mine. As a matter of fact, a shot in the brain, in the upper part of the heart, or properly placed in the spine instantly ends the life of a grizzly. Most hunters when facing a grizzly do not shoot accurately.

One day I saw three men fire from twelve to sixteen shots at a small grizzly bear on a mountain-side only a short distance away. That evening these men sincerely asserted that he must have weighed at least a ton—when he probably did not weigh more than five hundred pounds—and that though they shot him full of lead, he refused to die. I doubt whether a single one of their shots hit the grizzly. Most of the shots went wild, and some of them hit a rocky cliff about two hundred yards distant and fifty or sixty feet higher than the bear. At another time I saw a hunter kill four huge grizzly bears with just four successive shots. Of course he knew the vital point at which to aim, was a good shot, and had perfect self-control during the few seconds of shooting.

As a rule, the grizzly does not kill cattle or big game. There were buffalo-killing grizzlies, and an occasional one now kills cattle. These killers commonly slay right and left, often killing a dozen head in a short time, but they do not often kill big game. I have a number of times seen elk, deer, and mountain sheep feeding near a grizzly without showing the slightest concern.

The grizzly is an omnivorous feeder. He will eat anything that is edible,—fresh meat or carrion, bark, grass, grasshoppers, ants, fruit, grubs, and leaves. He is fond of honey and with it will consume rotten wood, trash, and bees,—stings and all. He is a destroyer of many pests that afflict man, and in the realm of economic biology should be rated high for work in this connection. I doubt whether any dozen cats, hawks, or owls annually catch as many mice as he. But in some localities the grizzly is almost a vegetarian. In western Montana and in the southern Selkirks of Canada he lives almost exclusively on plants and plant-roots, together with berries and bark.

All grizzlies are fond of fish and in some sections they become successful fishermen. Sometimes they capture fish by wading along a brook, and catching, with claws or teeth, the fish that conceal themselves beneath banks or roots. Commonly the bear makes a stand in driftwood on a bank, or on a log that has fallen into or across a stream. From this stand he knocks fish entirely out of the water with a lightning-like stroke of his paw. The bears that range along the water-sheds of the Columbia and its tributaries feed largely on fish, mostly salmon.

I saw a grizzly make a stand in the ripple of an Idaho stream, where he was partly concealed by a willow-clump. In about half an hour he knocked five large salmon out of the water. With a single stroke of his fore paw each fish was flung on the shore, fifteen or twenty feet away. He made only one miss. These salmon weighed between five and twenty pounds each.

One autumn day, along the timber-line in the Rocky Mountains, wild folk were feeding on the last of the season's berries. Birds were present in such numbers that it appeared like a cosmopolitan bird picnic. There were flocks of grouse and robins, numerous jays and camp-birds; and noisiest and liveliest of all were the Clarke crows. I watched the scene from the top of a tall spruce. This annual autumn feast is common to both bears and birds. In this region, and in the heights above, the bears sometimes fatten themselves before retiring for their long winter's sleep.

While I was up in the tree, out of the woods below a mother grizzly and her two cubs ambled into an opening and made their way slowly up the slope toward me. Mother Grizzly stopped near my tree to dig out some mice. Just after this operation she evidently caught a faint scent of me and instantly stood on tiptoe, all concentration. Motionless as a statue, she looked, listened, and gathered information with her nostrils; but just one whiff of danger was all that came to her through the calm air.

Presently she relaxed and stood for a moment on all fours before moving on. One of the cubs concluded to suckle. Either this violated an ancient grizzly custom or else it was something that in the face of danger was too thoughtless to be excused; at all events the mother knocked the cub headlong with a side swing of her left fore paw. He landed heavily some yards away and tumbled heels over head. The instant he rolled on his feet he sniffed the earth eagerly, as though a remarkable discovery had been made; and immediately he started to dig rapidly with his fore paws, as if some good thing were buried just beneath. He may have been only pretending, however. Without uncovering a thing, he presently raced forward to overtake Mother Grizzly.

The hibernating habits of the grizzly are not completely understood. The custom probably originated, as did the hibernation of other animals, from the scarcity of food. In a long acquaintance with the grizzly my study of his hibernation has brought scanty returns, though all that I have actually seen has been of the greatest interest.

The grizzly hibernates each winter, — "dens up" from three to four months. The length of time is determined apparently by latitude and altitude, by the snow-fall, weather conditions — whether severe or mild, — and the length of the winter; and perhaps, also, by the peculiarities or the condition of the individual animal. Commonly he hibernates in high altitudes, many going to sleep near or above the timber-line.

The place where he hibernates preferably is a natural cave or a large opening beneath rocks. If completely sheltered in a cave, he is commonly satisfied to lie on bare rocks, with nothing over him. In other places, where the snow might come in contact with him, he commonly crawls beneath a huge pile of trash, leaves, sticks, and roots. Snow had drifted deeply over each hibernating-place I have found.

That his winter-sleep is more or less restless is shown in the spring by his hairless hips and sides, the hair having been worn off during the winter. This probably is due to frequent turnings from side to side.

He is generally fat when he turns in for his winter's sleep; but usually he does not eat anything for a few days before going in. On the few occasions on which I was able to keep track of a bear for several days before he went to sleep he did not eat a single thing during the four or five days that immediately preceded retiring. I have examined a number of grizzlies that were killed while hibernating, and in every instance the stomach and intestines were entirely empty and clean. These facts lead me to think that bears do not eat just before hibernating.

Nor do they at once eat heartily on emerging. The instances in which I was able to watch them for the first few days after they emerged from winter quarters showed each time almost a fast. Those observed ate only a few ounces of food during the four or five days immediately after emerging. Each drank a little water. The first thing each ate was a few willow twigs. Apparently they do not eat heartily until a number of days elapse.

On one occasion I carefully watched a grizzly for six days after he emerged from his hibernating-cave. His winter quarters were at timber-line on Battle Mountain, at an altitude of nearly twelve thousand feet. The winter had been of average temperature but scanty snow-fall. I saw him, by chance, just as he was emerging. It was the first day of March. I watched him with a field-glass. He walked about aimlessly for an hour or more, then returned to his sleeping-place without eating or drinking anything.

The following morning he came forth and wandered about until afternoon; then he broke his fast with a mouthful of willow-twigs. Soon after eating these he took a drink of water. After this he walked leisurely about until nearly sundown, then made himself a nest at the foot of a cliff in the woods. Here he remained until late the following afternoon, apparently sleeping. Just before sundown he walked out a short distance, smelled of a number of things, licked the snow a few times, and then returned to his nest.

The next morning he went early for a drink of water and ate more willow-twigs. In the afternoon of this day he came on a dead bird,—apparently a junco,—which he ate. Another drink, and he lay down at the foot of a tree for the night. The next morning he drank freely of water, surprised a rabbit, which he entirely devoured, and then lay down and probably slept until noon the following day. On this day he found a dead grouse, and toward evening he caught another rabbit.

The following day he started off with more spirit than on any of the preceding ones. Evidently he was hungry, and he covered more distance that day than in all those preceding. He caught another rabbit, apparently picked up three or four dead birds, and captured a mouse or two.

Grizzlies are born about midwinter, while the mother is in the hibernating-cave. The number at birth is commonly two, though sometimes there is only one, and occasionally there are as many as four. The period between births is usually two years. Generally the young bears run with their mother a year and sleep in the cave with her the winter after their birth.

At the time of birth the grizzly is a small, blind, almost hairless, ugly little fellow, about the size of a chipmunk. Rarely does he weigh more than one pound! During the first two months he grows but little. When the mother emerges from the cave the cubs are often no larger than cottontail rabbits; but from the time of emergence their appetites increase and their development is very rapid.

They are exceedingly bright and playful youngsters. I have never seen a collie that learned so easily or took training so readily as grizzly bear cubs. My experience, however, is confined to five cubs. The loyalty of a dog to his master is in every respect equaled by the loyalty of a grizzly cub to his master. A grizzly, young or old, is an exceedingly sensitive animal. He is what may be called high-strung. He does unto you as you do unto him. If you are invariably kind, gentle, and playful, he always responds in the same manner; but tease him, and he resents it. Punish him or treat him unfairly, and he will become permanently cross and even cruel.

Grizzly bears show great variations in color. Two grizzlies of a like shade are not common, unless they are aged ones that have become grizzled and whitish. Among their colors are almost jet black, dark brown, buff, cinnamon, gray, whitish, cream, and golden yellow. I have no way of accounting for the irregularity of color. This variation commonly shows in the same litter of cubs; in fact it is the exception and not the rule for cubs of the same litter to be of one color. In the Bitter Root Mountains, Montana, I saw four cubs and their mother all five of which were of different colors.

The color of the grizzly has been and still is the source of much confusion among hunters and others who think all grizzlies are grayish. Other names besides grizzly are frequently used in descriptions of this animal. Such names as silver-tip, baldface, cinnamon, and range bear are quite common. Within the bounds of the United States there are just two kinds of bears,—the grizzly and the black; these, of course, show a number of local variations, and five subspecies, or races, of the grizzly are recognized. Formerly he ranged over all the western part of North America.

The great Alaskan bears are closely allied to the grizzly, but the grizzly that is found in the United States is smaller than most people imagine. Though a few have been killed that weighed a thousand pounds or a trifle more, the majority of grizzlies weigh less than seven hundred pounds. Most of the grizzly's movements appear lumbering and awkward; but, despite appearances, the grizzly is a swift runner. He is agile, strikes like lightning with his fore paws, and, when fighting in close quarters, is anything but slow. The life of a grizzly appears to be from fifteen to forty years.

In only a few localities is there any close season to protect him. Outside the National Parks and a few game preserves he is without refuge from the hunter throughout the year. It is not surprising that over the greater portion of his old territory he rarely is seen. He is, indeed, rapidly verging on extermination. The lion and the tiger are often rapacious, cruel, sneaking, bloodthirsty, and cowardly, and it may be better for other wild folk if they are exterminated; but the grizzly deserves a better fate. He is an animal of high type; and for strength, mentality, alertness, prowess, superiority, and sheer force of character he is the king of the wilderness. It is unfortunate that the Fates have conspired to end the reign of this royal monarch. How dull will be the forest primeval without the grizzly bear! Much of the spell of the wilderness will be gone.

The Rocky Mountain National Park

Extend a straight line fifty-five miles north west from Denver and another line sixty miles southwest from Cheyenne and these lines meet in approximately the centre of the Rocky Mountain National Park. This centre is in the mountain-heights a few miles northwest of Long's Peak, in what Dr. F. V. Hayden, the famous geologist, calls the most rugged section of the Continental Divide of the Rocky Mountains.

This Park is a mountain realm lying almost entirely above the altitude of nine thousand feet. Through it from north to south extends the Snowy Range,—the Continental Divide,—and in it this and the Mummy Range form a vast mountain Y. Specimen Mountain is the north end of the west arm of this Y, while Mummy Mountain is at the tip of the east arm. Mt. Clarence King on the south forms the base of the stem, while Long's Peak is against the eastern side of the stem, about midway.

Long's Peak, "King of the Rockies," is the dominating peak and rises to the altitude of 14,255 feet. There are ten or more peaks in the Park that tower above thirteen thousand, and upwards of forty others with a greater altitude than twelve thousand feet. Between these peaks and their out-jutting spurs are numerous cañons. The Park is from ten to eighteen miles wide, its greatest length is twenty-miles, and its total area is about three hundred and sixty square miles.

A line drawn around the Park on the boundary line would only in two or three places drop below the altitude of nine thousand feet. The area thus is high-lying and for the most part on edge. About one fifth of the entire area is above the limits of tree-growth. The peaks are rocky, rounded, and sharp. Here and there they are whitened by comparatively small snow and ice fields. From the summits the mountains descend through steeps, walls, slopes, terraces, tablelands, spurs, gorges, and mountain valleys.

This Park is a wilderness. Though entirely surrounded by settlers and villages, it is an almost unbroken wild. Many of its peaks are as yet unclimbed. There are pathless forests, unvisited gorges, unnamed lakes, and unknown localities.

Gray and red granite form the larger portion of its surface. Here and there are mixtures of schist, gneiss, and porphyry. The northwest corner is volcanic and is made up of rhyolite, obsidian, and lava. The Indians have a tradition concerning the volcanic activity of Specimen Mountain, though I doubt if this mountain has been active within a century. It is a dead or sleeping volcano. A part of its old crater-rim has fallen away, and brilliant flowers cover the cold ashes in the crater.

Dedication of Rocky Mountain National Park, September 4, 1915.
Courtesy Estes Park Museum.

Most of the territory was glaciated during the last ice age, and there still remain five small glaciers and a number of ice-fields. The Hallett Glacier is on the north shoulder of Hague's Peak, the Sprague Glacier on the south side of Stone's Peak, Tyndall Glacier between Flat-Top and Mt. Hallett, and Andrews Glacier in a cirque of Loch Vale, while an unnamed small one is at the bottom of the east precipice of Long's Peak.

There can hardly be found a greater and more closely gathered area of imposing, easily read glacial records than those which centre about Long's Peak. These works of the Ice King, both intact and partly ruined, have attracted the attention and study of a number of prominent geologists and glaciologists. Among these ice works Dr. Hayden and Dr. David Starr Jordan have climbed and wandered. Vernon L. Kellogg has here gathered material for a book, and Dr. Edward L. Orton, former State Geologist of Ohio, has spent many weeks here in study. Within a six-mile radius of the top of Long's Peak are more than thirty glacier lakes and perhaps twice as many lakelets or mountain tarns. Immediately south of the Peak, Wild Basin is literally filled with glacier records. To the north is Moraine Park; to the northwest, Glacier Gorge and Loch Vale; to the west, lying between the Peak and Grand Lake, there is a wondrous area of the Ice King's topography.

Bierstadt, St. Vrain, and Mills Moraines are imposing deposits of glacial débris. Of these Mills Moraine has been the most studied. It apparently holds the story of two widely separated ice ages. This moraine evidently was formed by the glacier which made the basin of Chasm Lake. It extends eastward from Long's Peak, its uppermost end being at twelve thousand five hundred feet. At timber-line its trend is toward the southeast. It is about one mile wide, five miles long, and in places apparently more than one thousand feet deep.

The ice-stream which piled the enormous Bierstadt Moraine took its rise on the west summit slope of Long's Peak. It flowed first toward the west, and in the upper amphitheatre of Glacier Gorge it united with the ice-stream from the north slope of Shoshone Peak and the stream off the eastern slope of Mt. McHenry. Although a part of this enlarged flow appears to have been thrust across the Continental Divide, the larger portion of it was deflected to the north through Glacier Gorge. Emerging from this gorge and enlarged by the ice-streams from Mt. Otis, Mt. Hallett, and other peaks in the Continental Divide, it flowed on to thrust against the eastern base of Flat-Top Mountain. This bent it to the east, and from this turning-point it began to unload its débris on Bierstadt Moraine. A part of its débris was dropped in a smaller parallel moraine on the opposite side of Glacier Creek, and finally a terminal moraine was piled against the western front of Green Mountain, where it almost united with the terminal part of the Moraine on the south side of Moraine Park.

The glaciers have formed and distributed much of the soil of this region. Above timber-line there are wide, sedgy meadows and tundras and dry, grassy moorlands. Everywhere on the heights where there is soil there is a growth of Arctic-Alpine vegetation. Above the limits of tree-growth are enormous ragged areas and tiny ledge gardens that are crowded with a variety of brilliantly colored wild blossoms.

The average altitude of the timber-line is about eleven thousand three hundred feet, nearly a vertical mile higher than the timber-line in the Alps. Timber-line the world over is a place of striking interest, but nowhere have I found or heard of a timber-line which exhibits so many telling features as does the forest-frontier on the eastern side of the Continental Divide. The prevailing tree on the drier slopes at timber-line is *Pinus flexilis,* the limber pine. In the moist places Engelmann spruce predominates, and in many of the moister places there are dwarfed and tangled growths of arctic willow, black birch, and aspen.

Among the least broken and most enchanting of the primeval forests of the Park are a few that are grand. One of these is between the head of Fall River and the Poudre; another is in Forest Cañon; one is in the southern part of Wild Basin; still another is on the western slope of Stone's Peak and Flat-Top Mountain. These forests are mostly Engelmann spruce, with a scattering of sub-alpine fir. Around the lower, warmer slopes grows the Western yellow pine, and on the cold lower slopes the Douglas spruce. There are a number of extensive lodge-pole pine forests. These are from thirty to one hundred and thirty years old. Lines of aspen adorn most streams; here and there where the soil is moist they expand into groves.

The wild-flower inhabitants of this great Park number more than a thousand species. Many of these are members of famous families,—famous for their antiquity upon the earth, for their delicate scent, for their intricate and artistic structure, and for their brilliant color.

The gentian family is represented by fifteen species, one of these being a fringed blue gentian, a Western relative of the fringed gentian celebrated by the poet Bryant. There are intricately-formed orchids. The silver and blue columbine is here at its best; it blossoms on the lower slopes in June, on the heights during September. The populous pea family, in yellow, white, and lavender, covers and colors extensive areas. Then there are asters, daisies, mariposa lilies, polemonium, wintergreen, forget-me-nots, black-eyed Susans, and numerous other handsome flower people. These flowers are scattered all over the Park except in places destitute of soil. I have found primroses, phlox, and mertensia on the summit of Long's Peak. In the heights above the limits of tree-growth there are scores of other blossoms.

More than one hundred species of birds nest in these scenes. Among these are the robin, the bluebird, the wren, the hermit thrush, the hummingbird, the golden eagle, the white-crowned sparrow, and that marvelous singer the solitaire. Among the resident birds are the ouzel, the crested and the Rocky Mountain jays, the chickadee, the downy woodpecker, and the magpie. The ptarmigan and the rosy finch are prominent residents in the heights above the timber-line.

Once the big-game population was numerous. But the grizzly has been almost exterminated, and only a few black bear remain. There are a few mountain lions and elk. Deer are fairly common, and in localities mountain sheep are plentiful and on the increase. Specimen Mountain probably is one of the places most frequented by mountain sheep. A number of times flocks of more than a hundred have been seen on this mountain. A scattering of wolves, coyotes, and foxes remain. Conies are numerous in the slide rock of the heights, and snowshoe rabbits people the forests. The Frémont, or pine, squirrels are scattered

Enos Mills at Park dedication
(left to right, Mills; hotel-owner and steamcar pioneer F. O. Stanley;
Colorado congressman Edward Taylor; and park advocate Mary Belle
King Sherman, "The National Park Lady").
Courtesy National Park Service—Rocky Mountain National Park.

throughout the woods. Lunch where you will, and the dear and confiding busy chipmunk is pretty certain to approach. The region appears to be above the snake line, and I have never seen a snake within the boundary. The streams and a number of the lakes have their population of rainbow and brook trout. Around the water's edge mink make their home.

The beaver has colonies large and small all over the park up to the limits of tree-growth. Houses, ponds, dams, tree-cuttings, canals, and other works of the beaver are here readily seen. Excellent opportunities are afforded to study beaver manners and customs and to comprehend the influence of his work in the conservation of soil and water.

Big game, and in fact all wild life, begin to increase in numbers and also to allow themselves to be seen from the instant they receive the complete protection which parks afford. This park will thus assure a multiplication of the various kinds of wild life which the region now contains. And this increased wild life, with no hunters to alarm, will allow itself to be readily seen.

There are only a few miles of road within the Park boundaries, but the Fall River Road, now under construction across the Continental Divide at Milner Pass, just south of Specimen Mountain, will be a wonderful scenic highway. Although there are a number of trails in the Park, so broken is the topography that most of the country a stone's throw away from them is unvisited and unknown.

A road skirts the western boundary of the Park and touches it at Grand Lake and Specimen Mountain. Another road closely parallels the eastern boundary-line, and from it a half-dozen roads touch the Park. This parallel road reaches the roads of Denver and of the plains through the Boulder, Left Hand, Big Thompson, and two St. Vrain cañons.

The drainage of the western half of the Park concentrates in the Grand River on the western boundary and reaches the Pacific Ocean through the Grand Cañon of Arizona. A number of streams rise in the eastern side. These assemble their waters in the Platte River out on the plains. In their upper course, all these streams start from the snows and come rushing and bounding down the roughest, steepest slopes.

The climate of the eastern slope is comparatively dry and mild. The winters are sunny, but little snow falls, and the winds are occasionally warm and usually extremely dry. Though only a few miles from the eastern slope, the western rarely receives a wind, and its snow-fall is more than double that of the eastern.

Numerous authors and artists have made long visits in this region, and its scenery has received their highest praise. Bierstadt, the artist, came here in 1870. A few years later he was followed by the famous authors Isabella Bird, Anna Dickinson, and Helen Hunt. Frederick H. Chapin visited the region in 1888 and wrote a splendidly illustrated book about it, called

"Mountaineering in Colorado." This was published by the Appalachian Club. In commenting upon the scenery of the region, Hayden, Father of the Yellowstone National Park, turned aside from scientific discussion in his geological report for 1875 to pay the following tribute to the scenic charm of this territory: —

"Not only has nature amply supplied this with features of rare beauty and surroundings of admirable grandeur, but it has thus distributed them that the eye of an artist may rest with perfect satisfaction on the complete picture presented. It may be said, perhaps, that the more minute details of the scenery are too decorative in their character, showing, as they do, the irregular picturesque groups of hills, buttes, products of erosion, and the finely moulded ridges — the effect is pleasing in the extreme."

Long's Peak is considered by mountain-climbers an excellent view-point. Standing aside one mile from the Continental Divide and rising above a large surrounding wonderland, its summit and upper slopes give splendid views and command a variety of scenes, near and far. While upon its slope, Mr. Chapin said: "I would not fail to impress on the mind of the tourist that the scenes are too grand for words to convey a true idea of their magnificence. Let him, then, not fail to visit them." It is an extremely rocky and rugged peak, but it is almost entirely free of snow and ice, so that climbing it is simply a day's work crowded with enjoyment and almost free from danger. Though it is two hundred and fifty feet lower than "the" highest peak in the Rocky Mountains and three hundred and fifty feet lower than Mt. Whitney, California, the highest peak in the United States, Long's Peak probably has a greater individuality than either. Alongside it stands Mt. Meeker, with an altitude of 14,000 feet. These sky towers are visible more than one hundred miles. The Indians of the Colorado and Wyoming plains used to call them the "Two Guides."

It is possible, if not probable, that Long's Peak was originally one thousand or even two thousand feet higher. The mass of this peak stands apart from the main range and embraces three other peaks. These are Mt. Meeker, Mt. Washington, and Storm Peak. All are united below thirteen thousand feet. They may once have been united in one greatly higher mass. Much of the débris in the vast Boulderfield and Mills Moraines and a lesser amount from the enormous Bierstadt and St. Vrain Moraines must have come from the summit slope of the Long's Peak group. No small part of this may have come from above thirteen thousand feet. An exceedingly small percentage of the glacial débris which surrounds Long's Peak would, if atop the Long's Peak group, elevate it two thousand feet higher.

The Glacier Gorge region, which lies just to the northwest of Long's Peak, probably has the most magnificent scenery in the Park. Here are clustered enormous glaciated gorges, great glaciated walls, alpine lakes, waterfalls, moraines, alpine flora, and towering peaks.

Wild Basin, a broken and glaciated region of twenty-five square miles, lies immediately south of the Peak. This basin is almost encircled by eight towering peaks, and the enormous St. Vrain Moraine thrusts out of its outlet and shows where the united ice-rivers formerly made their way from this basin. Within this wild area are lakes, forests, waterfalls, and a splendid variety of wild and lovely scenes.

The glacier lakes and wild tarns of this Park are one of its delights. Though most of these water fountains are small, they are singularly beautiful. They are in the middle-mountain zone, in a belt which lies between the altitudes of ten thousand and twelve thousand feet. There are more than a hundred of these, and their attractiveness equals that of any of the mountain lakes of the world.

The best known and most popular of these lakes are Fern and Odessa. These lie about twelve miles west of the village of Estes Park. Chasm Lake, on the east side of Long's Peak, is set in an utterly wild place. Its basin was gouged from solid granite by the old Long's Peak Glacier. Mt. Washington, Mt. Meeker, and Long's Peak tower above it, and around it these peaks have flung their wreckage in chaotic confusion. A glacier almost crawls into it, and the east precipice of Long's Peak, the greatest precipice in the Park, looms above it.

Long, Black, Thunder, Ouzel, and Poudre Lakes have charms peculiar to each, and each is well worth a visit. Lake Mills, in the lower end of Glacier Gorge, is one of the largest lakes in the Park. The largest lake that I know of in the Rocky Mountain

Timberline Cabin on Longs Peak, below the Boulder Field.
Built by Enos Mills for the overnight use of climbers in 1908.
Courtesy National Park Service.

National Park is Lake Nanita. This is about one mile long and half as wide, and reposes in that wilderness of wild topography about midway between Grand Lake and Long's Peak. There are mountain people living within eight or ten miles of this lake who have never even heard of its existence. Although I have been to it a number of times, I have never found even a sign of another human visitor. A member of the United States Geological Survey is the only individual I have ever met who had seen it.

As originally planned, the Park was to have more than twice its present area. I hope there may be early added to this region Mt. Audubon, Arapahoe Peak, and other territory to the south. The summit of Twin Peaks on the east would make another excellent addition. A part of the Rabbit Ear Range to the northwest, and Medicine Bow Mountains and the headwaters of the Poudre lying to the north, would make excellent park territory.

But even as it now stands, this splendidly scenic region with its delightful climate appears predestined to become one of the most visited and one of the most enjoyed of all the scenic reservations of the Government. In addition to its scenery and climate, it is not far from the geographical centre of the United States. A number of transcontinental railroads are close to it, and two railroads run within a few miles of its border. The Lincoln Highway is within twenty-miles of it, and six excellent automobile roads connect its edges with the outside world.

Each year visitors reach it in increasing numbers. During 1914 there were more than 56,000 of these, many of whom remained to enjoy it for weeks. It has a rare combination of those characteristics which almost every one wants and which all tired people need,—accessibility, rare scenery, and a friendly climate.

Grizzly Sagacity

One autumn day, while I was watching a little cony stacking hay for the winter, a clinking and rattling of slide rock caught my attention. On the mountain-side opposite me, perhaps a hundred yards away, a grizzly bear was digging in an enormous rockslide. He worked energetically. Several slabs of rock were hurled out of the hole and tossed down the mountain-side. Stones were thrown right and left. I could not make out what he was after, but it is likely that he was digging for a woodchuck.

After a short time only his shoulders showed above the scattered slide rock as he stood erect. Then he began piling the stones upon the edge of his deepening hole. The slope was steep and the stones had to be placed with care to prevent their tumbling back. After lifting into place one huge slab, he stood and looked at it for an instant and then slightly changed its position. On top of this stone he piled another large one, eyed it closely, shook it to see if it was solid, and finally shifted it a trifle. Had he not been wearing a grizzly-bear coat it would have been easy to believe that a powerful, careful, thoughtful man was eagerly digging that hole.

The keenness of the grizzly's sagacity and the workings of his rare wit were impressed upon me in a photographing experience that I had. Two other young fellows and I thought we could get a near-by photograph of an old grizzly that ranged near us. We entered his territory at three widely separated places and moved in concert toward the centre. We hoped that either one of us would be able to slip up close to the grizzly or else he, in running away, would come close to one of us.

Very soon one of the boys aroused the bear and started him running. The grizzly had evidently scented him half a mile away. Running in my direction, when within about a mile he discovered my presence, turned, and retreated six or seven miles into a remote corner of his territory. In this retreat he did not go within two miles of either of the other fellows.

Realizing that the bear had eluded us, we slightly separated and moved toward him. He did not wait to be cornered in a cañon. Late that day we followed his devious tracks and discovered his movements. We learned to our chagrin that he had doubled back in the cañon and come part way toward us. Then, climbing an out-thrusting ridge where he could see in all directions, he evidently had watched us when we passed up a grassy valley beneath him. After we were in the timber beyond he had descended to the valley. Then the most amazing turn came. Instead of running away in the opposite direction he had followed along close behind us! By the time we discovered all this the day was gone, and so was the bear. He had had an adventure.

Did the grizzly know we were unarmed? He might have used the same tactics in any case. Anyway, he easily kept out of our way, followed our moves, and had, perhaps, enjoyed our unsuccessful efforts.

I would give the grizzly first place in the animal world for brain-power. He is superior in mentality to the horse, the dog, and even the gray wolf. Instinct the grizzly has, but he also has the ability to reason. His ever-alert, amazingly developed senses are constantly supplying his brain with information—information which he uses, and uses intelligently. His powers of scent are exquisite. His ears hear faint sounds; they are continually on scout and sentinel duty. Wireless messages from long distances which his senses pick up are accurately received and their place of origin correctly determined.

The grizzly appears to guide his daily life with plan and forethought. He has the genius for taking pains. He is constantly alert and meets emergencies with brains. The following actions have impressed me with his keen mental processes.

A grizzly cub in Yellowstone Park found a big ham skin—a prized delicacy. Just as the little fellow was lifting it to his mouth a big bear appeared. He instantly dropped the ham skin, sat down on it, and pretended to be greatly interested in something in the edge of the woods.

Another young grizzly in the Yellowstone one day found a tin can that was open at one end and partly filled with fish. He raised it in his fore paws and peeped in, then deliberately turned the can upside down and shook it. Nothing came out. He shook again; no result. Then he proceeded just about as you or I might have done. He placed the can on the ground, open end down, and hammered the bottom of the can with a stone until the fish dropped out.

In a zoo one day, a piece of hard-tack that a grizzly bear wanted fell into the hands of a black bear. The black bear dipped the hard-tack in the water and then started to take a bite. Evidently it was too hard. He put it in the water again, and while it soaked gave his attention to something else. While the black bear was not looking, the grizzly, standing on the farther edge of the pool, stirred the water with a fore paw and started the hard-tack toward him on the waves. The instant the first wave touched the black bear he looked around, grabbed the precious hard-tack, which was rapidly floating away, and, pushing it to the bottom of the pool, put one hind foot upon it. How very like the mental processes of human beings!

One day in North Park, Colorado, I came upon the carcass of a cow that wolves had recently killed. It lay in a grassy opening surrounded by willow clumps. Knowing that bears were about, I climbed into the substantial top of a stocky pine near by, hoping that one would come to feast. A grizzly came at sundown.

When about one hundred feet from the carcass the bear stopped. Standing erect, with fore paws hanging loosely, he looked, listened, and carefully examined the air with his nose. The grizzly is eternally vigilant; he appears to feel that he is ever pursued. As the air was not stirring, I felt that he could not scent me in my tree-top perch. It may be, however, that he faintly caught my lingering scent where I had walked round the opening. After scouting for a minute or two with all his keen senses, he dropped on all fours and slowly, without a sound, advanced toward the willow clumps.

In places of possible ambush the grizzly is extremely cautious. He is not a coward, but he does not propose to blunder into trouble. When within thirty feet of the waiting feast this bear redoubled his precautions against surprise and ambush by walking round the carcass. Then, slipping stealthily to the edge of a thick willow clump, he flung himself into it with a fearful roar, instantly leaping out on the other side ready to charge anything that might start from the willows; but nothing started. Standing erect, tense in every muscle, he waited a moment in expectant attitude. Then he charged, roaring, through another willow clump, and another, until he had investigated every possible place of concealment near the carcass. Not finding an enemy, he at last went to the carcass.

When he had feasted for a few minutes he suddenly rose, snarled, and sniffed along my trail for a few yards. He uttered a few growling threats. That a grizzly cannot climb a tree is a fact in natural history which gave me immense satisfaction. But the bear returned to the carcass and finished his feast. Finally, having raked grass and trash over the remains, he doubled back on his trail and faded into the twilight.

Grizzlies often show courage and strategy by hiding and lying in ambush for a pursuing hunter. On one occasion I had been following a grizzly for a number of days, trying to get his photograph at short range. He knew I was in pursuit. Finally, he doubled back on his trail a short distance and crouched behind a log. His tracks as I followed them passed along the other side of this log, and continued plainly ahead of me across the top of a snow-covered moraine. But as I approached the log, the wind stirred the bear's fur and gave me warning.

A grizzly appears to understand that his tracks reveal his movements. I was once following one that had been wounded by a hunter to see where he went and what he did. He circled from his trail and came back to it over logs and rocks, which left no markings, and hid in a clump of fir trees. On seeing this possible place of ambush by the trail, I turned aside and climbed a pine to reconnoitre. When the bear realized that I had discovered him, he made off in anger.

Round the foot of Long's Peak I followed a bear through a shallow snow, hoping to overtake and photograph him. Most of the snow had melted off the logs and bowlders. After trailing him four or five miles I came to a bowlder where he had climbed up and looked around. Possibly he wished to see how close I was to him; possibly he was deciding just where he would carry out a plan for outwitting me. At any rate, he jumped from the bowlder, walked round it, traveled a short distance slowly, then set off on a run, going east. After I had followed his trail for more than a mile, his tracks ceased in a rocky, snowless area where his footprints did not show.

I thought I should find his tracks in the snow on the farther edge of the rocky space; but they were not there. Then, in the snow, I went entirely round the edge of the rocky space without seeing a track. Thinking that possibly the grizzly was hiding in this small rocky area, I at once cautiously circled every place behind which he might be concealed, but without finding him.

Out in the snow I made a larger circle and at last discovered his tracks. Entering the rocky space, he had turned abruptly to the left and traveled about one hundred feet. Then, from the rocks, he had made a long leap into a clump of bushes, from this leaped into another clump of bushes, and finally into the snow. He thus left the rocky place without leaving any telltale tracks within thirty feet of it.

He started westward—back toward the bowlder—alongside his first trail, and traveled for about a mile parallel to it and less than one hundred feet from it. Near the bowlder he waited in concealment at a point where he could watch his former trail, and evidently stayed there until I passed.

Then he traveled on a short distance to another small rocky area. Doubling in his tracks, he came back for one hundred feet or so in the trail he had thus made. Working toward his first trail, he hid his tracks by leaping among fallen timbers and bushes, and at last made a leap into his first trail by the bowlder, where he made many tracks in the snow. Along this old trail he traveled east again a short distance, stepping precisely in his former footprints.

Out of this trail he leaped upon the top of a low, snowless bowlder on the right, and from this upon another bowlder. He walked along a bare fallen log. Here I must have searched more than two hours before detecting two or three broken sticks, which gave me a clew to the direction he had taken. From the log he walked upon a cross log and then plunged through fifty or sixty feet of thicket which showed no trail. From where he had emerged on the farther side of the thicket there was little by which to trace him for the next quarter of a mile. He zigzagged over fallen logs and leaped upon snowless bowlders until he came to a tree leaning against a cliff. Up this tree he walked to a ledge, where, fortunately, there was a little snow which recorded his track. He followed the ledge to the top of the cliff and, leaving this, ran for four or five miles. It took me twenty-four hours to unravel the various tangles, and I finally gave up the idea of photographing him. Long before I arrived at the top of the cliff I had concluded that I was following a reasoning animal, one who might be more alert than I myself.

Though a grizzly has both speed and strength, he generally uses his wits and thus obtains the desired end in the easiest way. Three or four persons have told me that they have seen instances of a grizzly bear's taking the part of an acrobat. The bear, by this means, endeavored to attract the attention of cattle, with the idea of drawing them close and seizing one of them. Among his pranks he turned an occasional somersault, rolled over and over, and chased his tail.

A Utah grizzly killed about one thousand head of cattle in fifteen years. During this time there was a large reward offered for his death. Numerous attempts were made to capture him. Old hunters and trappers tried with rifles and traps; expeditions of men, horses, and dogs pursued him. All these years he lived on as usual in his home territory, made a kill every few days, and was seen only two or three times.

Another grizzly, eluding pursuers, slaughtered live stock freely, and managed to survive thirty-five years of concerted efforts to kill or capture him. There was a rich reward on his head.

There are similar accounts of Clubfoot, Three-Toes, and other outlaw grizzlies. All of these bears slaughtered cattle by the hundreds in their home territory, lived with heavy prices on their heads, and for years outwitted skillful hunters and trappers, escaping the well-organized posse again and again. Knowing many of the hunters and their skillful methods, and the repeated triumphs of other grizzlies over combinations and new contrivances, I am convinced that the grizzly bear is an animal who reasons.

When in a trap or cornered, a wounded grizzly sometimes feigns death. Apparently he considers his situation desperate and sees in this method the possibility of throwing his assailant off guard. Considering that need of feigning death is recent,—since the arrival of the white man with high-power rifle and insidious steel trap,—this strategy appears like a clear case of reasoning.

The grizzly is difficult to anticipate. His strategy usually defeats the hunter. One wounded bear may at once charge the hunter; the next may run from him; and the third may hold the ground defiantly. The grizzly meets what to us seem identical situations in unlike manner, and makes sudden changes in his habits without our seeing the cause for such changes. Quickly he makes the acquaintance of the new and promptly adjusts himself to it. If it is dangerous he avoids it, if advantageous he uses it.

Often in traveling to a distant place the grizzly goes on the run, but just as often he goes at slower speed. If plodding slowly, he conveys the impression of deliberating. He often appears to be thinking, and probably is. Though shuffling along, he is bound for a definite place with the intention of doing a definite thing. Suddenly he changes his mind and goes off in the opposite direction.

I have seen a bear hustling along, with his mind apparently made up; he is in a hurry to carry out some plan, to reach a given place, or see some particular thing. All at once he notices where he is and stops. He remembers that he intended to look at such and such a thing on the way but has neglected to do so. He hesitates a few moments, then goes back.

On rare occasions the grizzly walks along, perhaps in bountiful summer, thinking of nothing in particular, with head swinging slowly from side to side. Something arouses him; he may promptly retreat or he may investigate. You never know what a grizzly will do next or how he will do it, but everything he does is with fresh interest and delightful individuality.

An old grizzly pursued by wolves once gave me a fearful exhibition of nature. He came running across an opening in the southern end of North Park with several wolves close in pursuit. He acted as though away from home—hard pressed, bewildered, and in a strange territory. The wolves were crowding him closely as he reached the edge of the woods. With a sudden move he wheeled and struck at the one in the lead. Instantly the others were around him, snarling and snapping. The grizzly wheeled and stuck quickly to right and left, striking outward and downward somewhat after the fashion of a cat striking at a near-by object. Then he turned and ran on.

A few miles farther on he again crossed an opening. Fresh wolves were now in pursuit. I saw several of the pack lying down, panting and resting. The grizzly had no rest, he was hard pressed. At one place, closely crowded, he backed up in the corner of a cliff and here put up such a fight that he drove the wolves off for the time being. He killed one and badly injured two of them. Towards evening he took refuge in a denlike place for which he evidently had been heading. The following morning a number of the wolves were gone, but the others were waiting for the grizzly in front of the den.

A grizzly with three feet managed to maintain himself in a territory near my home, and I twice heard of his outwitting hunters and their hounds. The territory was occasionally invaded by trappers but he avoided their snares. Hunters with dogs finally drove him off his domain. Where he went, what struggles he had, what masterly retreats he made, what troubles he had in making a living, and what his final tragic end, I do not know. That he survived so long with one foot gone indicates that he was a bear of powers, a bear with a career, whose biography or autobiography would be full of action and adventure.

It cannot be stated too strongly that the grizzly is not a coward. Every drop of blood in his body is courageous. He has no fear. He is intelligent enough to know that man is a dangerous enemy—that it is almost suicidal for a bear to expose himself to man. There is no animal of the wilds whom he avoids. Man, with field-glasses, dogs, and a rifle that will kill at the distance of a mile, are odds too great for him. He wisely endeavors to avoid man, but if he cannot do so, when the fight comes he exhibits one hundred per cent of courage and efficiency.

Only a few generations ago the grizzly was instinctively courageous, never avoiding a foe; with courage he met every issue, almost invariably coming out triumphant. But when man is the issue, the grizzly, seeing more than one move ahead, has the wisdom and the greater courage to suppress the old instinctive trait, for its use would be ineffective.

For years I have watched, studied, and enjoyed the grizzly, have seen his actions under a variety of influences—fighting and playing, sleeping and food-getting. I have watched him when he was under normal influences and abnormal ones; when pursuer and when pursued; have kept him within the focus of my field-glasses for hours at a time, and have trailed for days with a camera this master animal.

The grizzly is so dignified and so strangely human-like that I have felt degraded every time I have seen him pursued with dogs. A few times I have outwitted him; more often he has outwitted me. We have occasionally met unexpectedly; sometimes each stared without alarm, and at other times each fled in an opposite direction. Sometimes the grizzly is guided by instinct, but more often his actions are triumphantly directed by reason.

Interior, Longs Peak Inn.
Courtesy Estes Park Museum.

Trailing
without a Gun

I had gone into Wild Basin, hoping to see and to trail a grizzly. It was early November and the sun shone brightly on four inches of newly fallen snow; trailing conditions were excellent. If possible I wanted to get close to a bear and watch his ways for a day or two.

Just as I climbed above the last trees on the eastern slope of the Continental Divide, I saw a grizzly ambling along the other side of a narrow cañon, boldly outlined against the sky-line. I was so near that with my field-glasses I recognized him as "Old Timberline," a bear with two right front toes missing. He was a silver-tip,—a nearly white old bear. For three days I followed Old Timberline through his home territory and camped on his trail at night. I had with me hatchet, kodak, field-glasses, and a package of food, but no gun.

The grizzly had disappeared by the time I crossed the cañon, but a clear line of tracks led westward. I followed them over the Divide and down into the woods on the other side. In a scattered tree-growth the tracks turned abruptly to the right, then led back eastward, close to the first line of tracks, as though Old Timberline had turned to meet anyone who might be following him.

The most impressive thing I had early learned in trailing and studying the grizzly was that a wounded bear if trailed and harassed will sometimes conceal himself and lie in an ambush in wait for his pursuer. I never took a chance of walking into such danger. Whenever the trail passed a log, bowlder, or bushes that might conceal a bear, I turned aside and scouted the ambush for a side view before advancing further.

Old Timberline's tracks showed that he had now and then risen on hind feet, listened, and turned to look back. He acted as though he knew I was following him, but this he had not yet discovered. All grizzlies are scouts of the first order; they are ever on guard. When at rest their senses do continuous sentinel duty, and when traveling they act exactly as though they believed some man was in pursuit.

Following along the trail and wondering what turn the grizzly would make next, I found where he had climbed upon a ledge in the edge of an opening, and had evidently stood for some seconds, looking and listening. From the ledge he had faced about and continued his course westward, heading for a spur on the summit of the Divide.

We were in what is now the southern end of the Rocky Mountain National Park. The big bear and myself were on one of the high sky-lines of the earth. We traversed a territory ten thousand to twelve thousand feet above sea-level, much of it above the limits of tree growth. There were long stretches of moorland, an occasional peak towering above us, and ridges long and short thrusting east and west, and cañons of varying width and depth were to be seen below us from the summit heights.

Crossing this spur of the Divide, the grizzly entered the woods. Here he spent so much time rolling logs about and tearing them open for grubs and ants that I nearly caught up with him. I watched him through the scattered trees from a rocky ledge until he moved on. This after a few minutes he did. As he came to an opening in the woods, I wondered whether he would go round it to the right or to the left. To my astonishment, without the least hesitation he sauntered across the opening, his head held low and swinging easily from side to side. But the instant he was screened by trees beyond, rising up, with fore paws resting against a tree, he peered cautiously out to see if he was being followed. When the next opening in the woods was reached, he went discreetly round it. You never know what a grizzly's next move will be nor how to anticipate his actions.

Old Timberline started down into a cañon as though to descend a gully diagonally to the bottom. I hastily made a short cut and was ready to take his picture when he should come out at the lower end. But he never came. After waiting some time, I back-tracked and found he had gone only a few hundred feet down the gully, then returned to the top of the cañon and followed along the rim for a mile. He had then descended directly to the bottom of the cañon and gone straight up to the top on the other side.

Autumn is the time when bears most search the heights for food. Old Timberline's trail headed again for the heights. When I next caught sight of him, he was digging above the tree-line, but as it was now nearly night, I went back a short distance into the woods and built a fire by the base of a cliff. Here all through the clear night I had a glorious view of the high peaks up among the cold stars.

Before daylight I left camp and climbed to the top of a tree-less ridge, thinking that the bear might come along that way. In the course of time he appeared, about a quarter of a mile east of me. After standing and looking about for a few minutes, he started along the ridge, evidently planning to recross the Continental Divide near where he had crossed the day before. As I could not get close to him from this point, I concluded to follow his trail of the preceding night and if possible find out what he had been doing.

A short distance below him I found his trail and back-tracked to a place which showed that he had spent the night near the entrance of a recently dug den. I learned some weeks later that this den was where he hibernated that winter. A short distance farther on I came to where he had been digging when I saw him the evening before. Evidently he had been successful. A few drops of blood on the snow showed that he had captured some small animal, probably a cony. From this point I trailed Old Timberline forward and eastward, and near noon I caught a glimpse of him on the summit of the Divide.

While roaming above timber-line he did not take the precaution to travel with his face in the wind. He could see toward every point of the compass. He was ambling easily along, but I knew that his senses were wide awake—that his sentinel nose never slept and that his ears never ceased to hear. Climbing to the very summit of a snow-covered ridge, he lay down with his back to the wind. Evidently he depended upon the wind to carry the warning scent of any danger behind him, while he was on the lookout for anything in front of him. Nothing could approach nearer than half a mile without his knowing it. He looked this way and that. After only a short rest he arose and started on again.

I hoped that some time I should be able to photograph Old Timberline at twenty-five or thirty feet. But at all times, too, I was more eager to watch him, to see what he was eating, where he went, and what he did. I was constantly trying to get as close as possible. Of course I had ever to keep in mind that he must not see, hear, nor scent me. I had to be particularly careful to prevent his scenting me. Often in hastening to reach a point of vantage I had to stop, note the topography, and change my direction, because a wind-current up an unsuspected cañon before me might carry news of my presence to the bear.

Near mountain-tops the wind is deflected this way and that by ridges and cañons. In a small area the prevailing west wind may be a north wind, and a short distance farther on it may blow from the southwest. Often, when the bear was somewhere in a cañon, I climbed entirely out of it, to avoid the likelihood of being scented, and scurried ahead on a plateau.

Usually I followed in the bear's trail, but sometimes I made short cuts. So long as Old Timberline remained on the moorland summit of this treeless ridge, I could not get close to him. But when he arose and started down the ridge, I hurried down the slope, hoping to get ahead and hide in a place of concealment near which he might pass. I kept out of sight in the woods and hastened forward for two miles, then climbed up and hid in a rock-slide on the rim of the ridge.

By and by I saw Old Timberline coming. When within five hundred feet of me he stopped and dug energetically. Buckets of earth flew behind, and occasionally a huge stone was torn out and hurled with one paw to the right or left. Once he stopped digging, rose on hind feet, and looked all around as though he felt that some one was slipping up on him. He dug for a few minutes longer and then again stood up and sniffed the air. Not satisfied, he walked quickly to a ledge from which he could see down the slope to the woods. Discovering nothing suspicious, he returned to his digging, stepping in his former footprints. He uncovered something in its nest, and through my glasses I saw him strike right and left and then rush out in pursuit of it. After nosing about in the hole where he had been digging, he started off again. He went directly to the ledge, walking in his former well-tracked trail, then descended the steep eastern slope of the Divide toward the woods. I hurried to the ledge from which he had surveyed the surroundings and watched him.

Arriving at a steep incline on the snowy slope, Old Timberline sat down on his haunches and coasted. A grizzly bear coasting on the Continental Divide! How merrily he went, leaning forward with his paws on his knees! At one place he plunged over a snowy ledge and dropped four or five feet. He threw up both fore paws with sheer joy. Soon he found himself exceeding the speed-limit. Looking back over one shoulder, and reaching out his paw behind him, he put on brakes; but as this did not check him sufficiently, he whirled about and slid flat on his stomach, digging in with both fingers and toes until he slowed down.

Then, sitting up on his haunches again, he set himself in motion by pushing along with rapid backward strokes of both fore paws. He coasted on toward the bottom. In going down a steep pitch of one hundred feet or more he either quite lost control of himself or let go from sheer enthusiasm. He rolled, tumbled, and slid recklessly along. Reaching the bottom, he rose on hind feet, looked about him for a few seconds, and then climbed halfway up the course for another coast. At the end of this merry sliding he landed on an open flat in the edge of the woods.

As it was nearly dark and I should not be able to see or follow the bear much longer, I concluded to roll a rock from the ledge down near him. Twice I noticed that he had paid no attention to rocks that broke loose above and rolled near him. But he heard this rock start and rose up to look at it. It stopped a few yards from him. He sniffed the air with nose pointing toward it and then went up and smelled it. Rearing up instantly, he looked intently toward the mountain-top where I was hidden. After two or three seconds of thought he turned and ran. Evidently the stone had carried my scent to him. It was useless to follow him in the night.

The next morning I left camp and followed Old Timberline's trail through the woods. He had run for nearly ten miles almost straight south until coming to a small stream. Then for some distance he concealed, involved, and confused his trail with a cleverness that I have never seen equaled. Most animals realize that they leave a scent which enables other animals to follow them, but the grizzly is the only animal that I know who appears to be fully aware that he is leaving telltale tracks. He will make unthought-of turns and doublings to walk where his tracks will not show, and also tramples about to leave a confusion of tracks where they do show.

Arriving at the stream, the bear crossed on a fallen log and from the end of this leaped into a bushy growth beyond. I made a détour, thinking to find his tracks on the other side of the bushes, and I threw stones into the bushes, not caring to go into them. Both tracks and grizzly seemed to have vanished. I went down stream just outside the bushes bordering it, expecting every instant to find the grizzly's tracks, but not finding them. Then I returned to the log on which he had crossed the stream, and from which he had leaped into the bushes.

Examining the tracks carefully, I now discovered what I had before overlooked. After leaping into the bushes the bear had faced about and leaped back to the log, stepping carefully into his former tracks. From the log he had entered the water and waded up stream for a quarter or a mile. Of course not a track showed. At a good place for concealing his trail he had leaped out of the water into a clump of willows on the north bank. From the willows he made another long leap into the snow and then started back northward, alongside his ten-mile trail and one hundred feet from it, as though intending to return to the place where I had rolled the stone down the slope near him.

I did not discover all this at once, however. In my search for his trail I went up stream on the north side and passed, without noticing, the crushed willows into which he had leaped. Crossing to where the bank was higher, I started back down stream on the other side, and in doing so chanced to look across and see the crushed clump of willows. But it took me hours to untangle this involved trail.

When I had followed the tracks northward for more than a mile, the trail vanished in a snowless place. Apparently the grizzly had planned in advance to use this bare place, because the moves he made in it were those most likely to bewilder the pursuer. He did three things which are always more or less confusing and even bewildering to the pursuer, be he man or dog. He changed his direction, he left no tracks, and he crossed his former trail, thereby mixing the scents of the two. He confused the nose, left no record for the eye, and broke the general direction.

Unable to determine the course the bear had taken across this trackless place, I walked round it, keeping all the time in the snow. When more than halfway round I came upon his tracks leaving the bare place. Here he had changed his direction of travel abruptly from north to east, crossed his former trail, gone on a few yards farther, and then abruptly changed from east to north.

I hurried along his tracks. After a few miles I saw where perhaps the night before he had eaten part of the carcass of a bighorn. To judge from tooth marks, the sheep had been killed by wolves. The trail continued in general northward, parallel to the summit and a little below it. As I followed, the tracks approached timber-line, the trees being scattered and the country quite open.

Suddenly the trail broke off to the right for five or six hundred feet into the woods, as though Old Timberline had remembered an acquaintance whom he must see again. He had hustled along straight for a much-clawed Engelmann spruce, a tree with bear-claw and tooth marks of many dates, though none were recent. Old Timberline, apparently, had smelled the base of the tree and then risen up and sniffed the bark as high as his nose could reach. He had neither bitten nor clawed. Then he had gone to two near-by trees, each of which had had chunks bitten or torn out, and here smelled about.

Retracing his tracks to where the trail had turned off abruptly, the bear resumed his general direction northward. When he stopped on a ridge and began digging, I hurried across a narrow neck of woods and crept up as close as I dared. A wagonload of dirt and stones had been piled up. While I watched the digging, a woodchuck rushed out, only to be overtaken and seized by the bear, who, having finished his meal, shuffled on out of sight.

I followed the trail through woods, groves, and openings. After an hour or more without seeing the grizzly, I climbed a cliff, hoping to get a glimpse of him on some ridge ahead. I could see his line of tracks crossing a low ridge beyond and felt that he might still be an hour or so in the lead. But, in descending from the cliff, I chanced to look back along my trail. Just at that moment the bear came out of the woods behind me. He was trailing me!

I do not know how he discovered that I was following him. He may have seen or scented me. Anyway, instead of coming directly back and thus exposing himself, he had very nearly carried out his well-planned surprise when I discovered him. I found out afterwards that he had left his trail far ahead, turning and walking back in his own footprints for a distance, and trampling this stretch a number of times, and that he had then leaped into scrubby timber and made off on the side where his tracks did not show in passing along the trampled trail. He had confused his trail where he started to circle back, so as not to be noticed, and slipped in around behind me.

But after discovering the grizzly on my trail I went slowly along as though I was unaware of his near presence, turning in screened places to look back. He followed within three hundred feet of me. When I stopped he stopped. He occasionally watched me from behind bushes, a tree, or a bowlder. It gave me a strange feeling to have this big beast following and watching me so closely and cautiously. But I was not alarmed.

I concluded to turn tables on him. On crossing a ridge where I was out of sight, I turned to the right and ran for nearly a mile. Then, circling back into our old trail behind the bear, I traveled serenely along, imagining that he was far ahead. I was suddenly startled to see a movement of the grizzly's shadow from behind a bowlder near the trail, only three hundred feet ahead. He was in ambush, waiting for me! At the place where I left the trail to circle behind him, he had stopped and evidently surmised my movements. Turning in his tracks, he had come a short distance back on the trail and lain down behind the bowlder to wait for me.

I went on a few steps after discovering the grizzly, and he moved to keep out of sight. I edged toward a tall spruce, which I planned to climb if he charged, feeling safe in the knowledge that grizzlies cannot climb trees. Pausing by the spruce, I could see his silver-gray fur as he peered at me from behind the bowlder, and as I moved farther away I heard him snapping his jaws and snarling as though in anger at being outwitted.

Just what he would have done had I walked into his ambush can only be guessed. Hunters trailing a wounded grizzly have been ambushed and killed. But this grizzly had not even been shot at nor harassed.

Generally, when a grizzly discovers that he is followed, or even if he only thinks himself followed, he at once hurries off to some other part of his territory, as this one did after I rolled the stone. But Old Timberline on finding himself followed slipped round to follow me. Often a grizzly, if he feels he is not yet seen,—that his move is unsuspected,—will slip round to follow those who are trailing him. But in no other case that I know of has a bear lingered after he realized that he was seen. After Old Timberline discovered that I had circled behind him, he knew that I knew where he was and what he was doing.

But instead of running away he came back along the trail to await my coming. What were his intentions? Did he intend to assault me, or was he overcome with curiosity because of my unusual actions and trying to discover what they were all about? I do not know. I concluded it best not to follow him farther, nor did I wish to travel that night with this crafty, soft-footed fellow in the woods. Going a short distance down among the trees, I built a rousing fire. Between it and a cliff I spent the night, satisfied that I had had adventure enough for one outing.

Trailing is adventurous. Many of the best lessons of woodcraft that I have learned, several of the greatest and most beneficial outings that I have had, were those during which I followed, sometimes day and night, that master of strategy, the grizzly bear. A few times in trailing the grizzly I have outwitted him, but more frequently he has outwitted me. Every grizzly has speed, skill, and endurance. He has mental capacity and often shows astounding plan, caution, courage, and audacity.

Trailing without a gun is red-blooded life, scouting of the most exacting and manly order. The trailer loses himself in his part in the primeval play of the wilderness. It is doubtful if any other experience is as educational as the trailing of the grizzly bear.

Why We Need National Parks

The Piute Indians have a legend which says that just at the close of creation the woman was consulted. She at once called into existence the birds, the flowers, and the trees. That is the kind of a woman with whom to start a world. We still need park places full of hope and beauty, with birds, flowers, and trees, that with their help we may live long and happily and harmoniously upon a beautiful world.

Scenic parts of this poetic and primeval world—parts rich in loveliness and grandeur—are saved for us in our National Parks. The National Parks and Monuments are filled with Nature's masterpieces, and contain splendid scenic and scientific features not elsewhere to be seen. The traveler might spend a lifetime in them without exhausting even their best attractions.

A National Park is an island of safety in this riotous world. Splendid forests, the waterfalls that leap in glory, the wild flowers that charm and illuminate the earth, the wild sheep of the sky-line crags, and the beauty of the birds, all have places of refuge which parks provide.

A National Park is a fountain of life. It is a matchless potential factor for good in national life. It holds within its magic realm benefits that are health-giving, educational, economic; that further efficiency and ethical relations, and are inspirational. Every one needs to play, and to play out of doors. Without parks and outdoor life all that is best in civilization will be smothered. To save ourselves, to prevent our perishing, to enable us to live at our best and happiest, parks are necessary. Within National Parks is room—glorious room—room in which to find ourselves, in which to think and hope, to dream and plan, to rest and resolve.

Nature, like our best friends, will have us do our best. King Lear led the typical purposeless indoor life. He was surrounded with pomp and senseless ceremony. He was in the midst of enemies of sincerity and individuality. He decayed. He was turned outdoors. Across the stormy moor he wandered, followed by his faithful Fool. At the door of the hovel he hesitated. Urged by the Fool, he agreed to take shelter inside. In a brief time with Nature on the moor he had become acquainted with himself and had developed universal sympathy. Standing in the storm at the entrance to the hovel, he uttered this noble cry of compassion:—

> Poor naked wretches, wheresoe'er you are,
> That bide the pelting of this pitiless storm,
> How shall your houseless heads and unfed sides,
> Your loop'd and window'd raggedness, defend you
> From seasons such as these?

National Parks provide climate for everybody and scenery for all. If we play in the scenes where fairies live, for us all will be right with the world. Parks give purpose, noble purpose, to life. They are the "Never-Never-Land" in which we shall ever be growing, but never grow up.

Early Tourists in Rocky Mountain National Park.
Courtesy National Park Service—Rocky Mountain National Park.

The great peaks with age-old ice and snow, the mountain-high waterfalls that rush and roar, the waveless lakes that show the cloud and the blue, the waves of wind that shake the stead-fast trees, the songs of birds that ring through the wilderness, the many-colored flowers and glorious sunsets—these waken and inspire us. We are glad to be living, and life's duties are done with happiest hands. We need these enchanted places. I am thankful to the pioneers who saw the wilderness scenes and were thoughtful enough to save the National Parks for us.

Robert Louis Stevenson says, "A man's most serious business is his amusements"; and some one else has said:—

> We need more plain pleasures, for recreation rightly used is a resource for the common purposes of daily life that is entitled to rank with education, with art, with friendship. It is one of the means ordained for the promotion of health and cheerfulness and morality. Vice must be fought by welfare, not restraint; and society is not safe until to-day's pleasures are stronger than its temptations. Amusement is stronger than vice and can strangle the lust of it. Not only does morality thus rest back on recreation, but so does efficiency. One half of efficiency and happiness depends upon vitality, and vitality depends largely upon recreation, especially the simple recreation of the open air.

How and where people play determines the character of individuals and the destiny of their country. Success in life-work depends upon play and relaxation. Blue Monday did not originate outdoors. It is doubtful if any other influence produces so many good habits as a park. Parks keep a nation hopeful and young.

The better and stronger nation of the future will be a park-using nation. Many wrecked nations have tried to get along without outdoor parks and recreation places. It is but little less than folly to spend millions on forts and warships, on prisons and hospitals, instead of giving people the opportunity to develop and rest in the sane outdoors.

The population of the United States now numbers a hundred millions and is growing with amazing rapidity. The harassing, exacting life of to-day makes outdoor life more important than ever before. Even in the country, more play places are needed. Most of the park-like places in the country have fallen into private hands to the exclusion of the public, but in every State in the Union a number of scenic places are available. These might well be secured by the public and made into city and county, state and national parks.

The intensity of love for native land depends chiefly upon the loveliness of its landscapes—upon its scenery. The great scenic places of a land should be owned by the public and often seen by the public. We cannot love an ugly country. Beauty satisfies the world's great longing. Hatred and prejudice may be taught, but the love of land must be inspired—and inspired by the scenic loveliness of that land. "The beautiful is as useful as the useful." Some time a Secretary of Parks and Recreation may be the most honored member of the President's Cabinet.

Develop National Parks, and there is no danger that the people will fail to use them. They will help us to build a vast travel industry. In each of the years immediately preceding the European war, more than half a million Americans went to Europe. Each individual spent not less than a thousand dollars, a total of five hundred million dollars—this exclusive of large sums spent for works of art, jewelry, and clothing. Why should not such vast expenditures be made in our own country instead of in foreign lands? Scenery is an asset, and parks, multiplied and properly managed, would greatly help to keep our money at home as well as to educate and refine our people.

The existing National Parks—and there will be others—are a vast undeveloped resource of enormous potential value. They are a golden field that will grow the more with reaping! The Parks have the power to change and better the habits of a nation. They may arouse in us the desire to spend most of our spare time, and lead to the fashion of holding most of our social gatherings, outdoors.

Lack of national unity is perilous. A nation divided against itself is not strong. Internal strife sometimes is worse than foreign war. The people of the United States are united in name, but are they doing good team-work? The mingling of people from all quarters in their own great National Parks means friendly union. The Westerner ought to know the Easterner;

the Easterner should be acquainted with the Westerner, and he ought also to see the magnificent distances in the West. Travel to National Parks will promote such acquaintance in the happiest circumstances. Greatly it would help the general welfare of the nation if the citizens of the United States were better acquainted with their own country, its resources, its people, and its problems. The debates on various public measures in Congress show a lack of national unity that arises from a lack of national information. A people united is a nation well prepared.

I sometimes think that getting really acquainted with some-person, or with some fact, is a great event. There is nothing like acquaintance for promoting friendship, sympathy, and coöperation. To bring the capitalist and the laborer—all classes—together in the Park's august scenes, is bound to encourage acquaintance and to prevent misunderstandings. All this means unity, friendship, and will keep war drums in the background.

He who feels the spell of the wild, the rhythmic melody of falling water, the echoes among the crags, the bird-songs, the wind in the pines, and the endless beat of wave upon the shore, is in tune with the universe. And he will know what human brotherhood means; will understand the heart of the democratic poet who declares, "A man's a man for a' that."

In Nature's ennobling and boundless scenes, the hateful boundary-lines and the forts and flags and prejudices of nations are forgotten. Nature is universal. She hoists no flags of hatred. Wood-notes wild contain no barbaric strains of war. The supreme triumph of parks is humanity. And as I have said elsewhere, some time it may be that an immortal pine will be the flag of a united and peaceful world.

John Muir felt that National Parks were the glory of the country and should make this country the glory of the earth. I feel certain that if Nature were to speak she would say, "Make National and State Parks of your best wild gardens, and with these I will develop greater men and women."

The Trail

National Parks will insure the perpetuation of the primitive and poetic pathway, the Trail.

The trail is as old as the hills. In every wild corner of the world it is the dim romantic highway through "No Man's Land." Ever intimate with the forest and stream, this adventurous and primitive way has an endless variety. Its scenes shift and its vistas change. It has the aroma of the wilderness. It always leads to a definite place over a crooked and alluring way. With eager haste it may go straight to some poetic point, but usually it winds with many a delightful delay. I think of it as watching the white cascades, listening to the echoes, delaying by the lonely shore, spending hours in the forest primeval, leisurely crossing the grassy, sun-filled glades, skirting the time-stained crags and vanishing into the heights, looking down into the valley, and tarrying where artists would linger. Somewhere it leads to a lake.

At the primitive beaver house it takes a look as it crosses the expanded brook upon the beaver dam. A fallen tree gives it a way across the river. In a gorge it hears the ouzel from the rocks pour forth his melody—joyous notes of happy, liquid song.

It crosses a moraine to examine the useful débris that the Ice King formed while he was sculpturing the mountains and giving lines to the landscape. Clouds bound for definite ports in the trailless sky adorn its realm with floating shadows. It passes a picturesque old landmark, a pine of a thousand years. In this one spot the ancient pine has stood, an observing spectator, while the seasons and the centuries flowed along. His autobiography is rich in weather lore, full of adventures, and filled with thrilling escapes from fires, lightning, and landslides. During his thousand years, strange travelers and processions have passed along. He often saw victor and victim and the endless drama of the wilderness.

The trail is followed by wild life, and along it the wild flowers fill the wild gardens. It has the spirit of the primal outdoors. It extends away ever to the golden age. Many a night this way across the earth is as thick with fireflies as the great Milky Way across the sky with stars. The moon, the white aspens, and the dark spruces pile it with romantic shades, and on a sunny day it is often touched by the fleeting shadow of an eagle in the sky.

This old acquaintance would have you carry your own pack, and, like your best friend, expects your best on every occasion. The trail compels you to know yourself and to be yourself, and puts you in harmony with the universe. It makes you glad to be living. It gives health, hope, and courage, and it extends that touch of nature which tends to make you kind. This heroic way conducted our ancestors across the ages. It should be preserved. It has for us the inspiration of the ages.

A dim trail led our wandering primeval ancestors out from the twilight. It was a trail ever winding, shadowy, and broken, but ever under the open sky and ever from "yesterday's seven thousand years." It had its beginning in the walks of beasts that prowled the solemn primeval forests. Over it our half-lost ancestors painfully advanced. A fallen tree was their first bridge and a floating log their first boat. They wondered at the strange alternating day and night at which we still wonder. With joy they watched the shining dawn, and with fear and dread they saw the dusk of dying day. They learned the endless procession of seasons. The mysterious movements of wind and water aroused their curiosity, and with childlike interest they followed the soft and silent movements of the clouds. The wide and starry sky appealed strangely, strongly, to their imagination, and in this luminous field of space their fancy found a local habitation and a name for the thousand earthly fears and factors of their lives.

They dared the prairie, climbed the hills, but long kept close to the forest.

After hard and fearful ages—after "a million years and a day"—the camp-fire came at last. This fragment of the Immortal Sun conquered the cold and the night, and misery and dread gave way to comfort and hope. No more the aspen trembled. It became a dancing youth, while the strange, invisible echo was a merry hiding child. The fireflies changed to fairies, and Pan commenced to pipe the elemental melody of the wild.

Nature ever shouted her pictures and interested her children in fairylands. Winter, cold and leafless; spring, full of song and

Tourists at Longs Peak Inn.
Courtesy Estes Park Museum.

promise; the generous wealth of summer; and autumn with its harvest and color, came and disappeared, and came again through all the mysterious years. Lightning, the echo, with roar and whisper of the viewless air, the white and lonely moon, the strange eclipse, the brilliant and fleeting rainbow,—Nature's irised silken banner—the mystery of death, these seeds of thought bloomed into the fanciful, beautiful myths and legends that we know.

Once, like a web of joy, trails overspread all the wild gardens of the earth. The long trail is gone, and most others are cut to pieces and ruined. The few broken remnants are but little used.

The traveler who forgets or loses the trail will lose his way, or miss the best of life. The trail is the directest approach to the fountain of life, and this immortal way delays age and commands youth to linger. While you delay along the trail, Father Time pauses to lean upon his scythe. The trail wanders away from the fever and the fret, and leads to where the Red Gods call. This wonderful way must not be buried and forgotten.

Snow-blinded
on the Summit

As I climbed up out of the dwarfed woods at timberline in the Rocky Mountains, and started across the treeless white summit, the terrific sun glare on the snow warned me of the danger of snow-blindness. I had lost my snow glasses. But the wild attractions of the heights caused me to forget the care of my eyes and I lingered to look down into cañons and to examine magnificent snow cornices. A number of mountain sheep also interested me. Then for half an hour I circled a confiding flock of ptarmigan and took picture after picture.

Through the clear air the sunlight poured with burning intensity. I was 12,000 feet above the sea. Around me there was not a dark crag nor even a tree to absorb the excess of light. A wilderness of high, rugged peaks stood about—splendid sunlit mountains of snow. To east and west they faced winter's noonday sun with great shadow mantles flowing from their shoulders.

As I started to hurry on across the pass I began to experience the scorching pains that go with seared, sunburnt eyes—snow-blindness. Unfortunately, I had failed to take even the precaution of blackening my face, which would have dulled the glare. At the summit my eyes became so painful that I could endure the light only a few seconds at a time. Occasionally I sat down and closed them for a minute or two. Finally, while doing this, the lids adhered to the balls and the eyes swelled so that I could not open them.

Blind on the summit of the Continental Divide! I made a grab for my useful staff which I had left standing beside me in the snow. In the fraction of a second that elapsed between thinking of the staff and finding it my brain woke up to the seriousness of the situation. To the nearest trees it was more than a mile, and the nearest house was many miles away across ridges of rough mountains. I had matches and a hatchet, but no provisions. Still, while well aware of my peril, I was only moderately excited, feeling no terror. Less startling incidents have shocked me more, narrow escapes from street automobiles have terrified me.

It had been a wondrous morning. The day cleared after a heavy fall of fluffy snow. I had snowshoed up the slope through a ragged, snow-carpeted spruce forest, whose shadows wrought splendid black-and-white effects upon the shining floor. There were thousands of towering, slender spruces, each brilliantly laden with snow flowers, standing soft, white, and motionless in the sunlight. While I was looking at one of these artistically dec-orated trees, a mass of snow dropped upon me from its top, throwing me headlong and causing me to lose my precious eye-protecting snow glasses. But now I was blind.

With staff in hand, I stood for a minute or two planning the best manner to get along without eyes. My faculties were in-tensely awake. Serious situations in the wilds had more than once before this stimulated them to do their best. Temporary blindness is a good stimulus for the imagination and the mem-ory—in fact, is good educational training for all the senses. However perilous my predicament during a mountain trip, the possibility of a fatal ending never even occurred to me. Looking back now, I cannot but wonder at my matter-of-fact attitude concerning the perils in which that snow-blindness placed me.

I had planned to cross the pass and descend into a trail at tim-berline. The appearance of the slope down which I was to travel was distinctly in my mind from my impressions just before darkness settled over me.

Off I slowly started. I guided myself with information from feet and staff, feeling my way with the staff so as not to step off a cliff or walk overboard into a cañon. In imagination I pictured myself following the shadow of a staff-bearing and slouch-hatted form. Did mountain sheep, curious and slightly suspicious, linger on crags to watch my slow and hesitating advance? Across the snow did the shadow of a soaring eagle coast and circle?

I must have wandered far from the direct course to timber-line. Again and again I swung my staff to right and left hoping to strike a tree. I had travelled more than twice as long as it should have taken to reach timberline before I stood face to face with a low growing tree that bristled up through the deep snow. But had I come out at the point for which I aimed—at the trail? This was the vital question.

The deep snow buried all trail blazes. Making my way from tree to tree I thrust an arm deep into the snow and felt of the bark, searching for a trail blaze. At last I found a blaze and going on a few steps I dug down again in the snow and examined a tree which I felt should mark the trail. This, too, was blazed.

Feeling certain that I was on the trail I went down the mountain through the forest for some minutes without searching for another blaze. When I did examine a number of trees not another blaze could I find. The topography since entering the forest and the size and character of the trees were such that I felt I was on familiar ground. But going on a few steps I came out on the edge of an unknown rocky cliff. I was now lost as well as blind.

During the hours I had wandered in reaching timberline I had had a vague feeling that I might be travelling in a circle, and might return to trees on the western slope of the Divide up which I had climbed. When I walked out on the edge of the cliff the feeling that I had doubled to the western slope became insistent. If true, this was most serious. To reach the nearest house on the west side of the range would be extremely difficult, even though I should discover just where I was. But I believed I was somewhere on the eastern slope.

I tried to figure out the course I had taken. Had I, in descending from the heights, gone too far to the right or to the left? Though fairly well acquainted with the country along this timberline, I was unable to recall a rocky cliff at this point. My staff found no bottom and warned me that I was at a jumping-off place.

Increasing coolness indicated that night was upon me. But darkness did not matter, my light had failed at noon. Going back along my trail a short distance I avoided the cliff and started on through the night down a rocky, forested, and snow-covered slope. I planned to get into the bottom of a cañon and follow downstream. Every few steps I shouted, hoping to attract the attention of a possible prospector, miner, or woodchopper. No voice answered. The many echoes, however, gave me an idea of the topography—of the mountain ridges and cañons before me. I listened intently after each shout and noticed the direction from which the reply came, its intensity, and the cross echoes, and concluded that I was going down into the head of a deep, forest-walled cañon, and, I hoped, travelling eastward.

For points of the compass I appealed to the trees, hoping through my knowledge of woodcraft to orient myself. In the study of tree distribution I had learned that the altitude might often be approximated and the points of the compass determined by noting the characteristic kinds of trees.

Cañons of east and west trend in this locality carried mostly limber pines on the wall that faces south and mostly Engelmann spruces on the wall that faces the north. Believing that I was travelling eastward I turned to my right, climbed out of the cañon, and examined a number of trees along the slope. Most of these were Engelmann spruces. The slope probably faced north. Turning about I descended this slope and ascended the opposite one. The trees on this were mostly limber pines. Hurrah! Limber pines are abundant only on southern slopes. With limber pines on my left and Engelmann spruces on my right, I was now satisfied that I was travelling eastward and must be on the eastern side of the range.

To put a final check upon this—for a blind or lost man sometimes manages to do exactly the opposite of what he thinks he is doing—I examined lichen growths on the rocks and moss growths on the trees. In the deep cañon I dug down into the snow and examined the faces of low-lying boulders. With the greatest care I felt the lichen growth on the rocks. These verified the information that I had from the trees—but none too well. Then I felt over the moss growth, both long and short, on the trunks and lower limbs of trees, but this testimony was not absolutely convincing. The moss growth was so nearly even all the way around the trunk that I concluded that the surrounding topography must be such as to admit the light freely from all quarters, and also that the wall or slope on my right must be either a gentle one or else a low one and somewhat broken. I climbed to make sure. In a few minutes I was on a terrace—as I expected.

Possibly back on the right lay a basin that might be tributary to this cañon. The reports made by the echoes of my shoutings said that this was true. A few minutes of travel down the cañon and I came to the expected incoming stream, which made its swift presence heard beneath its cover of ice and snow.

A short distance farther down the cañon I examined a number of trees that stood in thick growth on the lower part of what I thought was the southern slope. Here the character of the moss and lichens and their abundant growth on the northerly sides of the trees verified the testimony of the tree distribution and of previous moss and lichen growths. I was satisfied as to the points of the compass. I was on the eastern side of the Continental Divide travelling eastward.

After three or four hours of slow descending I reached the bottom. Steep walls rose on both right and left. The enormous rock masses and the entanglements of fallen and leaning trees made progress difficult. Feeling that if I continued in the bottom of the cañon I might come to a precipitous place down which I would be unable to descend, I tried to walk along one of the side walls, and thus keep above the bottom. But the walls were too steep and I got into trouble.

Out on a narrow, snow-corniced ledge I walked. The snow gave way beneath me and down I went over the ledge. As I struck, feet foremost, one snowshoe sank deeply. I wondered, as I wiggled out, if I had landed on another ledge. I had. Not desiring to have more tumbles, I tried to climb back up on the ledge from which I had fallen, but I could not do it. The ledge was broad and short and there appeared to be no safe way off. As I explored again my staff encountered the top of a dead tree that leaned against the ledge. Breaking a number of dead limbs off I threw them overboard. Listening as they struck the snow below I concluded that it could not be more than thirty feet to the bottom.

I let go my staff and dropped it after the limbs. Then, without taking off snowshoes, I let myself down the limbless trunk. I could hear water running beneath the ice and snow. I recovered my staff and resumed the journey.

In time the cañon widened a little and travelling became easier. I had just paused to give a shout when a rumbling and crashing high up the righthand slope told me that a snowslide was plunging down. Whether it would land in the cañon before me or behind me or on top of me could not be guessed. The awful smashing and crashing and roar proclaimed it of enormous size and indicated that trees and rocky débris were being swept onward with it. During the few seconds that I stood awaiting my fate, thought after thought raced through my brain as I recorded the ever-varying crashes and thunders of the wild, irresistible slide.

With terrific crash and roar the snowslide swept into the cañon a short distance in front of me. I was knocked down by the outrush or concussion of air and for several minutes was nearly smothered with the whirling, settling snow-dust and rock powder which fell thickly all around. The air cleared and I went on.

I had gone only a dozen steps when I came upon the enormous wreckage brought down by the slide. Snow, earthy matter, rocks, and splintered trees were flung in fierce confusion together. For three or four hundred feet this accumulation filled the cañon from wall to wall and was fifty or sixty feet high. The slide wreckage smashed the ice and dammed the stream. As I started to climb across this snowy débris a shattered place in the ice beneath gave way and dropped me into the water but my long staff caught and by clinging to it I saved myself from going in above my hips. My snowshoes caught in the shattered ice and while I tried to get my feet free a mass of snow fell upon me and nearly broke my hold. Shaking off the snow I put forth all my strength and finally pulled my feet free of the ice and crawled out upon the débris. This was a close call and at last I was thoroughly, briefly, frightened.

As the wreckage was a mixture of broken trees, stones, and compacted snow I could not use my snowshoes, so I took them off to carry them till over the débris. Once across I planned to pause and build a fire to dry my icy clothes.

With difficulty I worked my way up and across. Much of the snow was compressed almost to ice by the force of contact, and in this icy cement many kinds of wreckage were set in wild disorder. While descending a steep place in this mass, carrying snowshoes under one arm, the footing gave way and I fell. I suffered no injury but lost one of the snowshoes. For an hour or longer I searched, without finding it.

The night was intensely cold and in the search my feet became almost frozen. In order to rub them I was about to take off my shoes when I came upon something warm. It proved to be a dead mountain sheep with one horn smashed off. As I sat with my feet beneath its warm carcass and my hands upon it, I thought how but a few minutes before the animal had been alive on the heights with all its ever wide-awake senses vigilant for its preservation; yet I, wandering blindly, had escaped with my life when the snowslide swept into the cañon. The night was calm, but of zero temperature or lower. It probably was crystal clear. As I sat warming my hands and feet on the proud master of the crags I imagined the bright, clear sky crowded thick with stars. I pictured to myself the dark slope down which the slide had come. It appeared to reach up close to the frosty stars.

But the lost snowshoe must be found, wallowing through the deep mountain snow with only one snowshoe would be almost hopeless. I had vainly searched the surface and lower wreckage projections but made one more search. This proved successful. The shoe had slid for a short distance, struck an obstacle, bounced upward over smashed logs, and lay about four feet above the general surface. A few moments more and I was beyond the snowslide wreckage. Again on snowshoes, staff in hand, I continued feeling my way down the mountain.

My ice-stiffened trousers and chilled limbs were not good travelling companions, and at the first cliff that I encountered I stopped to make a fire. I gathered two or three armfuls of dead limbs, with the aid of my hatchet, and soon had a lively blaze going. But the heat increased the pain in my eyes, so with clothes only partly dried, I went on. Repeatedly through the night I applied snow to my eyes trying to subdue the fiery torment.

From timberline I had travelled downward through a green forest mostly of Engelmann spruce with a scattering of fir and limber pine. I frequently felt of the tree trunks. But a short time after leaving my camp-fire I came to the edge of the extensive region that had been burned over. For more than an hour I travelled through dead standing trees, on many of which only the bark had been burned away; on others the fire had burned more deeply.

Pausing on the way down I thrust my staff into the snow and leaned against a tree to hold snow against my burning eyes. While I was doing this two owls hooted happily to each other and I listened to their contented calls with satisfaction.

Hearing the pleasant, low call of a chickadee I listened. Apparently he was dreaming and talking in his sleep. The dream must have been a happy one, for every note was cheerful. Realizing that he probably was in an abandoned woodpecker nesting hole; I tapped on the dead tree against which I was leaning. This was followed by a chorus of lively, surprised chirpings, and one, two, three!—then several—chickadees flew out of a hole a few inches above my head. Sorry to have disturbed them I went on down the slope.

At last I felt the morning sun in my face. With increased light my eyes became extremely painful. For a time I relaxed upon the snow, finding it difficult to believe that I had been travelling all night in complete darkness. While lying here I caught the scent of smoke. There was no mistaking it. It was the smoke of burning aspen, a wood much burned in the cook-stoves of mountain people. Eagerly I rose to find it. I shouted again and again but there was no response. Under favourable conditions, keen nostrils may detect aspen-wood smoke for a distance of two or three miles.

The compensation of this accident was an intense stimulus to my imagination—perhaps our most useful intellectual faculty. My eyes, always keen and swift, had ever supplied me with almost an excess of information. But with them suddenly closed my imagination became the guiding faculty. I did creative thinking. With pleasure I restored the views and scenes of the morning before. Anyone seeking to develop the imagination would find a little excursion afield, with eyes voluntarily blindfolded, a most telling experience.

Down the mountainside I went, hour after hour. My ears caught the chirp of birds and the fall of icicles which ordinarily I would hardly have heard. My nose was constantly and keenly analyzing the air. With touch and clasp I kept in contact with the trees. Again my nostrils picked up aspen smoke. This time it was much stronger. Perhaps I was near a house! But the whirling air currents gave me no clue as to the direction from which the smoke came, and only echoes responded to my call.

All my senses worked willingly in seeking wireless news to substitute for the eyes. My nose readily detected odours and smoke. My ears were more vigilant and more sensitive than usual. My fingers, too, were responsive from the instant that my eyes failed. Delightfully eager they were, as I felt the snow-buried trees, hoping with touch to discover possible trail blazes. My feet also were quickly, steadily alert to translate the topography.

Occasionally a cloud shadow passed over. In imagination I often pictured the appearance of these clouds against the blue sky and tried to estimate the size of each by the number of seconds its shadow took to drift across me.

Mid-afternoon, or later, my nose suddenly detected the odour of an ancient corral. This was a sign of civilization. A few minutes later my staff came in contact with the corner of a cabin. I shouted "Hello!" but heard no answer. I continued feeling until I came to the door and found that a board was nailed across it. The cabin was locked and deserted! I broke in the door.

In the cabin I found a stove and wood. As soon as I had a fire going I dropped snow upon the stove and steamed my painful eyes. After two hours or more of this steaming they became more comfortable. Two strenuous days and one toilsome night had made me extremely drowsy. Sitting down upon the floor near the stove I leaned against the wall and fell asleep. But the fire burned itself out. In the night I awoke nearly frozen and unable to rise. Fortunately, I had on my mittens, otherwise my fingers probably would have frozen. By rubbing my hands together, then rubbing my arms and legs, I finally managed to limber myself, and though unable to rise, I succeeded in starting a new fire. It was more than an hour before I ceased shivering; then, as the room began to warm, my legs came back to life and again I could walk.

I was hungry. This was my first thought of food since becoming blind. If there was anything to eat in the cabin, I failed to find it. Searching my pockets I found a dozen or more raisins and with these I broke my sixty-hour fast. Then I had another sleep, and it must have been near noon when I awakened. Again I steamed the eye pain into partial submission.

Going to the door I stood and listened. A camp-bird only a few feet away spoke gently and confidingly. Then a crested jay called impatiently. The camp-bird alighted on my shoulder. I tried to explain to the birds that there was nothing to eat. The prospector who had lived in this cabin evidently had been friendly with the bird neighbours. I wished that I might know him.

Again I could smell the smoke of aspen wood. Several shouts evoked echoes—nothing more. I stood listening and wondering whether to stay in the cabin or to venture forth and try to follow the snow-filled roadway that must lead down through the woods from the cabin. Wherever this open way led I could follow. But of course I must take care not to lose it.

In the nature of things I felt that I must be three or four miles to the south of the trail which I had planned to follow down the mountain. I wished I might see my long and crooked line of footmarks in the snow from the summit to timberline.

Hearing the open water in rapids close to the cabin, I went out to try for a drink. I advanced slowly, blind-man fashion, feeling the way with my long staff. As I neared the rapids, a water ouzel, which probably had lunched in the open water, sang with all his might. I stood still as he repeated his liquid, hopeful song. On the spot I shook off procrastination and decided to try to find a place where someone lived.

After writing a note explaining why I had smashed in the door and used so much wood, I readjusted my snowshoes and started down through the woods. I suppose it must have been late afternoon.

I found an open way that had been made into a road. The woods were thick and the open road-way readily guided me. Feeling and thrusting with my staff, I walked for some time at normal pace. Then I missed the way. I searched carefully, right, left, and before me for the utterly lost road. It had forked, and I had continued on the short stretch that came to an end in the woods by an abandoned prospect hole. As I approached close to this the snow caved in, nearly carrying me along with it.

Confused by blinded eyes and the thought of oncoming night, perhaps, I had not used my wits. When at last I stopped to think I figured out the situation. Then I followed my snowshoe tracks back to the main road and turned into it.

For a short distance the road ran through dense woods. Several times I paused to touch the trees each side with my hands. Then I emerged from the woods, the pungent aspen smoke said that I must at last be near a human habitation. In fear of passing it I stopped to use my ears. As I stood listening, a little girl gently, curiously, asked:

"Are you going to stay here to-night?"

Enos Mills off on a Lecture Tour.
Courtesy Estes Park Museum.

A Day with
a Nature Guide

One morning six variously attired people, four men and two women, started from a hotel in the Rocky Mountain National Park with a nature guide. An auto whirled them to the end of the road far up the mountainside from whence they continued afoot. They were bound for one of the eternal snowdrifts on Long's Peak.

The essence of nature guiding is to travel gracefully rather than to arrive. This guide tactfully put two or three at ease by convincing them that in the United States the belief in ferocious animals is a superstition. "And no one" he continued, "in this locality has ever been attacked by a wild animal." The day was perfect, but so interestingly did the guide describe experiences in storms that everyone hoped to be Rain-in-the-Face before evening.

The guide was jollied for being silent. These people, true to the customs of the day, asked for rubber-neck specialties and demanded where their megaphone artist was. They were climbing in a V-shaped cañon, travelling west. Presently the guide pointed out that the right or north wall rises steeply in the sun and is covered with a scattered growth of stocky, long-armed pines. The left or south wall, which faces north, has a crowded growth of short-armed, tall spruces. In the bottom of the cañon between these closely approaching, but unlike forests is a lively stream with a few accompanying firs, willows, and flowers.

Each member of the party remembered something of plant distribution and each contributed something to the discussion concerning plant zones, slope exposures, temperature, and moisture—the determinism of ecological influences. When the scraps of information ceased the guide added that each cañon wall also had its special kinds of insect and mammal life, and that each of these tree species had its peculiar insect enemies and its bird and animal neighbours. Then, too, each individual bird and animal, every pair or flock claimed a small bit of territory and commonly lived closely within this, likewise insisting on neighbours keeping within their own reservation.

The nature guide is at his best when he discusses facts so that they appeal to the imagination and to the reason, gives flesh and blood to cold facts, makes life stories of inanimate objects. He deals with principles rather than isolated information, gives biographies rather than classifications. People are out for recreation and need restful, intellectual visions, and not dull, dry facts, rules, and manuals. What the guide says is essentially nature literature rather than encyclopedia natural history.

This party being interested in the distribution of plant and animal life, and in erosion, the guide made these the features of the day's excursion. In a mountain region widely varying life zones are seen side by side; and two or three types of erosion may, in places, be seen from one view point—the wear and tear on the earth's surface by many forces stands out unmistakably.

All that the guide said concerning erosion could be set down under the heading: The Biography of a Cañon. The various forces of erosion—running water, frost, ice, and acid, each at work in its respective place with distinctive tools—were prying, wedging, cutting the cañon wider and deeper. Roots wedged the rocks and dissolved them with acids, but at the same time helped also to resist these tireless forces, placing a binding, holding network of fibres. Gravity handled the transportation of dislodged material.

Each species of plant and animal is of orderly distribution and is found in the places that furnish it the necessities of life. On the middle slopes of the Rocky Mountains are trees, flowers, and animals that are not found a thousand feet farther up the slopes nor down the slopes a thousand feet in the foothills. The guide's discussion was the autobiography of each species—The Story of My Life, or How I Came to Be Where I Am and What I Am. In this each plant and animal gave its adventures, its customs, its home territory, its climatic zone, and all the endless and insistent play of the radical and romantic forces of evolution, environment, and ecology.

A few popular and scientific names of species were learned but the guide was reticent about giving classifications. His chief aim was to arouse a permanent interest in nature's ways, and this by illuminating big principles.

Climbing silently out of the cañon up a moderate slope just under timberline, this party halted among the trees for a few minutes on the edge of a small, grassy opening. A deer and her two spotted fawns walked out into view, then went across into the woods.

All turned aside and followed a porcupine that was lumbering across the opening, ignoring their presence. The guide remarked that there may have been a time when the porcupine threw his quills, standing up and hurling them, he imagined, like a primitive man a spear, but that the present development of this animal would prevent the quills being thrown more than three or four inches. However, the other woods fellows make it their business to keep out of his way. He has long been known as "the stupidest fellow in the woods": he is the only one who never appears to play, who has no interest in natural history, in nature guides, nor in the world. Being so well shielded and having an inexhaustible food supply in the boundless forests, he has not developed his wit.

Up and on the party went, except a man and woman who lingered to watch porky. In the edge of the woods the guide stopped to wait for the stragglers. But plainly panic-stricken at being separated from the party, they were just disappearing in the woods, headed north. Asking the others not to stir until he returned the guide dashed after them.

On reuniting the party the guide discussed the necessity of all staying together. "Most people," he said, "are easily confused and lose their direction. Thus it is bad for one to forge ahead, or to turn aside, or to stay behind. Moving together is absolutely necessary for the happiness of the party.

"Once," he continued, "a capable fellow said he would go ahead and wait for us at the foot of a near-by cliff. He never reached the cliff. While looking for him others of the party scattered and each and all were lost, and remained out over night."

A little before noon they walked out of the uppermost edge of the woods among the dwarfed trees and distorted groves at timberline—an aged and battered forest, small and strange. They were above the altitude of eleven thousand feet.

While they were resting the guide called attention to the abundance of paint brush—variously called the painted cup and Indian paint brush—which was growing near by. "Digging down to the roots of this plant parasite," he said, "you will find the roots of one specimen clasped over the roots of another. Of course its parasitic habits have given in part the form to its leaves and bracts." The mountain climbers at once asked for stories about the character and habits of other flowers and of the trees.

Beyond them on the edge of an Arctic moorland lay a snow-field about two blocks long. It appeared somewhat like uncut marble. Stained with rock dust, inlaid with wind-blown beetles and grasshoppers, its granular material lay melting in the sun. A bright flower border encircled it. It was made up of flowers of many kinds and colours, flowers with and without perfume, flowers dwarfed, and flowers on tall, stately stalks. In small compass was a variety of soil, moisture, and temperature conditions. The soil along the upper edges of the snowfield was coarse and dry; below, fine and moist. Each species of plants was occupying the peculiar place in which it could best flourish, or from which it could exclude competitors. It was determinism—conditions determining the distribution.

It probably is true that many of these flowers were developed around the Arctic Circle. The guide recounted the great Ice Age story—how plant and bird and animal life had been swept southward by the irresistible, slow-moving glacier. On the mountains the seeds grew, found a home; so, too, the ptarmigan, in conditions somewhat similar to the old home in the Arctic. In this new colony these birds and flowers still maintain the traditions of their respective old families.

"I am disappointed in finding bird life so rare," said one man of the party. "I have seen only one bird this morning." The guide remarked that he had seen at least twelve species of birds, and that directly before them at that moment were three species in plain sight. Why had he seen but a single bird? His eyes had not been trained to see. A day with a nature guide may help to train the eyes and all the senses.

A picnic party usually does much talking and more eating. A sight-seeing party often does things by the book and talks by comparison. A botany or a birding party is absorbed in details. But a nature guided party is vastly different from these: all of the party have a broad outdoor interest. They are not in a hurry, they are in a mood to be human. They make intimate friendships while getting acquainted with nature. One day's companionship in the wilds often better acquaints people with each other than years of ordinary association. The members of a nature guided party take on a wider, happier outlook. All are glad to be living.

The Bighorn, or wild mountain sheep, was seen at close range. Why these animals live in the heights among the peaks the year round is a story that ever stirs. Their scene-commanding, wild environment has exacted of them alertness, positiveness, sharp eyes, and the ability to play safely where there is much space and little substance beneath them. The interest in the lives of these vigorous animals was ever spontaneous. This, like all other subjects, was kept well out of the category of weights and measures; everything that might have been told about the dissected animal was left unsaid; dry bones were not measured, nor the scientific name from the tomb of dead language mentioned.

Knowing the way is now a minor guiding necessity. Mental development and character are the essentials of a successful guide. He needs to have a wide range of knowledge and to be capable of tactfully imparting this directly and indirectly.

The world is beginning to appreciate the necessity of an outside interest. Fortunate is the individual who has a nature hobby. Such an interest is known to improve health, lengthen life, and increase efficiency. An excursion with a nature guide may give any individual a new or a better hobby. Each person receives a chapter in a natural history story that makes him eager for other chapters which he may find anywhere outdoors.

Dr. Liberty H. Bailey strikes the keynote, I think, of nature guiding at a number of points in his "The Nature-Study Idea." At one place in this he says, "I like the man who has had an incomplete course. A partial view, if truthful, is worth more than a complete course, if lifeless. If the man has acquired a power for work, a capability for initiative and investigation, an enthusiasm for the daily life, his incompleteness is his strength. How much there is before him! How eager his eye! How enthusiastic his temper! He is a man with a point of view, not a man with mere facts. This man will see first the large and significant events; he will grasp relationships; he will correlate; later, he will consider the details."

Timberline, what determines it, and the species of trees that compose it; beavers, their part in conservation and their influence on the settlement and exploration of America; parasitic plants; the story of soil; the birth, life, and death of a lake; the home territory of animals; wind, the great seed-sower are some of the many possible interests of the trail.

A few people for years have practised nature guiding occasionally. It has made good and it has a place in national life. It carries with it health, mental stimulus, and inspiration. Recently nature guiding was given a definite place in the national parks by the Government licensing a number of nature guides to conduct people through the wilds. Nature ever is liberalizing, and the nature guide is one of the forces moving for the newer education and for the ideal of internationalism.

Nature guiding is not like sight-seeing or the scenery habit. The guide sometimes takes his party to a commanding viewpoint or a beautiful spot. But views are incidental. The aim is to illuminate and reveal the alluring world outdoors by introducing determining influences and the respondent tendencies. A nature guide is an interpreter of geology, botany, zoölogy, and natural history.

This guide listened courteously to those who wanted to display their own information—even to those who indulged in nature-faking or told stories that were whoppers; but he carefully avoided following their example. Local natural history he often related, and he was sure of an interested audience, for everyone enjoys local colour and is glad to have past incidents brought to life. He was a true guide. He had the utmost consideration for those in his care, and a quick eye for the interesting and the beautiful. He had the faculty of being entertaining, instructive, watchful, and commanding, all without his party realizing it. He held the climbers together, keeping everyone alert and in good humour; he is doing a distinct and honourable work for the world.

Children enthusiastically enjoy a day with a nature guide and fortunate the child who can have a number of these excursions. They are thought-compelling, interest-arousing. Children are led after the manner of old people. They must not be talked down to. The guide may enter a little more intimately into their joys, perhaps, making slight re-adjustments to their tastes. As a rule, the imagination of children is more readily and definitely fired than that of older people.

Climbing a high peak is an excellent experience for any child. A thousand movies of mountain climbers, a thousand stories by the climbers themselves, weeks in school, and numerous other experiences cannot do for the child what one day's effort in the heights will do for him. Mountain climbing has rare richness which cannot be transferred, but which any child may make his own in a day.

The climb should be made with a nature guide. One other individual or child might go along, but it would be better for the child to have only the guide to interrupt his stirring thoughts. A day of this kind will do much for the child's imagination and mental resourcefulness, and give a landmark to his mental horizon that will stand out through life.

In this the Age of Movies it will be a fortunate child who has interest in the fundamentals; who is rich through knowing the principles of Nature. An interest in flowers, birds, animals, or geology calls for outdoor excursions, for initiative, gives breadth of view, and is a life-long resource within. The movies will be improved, but even at their best they can never do for a child what an outdoor interest will enable him to do more beneficially for himself.

One day a guide was out with several children under eight years of age. They became interested in a double-topped spruce. They learned that the original tree-top was broken off and that the two topmost twigs then bent upward and raced for leadership. They had run a dead heat, as it were, and continued rival leaders. During the remainder of the day the children often spotted a double- topped tree. The cones of trees were noticed, and of course the cones of the balsam fir caused comment because these stood erect upon the limbs instead of hanging down from them.

In a small area, where a forest fire had swept fifteen years before, a few trees had survived. An examination of two of these revealed old fire scars. One of the scars indicated that the tree had been injured by the fire of fifteen years before and by another fire eighty-seven years previous. A few young aspens and thousands of young lodgepole seedlings were starting. Why the lodgepole pines were growing here brought out a discussion concerning the trees that commonly were the first to appear in a cleared or burned-over area. Only a few species of young trees thrive in the sunlight; others need shade in which to start. This principle appealed to the children. An old seed-hoarding lodgepole on the edge of the burned area was surrounded and examined. It had borne a crop of cones each year for seventeen years. All of these cones, unopened, clung thickly over its limbs.

A few days before the guide had led a party of older people over precisely the route followed by these children. He had talked to both parties similarly, but apparently the children had more deep and lasting enjoyment out of the day.

Who would not be delighted to go with a John Burroughs or a John Muir, to be personally conducted to woods, lakes, and streams by anyone who bubbled over with stories about birds, their home life and their travels, chipmunks and their children, and all the other stories and secrets of the wilderness?

It is splendid to have thousands of men, women, and children coming home each year from their vacations talking of the habits and customs of the animals and plants with which they became acquainted on their enjoyable yet purposeful holidays.

Nature guiding need not be confined to national parks. There might well be nature guides in every locality in the land. Fabre has shown monsters and hundreds of little, stirring people co-operating or battling in every growth-filled space. City parks and the wild places near cities and villages are available to thousands of people and are excellent places for the cultural and inspiring excursions with nature guides. Ere long nature guiding will be an occupation of honour and distinction. May the tribe increase!

Harriet–
Little Mountain Climber

Little Harriet Peters, a six-year-old friend of mine, was listening intently to the comments of the climbers whom I had just guided to the summit of Long's Peak. They were describing their trip to a number of others. Presently Harriet turned to me and asked what birds and animals lived on the top of this high peak of the Rockies.

Often I had been asked what could be seen from the top of the Peak; many people were curious about the size of the summit; most interested climbers wanted to know how long it took to go up and back; but never before had anyone asked what lived there.

When the mountain-climbing discussion ended this little girl very soberly asked if I would some time take her to the top of Long's Peak.

"Yes," I replied, "just as soon as we feel that you can go up and back easily. It is a long, steep climb."

Then she wanted to know: "Is it uphill all the way?"

I had early become interested in Harriet, she was so alert, so quiet, and always so cheerful and wide awake. She often went off alone to climb the near-by trails, or for a ride on her burro. Of course she enjoyed playing with other children. Though she had never been to school she had learned to read, and every day out of doors she appeared to be learning new things.

She was constantly surprising me by asking a lively and original question which showed that she saw many of the interesting things around her and wondered about them.

"How do beavers sharpen their teeth?" she asked one day. We had returned a few hours before from a visit to a beaver colony, where we had seen a number of large, dead trees whose hard wood showed the marks of the beavers' gnawing. Harriet really

179

wanted to get on top of Long's Peak; she was curiously, thoughtfully interested in the things to be seen on the summit of this rocky, snowy landmark that towered so grandly 14,255 feet into the sky. Although I had never taken anyone so young I was eager to go up with her.

One autumn day, just after Harriet was eight years of age, we went up. We started off on horseback. The trail begins in a mountain valley, 9,000 feet above sea level. The Peak rises in the sky one mile higher. After galloping a short distance we walked our ponies so that they might breathe for a stretch before taking another gallop. Harriet wanted to know why it was we slowed down when we might have galloped to the steeper part of the trail. Why I tightened the saddle cinches also called for an explanation.

"A person who walks with a loose shoe receives a blistered foot, and a horse ridden with a loose saddle receives a blistered back," I told her.

Most of the time Harriet was silent, observing, and thoughtful, but occasionally she asked a definite question about the things near by. She was interested in the new and unusual objects along the way. The lodgepole pine, perhaps because of its name, caused her to ask many questions. She wanted to know if Arkansas pine, such trees as she saw in her Arkansas home, also lived in the Rocky Mountains. She asked the name of the trees growing in groups near the lively brook along which we were riding. These were young balsam fir trees and the purple cones that stood upon the topmost limbs not far above her head attracted her attention.

She had remembered hearing that up the mountain-side there were species of trees that did not live in the valley, and that at the timberline, where the forest edge is farthest up the mountain, lived still other kinds of trees. While travelling westward in a cañon I pointed out the scattered limber pines growing on the north wall, in the sun, and the dense, tall growth of Engelmann spruce on the shady, opposite wall. She was interested that these two kinds of trees were living so close together, and yet one species kept on the warmer, drier side of the cañon and the other on the cooler, moister slope, while the firs grew only along the stream.

We saw a number of chipmunks eating the scarlet berries of the low-growing kinnikinick. They allowed us to ride close to them, and appeared so tame that Harriet asked:

"If we had time to stop would they let me play with them like the chipmunks around your cabin?"

The night before had been stormy on the upper mountain slopes. Harriet was surprised that there were a few inches of snow here and none down below. She was riding ahead that she might better see the fresh tracks of the birds and animals in the trail. There were many rabbit tracks clean-cut and splashed. It looked as though they had had a game. Suddenly my pony bumped into Harriet's who had stopped and turned to ask:

"Have some bare-footed children and their mother been up the trail this morning?"

A line of big tracks came out of the woods on the left and followed the trail up the mountain. How strangely like the tracks of bare-footed children and an old person; the tracks of a mother bear and two cubs! Slowly, quietly, not even whispering, we rode up the mountain hoping to see them. We were scolded by a pine squirrel for moving so cautiously. We saw where the bears had eaten blueberries in the snow; but there were no bears.

At timberline, 11,000 feet above sea level, all of the trees were small; yet they did not look like young trees, but appeared aged, storm-beaten, and strange. Many of them really were hundreds of years old, yet so tiny that Harriet could reach to the top of them. Many were not so tall as she.

"My doll would like to climb them but they are too small for me to climb," she said.

We tied our ponies and rambled along this strange edge of the forest. There were pines, firs, spruces, dwarfed birch and aspen, and Arctic willow.

"Why," Harriet asked, "do these little people live up here on the cold mountain-side?"

Magpies, camp-birds, and Clarke's nutcrackers were numerous, having a nutting picnic. All were having great fun, but the nutcrackers were getting most of the nuts, pecking holes in the pine cones, and busily eating the large, almost ripened fruit, and calling noisily. One of the camp-birds alighted upon Harriet's shoulder, curious to know if she had something for him to eat.

They are perhaps the most sociable and the best-known birds in the western mountains.

About nine o'clock the sun came out and the snow began to melt. The remainder of the day was calm and warm. No air stirred. On the Arctic moorlands above the timber line we watched carefully, hoping to see the Bighorn. We did not see even the track of one. But we came upon a flock of ptarmigan. These birds had already laid off most of their light brown summer clothes and were dressed in almost pure white.

The last three miles of the seven steep, winding miles to the summit are entirely above the limits of tree growth, among rocky crags and old snow-fields, with most of the trail over either solid or broken rock.

On Boulderfield, five miles from our starting point, we tied our ponies to rocks in the shelter of large boulders and continued upward on foot. Harriet was a sure-footed climber. As we started across this mile stretch of glacial moraine I told her that expert mountaineers travel slowly, always look before making a step, and stop for talking or looking around. Occasionally we rested, and sometimes we lay down upon a flat boulder and thoroughly relaxed.

At about 13,000 feet, while we were thus resting, there came a strange, chirpy squeak. Harriet heard it repeated a number of times before asking what it was. Presently a little animal resembling a rabbit somewhat, but more nearly like a guinea pig, ran in front of us, carrying in its mouth a few blades of coarse grass and one or two tiny Arctic plants. It was the mountain cony.

"Was he squealing because something bit his ears off?" Harriet asked. The cony's short ears do appear as though clipped.

I told her that the cony is called the "haymaker of the heights"; each autumn he gathers small haycocks of plants and stores them among the boulders for his winter food.

"Why doesn't he go down the mountain and live by the brook where there is more hay?" was another question that I could not answer.

About a thousand feet below the top of the Peak we turned aside for a drink from a tiny spring, the last water on the way up. Here we lingered several minutes. Harriet gathered a double handful of snow and carried it to the spring that she might send more water down the Mississippi to New Orleans. Then of the wet snow she made a dam on the rocks where the water flowed from the spring.

Leaving this place we did steep rock climbing over a few hundred feet to the Narrows. In places Harriet walked in front of me; but most of the time she was behind, and always close. By listening carefully I could tell that all was well with her without looking back. At no time were we roped together. In a few places I helped her, but most of the time she walked alone.

A few snow-drifts and ice-piles remain on the head and shoulders of the Peak all summer. The upper two thousand feet is almost solid rock; there are cracks, ledges, and shattered places, with a pinnacle and shattered rock around its base. Here and there was a beauty spot—a tiny bed of soil covered with grass and flowers in the midst of rocky barrenness.

From the Narrows, a little below the summit, we saw two eagles soaring and circling about in the air two or three thousand feet above us. A few times their shadows dashed by us. The Narrows is a ledge, a shelf-like stretch of the trail, on the edge of a precipice. There is no banister here, but one is needed. Many grown people have stopped at this point, but Harriet walked across without saying a word.

Up the "Home Stretch"—the last climb to the top—the slope is extremely steep and the rock solid. Here many people call out "safety first" and go up on all fours, but Harriet, who was in front of me, walked up swinging her arms and humming softly to herself.

We arrived at the summit of the Peak a little after twelve o'clock, five hours from the time we started. The broken summit surface is nearly level, and strewn with slabs and angular chunks of pink granite, from sand and coarse gravel up to blocks several feet across. The instant we stepped on the top I said to Harriet:

"Now you are here, what do you think of it?"

She stood for nearly a minute looking around without saying a word, then asked:

"Where did all the rocks come from?"

Harriet was surprised to find the top so large. There was just about room to give all the players in a baseball game a place to stand, with the batter, first baseman, and out-fielders all standing on the edge. We walked around the top, keeping close to the edge. In most places it dropped off steeply for a hundred feet. The east side is a perpendicular wall more than a thousand feet high. There were many cracked and loose stones on the edge; many were almost ready to fall overboard, as numerous others had already done. Plainly the top of the Peak had once been much larger. Just as we were sitting down to eat our lunch Harriet asked:

"How big was the top once?"

We sat in a safe place near the edge of a precipice where we could look down into Chasm Lake—a glacier-made basin—2,000 feet below us. The water, though clear, appeared as green as any emerald ink you have ever seen.

A half-tamed ground-hog, that in summer lived upon the summit, came forth to have scraps of our lunch. A flock of rosy finches alighted near us. A humming-bird flew over without stopping. A number of butterflies circled about in the calm, sunny air. Harriet asked if there were always the same animals on the summit. I told her I had seen Bighorn sheep tracks and mountain lion tracks there. Just once—when I was up with another little girl—I had seen a cotton-tail rabbit on the top, but I could not understand how he came to be there. Blue-birds, robins, ptarmigan, eagles, and weasels sometimes come to the summit.

We looked at the many-coloured lichens upon the rocks and at the green leaves of the purple primrose and the stalks of the yellow avens. They were growing in little patches of sand between rock slabs. Harriet asked where the plants and the mountain-top birds came from. I told her that a number of the same plants and animals were found in the far north around the Arctic Circle. At one time, many thousand years before, the Ice King had sent his glaciers a few thousand miles from the north, driving Arctic plants down on the moving ice and ptarmigan in front of it. These plants and birds had made their home on the mountain tops and remained after the ice melted away.

Harriet's aunt had told her that the Alps are much colder and snowier than the Rocky Mountains. No one lives as high in the

Alps as the mountain valley where we were living; timberline—
the forest edge—is at 6,500 feet there, and no plants or birds live
above the altitude of 9,000 feet.

As we stood for a moment before beginning the descent
Harriet turned and looked silently at the far-distant, magnificent
views to the north, south, east, and west. Not a question was
asked and I have often wondered what impression they made
upon her.

After having a little more than an hour on the top of the Peak
we started slowly homeward. When a little below the altitude of
12,000 feet we dismounted and searched among the boulders for
the columbine. Luckily we found a beautiful specimen with its
silver and blue petals waving on a slender stalk that stood several inches higher than Harriet's head. The columbine is the state
flower of Colorado, having been selected by a majority vote of
the school children, and is mentioned for our national flower.

Harriet looked again and again at the strange little trees at
timberline and watched eagerly for the bears. We talked about
the things we had seen. She asked many questions about the
trips other climbers had made, and I told her of experiences on
rainy days, on snowy days, and on wintry days. She was most
interested in my moonlight climbs and wished she might some
time go up at night.

Of the two hundred and fifty-odd trips which I made as a
guide to the summit of this great old Peak, the trip with Harriet
is the one I like best to recall; and I am sure, too, should Harriet
live three score and ten years she will remember the day of her
successful climb to the summit of Long's Peak.

This climb, as I remember, was in September, 1905. Some
years later I heard that Harriet was graduated from a girls' college in Texas. I often wonder what has become of her.

The Development of a Woman Guide

A number of nature guides are women. Their number will increase. Their work is identical with that of men guides. In this chapter are glimpses of some of the field experiences and some of the driving forces of environment that resulted in producing one woman nature guide. The name of this woman is omitted at her request.

"She's the woman who made the fifteen-mile moonlight walk across the mountains in the snow," said one of the waiting group, as a young lady in knickerbockers, having adjusted the snowshoes strapped across her shoulders, left the post office.

"Oh," said another, "that was nothing compared with the thirty-mile trip which she made alone across the Range."

"Evidently she is a woman with a purpose in life," remarked the postmaster, looking out the window at the graceful figure swinging easily up the street. "She came out here from the East last fall determined to become a good mountaineer, and took up a homestead near MacGregor Pass. She knows college and business life and her own mind, and apparently she knows how to walk and enjoy it. Undoubtedly she will make good in her ambitions to succeed out of doors."

This homesteader had seen twenty-seven summers and life had agreed with her. Her hair was red, and so, too, were her cheeks. She was five feet five, and weighed about one hundred and twenty. She had walked down to the village this November afternoon from her cabin four miles away, to get the week's accumulated mail and a few provisions. Darkness was already settling down over the pine-purpled mountains when she stopped to make a call. But she was not afraid of the dark—rather, she enjoyed night walks and walks in all weather.

"It is too late for you to think of going home to-night," said Mrs. Pond when her caller began adjusting her shoulder pack. "It will be dark before you can reach the cañon. Stay with us and go to Mrs. Samuel's card party."

"No," was the reply, "I must get home."

Then Mr. Pond came in to offer hospitality and advice and to enter objections against her going. He remarked that bears had been recently seen near the cañon.

"Well, I'll certainly start at once," said the homesteader, smiling; "I have been wishing I might see a bear."

Estes Park Village, ca. 1908.
Courtesy Estes Park Museum.

And off she started alone through the snow. And why had this young woman given up business to mountaineer?

A consulting decorator for a nation-wide business firm and in love with her job, she overworked and eventually had a nervous breakdown. During the months of enforced rest she had had time to think, and did so. Many things in business life, she had decided, were wearing without seeming really necessary or worth while. Once in a routine of work, the average individual ceases to grow—ceases to be the architect of his own fate. She found herself wishing to get away from the city with its exacting demands, to a simple form of existence where money, people, and society were secondary. Then came the opportunity to homestead.

It was dark when she reached home from the village. After building a fire she sat down to read her letters. One was from the New York classmate whom she had invited to share her cabin and her mountain experiences. Her distressed artist friend, after thinking over the matter for a number of weeks, at last wrote:

"You are nearly as crazy—yes, I guess you are a little farther gone than I am. Your letter thrilled me to death, I assure you, but being East in a comfortable, steam-heated home, two stories up, I can't help but wonder how it could be done, and we come out of it alive. I always did and always shall want to come West, but I must say I never quite worked myself up to thinking I could really enjoy living in the midst of the great unknown in a log cabin with one other person, and that person no stronger than myself, with no conveniences, and likely to be completely buried in snow at any minute.

"Now, if this hadn't been actually put before me as a proposition, my theorizing might picture it as the most wonderful experience I could wish for—yes, I should *love* to be snowed in and have wolves howl outside, and get the whole atmosphere thoroughly absorbed into my system, as you probably have done already. . . . I wonder if you have sort of gone crazy about the place, the way those wanderers do who go into the mountains and never come back. If so, I think you need a guardian. You must have some strong person with you, and a dog, a big dog. Where is the nearest doctor? Facts are not pleasant things to rub into your dreams when you're dreaming, but they're mighty pleasant things when you're living."

The wild predictions of the city lady, who had no knowledge of the romance of homesteading, and was without sympathy for the simple, splendid life that may be lived in the mountain frontier, did not come true.

City people and others have listed several absolute necessities for every homesteader: a gun, a dog or a cat, a sewing machine, a victrola, a telephone, a burro, and, of course, a companion, This independent, individual homesteader possessed none of these so-called essentials, but she had a greater possession than they could have given her. She had "Happiness." In these lines you have a good glimpse of her life and of herself during her first winter of homesteading:

HAPPINESS

My lot is a strangely happy one,
    Though far from the busy mart;
I live on my homestead all alone,
    With ever a song in my heart.

And if perchance I tire of home
    Away and away I go—
To gypsy by a stony brook,
    Or camp-fire in the snow.

When wily wind blows fierce and strong,
    Or cloud and mist allure,
I don my very oldest togs,
    And picnic then for sure.

My thoughts are as free as the mountain air,
    And never a care have I:
Where I live alone in a little hut
    And not even the road goes by!

In this mountain frontier neighbours are separated by magnificent distances. Yet this young woman visited all her homestead neighbours, journeying from two to sixteen miles on foot. Last Christmas she and one of the other women homesteaders who lived fifteen miles away walked to a midway place and had a merry camp-fire lunch among the pines. Alone she explored the forests and cañons. She climbed peaks, studied trees, and watched birds, beavers, mountain sheep, and other wild life. All alone, winter as well as summer; she made excursions, camping wherever night overtook her. Sometimes, too, she tramped by moonlight.

Many an evening in a wind-sheltered nook in the woods she cooked a scanty supper in the edge of a friendly camp-fire. After supper, if there was sufficient wood at hand for the night, she sat for a time watching the fire and thinking such thoughts as a lone, outdoor woman thinks. Often she wandered from the fire, better to have a look at the starry landmarks in the wide and trail-less sky. After a few hours of perfect sleep in a sleeping bag she rose early and eagerly watched for the fires of sunrise from some commanding crag.

Her homestead consists of one hundred and twenty acres of mountain scenery, much of which is on edge. The hind is covered with scattered growths of western yellow pine, Douglass spruce, and quaking aspen—the fairy aspen of which she has written so charmingly. A granite cliff towers several hundred feet above the house. From her front door you look westward up Fall River cañon, and beyond where the snowy peaks of the Continental Divide go far up into the sky. In front of the house is a garden of a few acres. Just outside her window is a table for birds. Chickadees and camp-birds were the only callers while I watched. Occasionally wild mountain sheep and deer confidingly follow an old game trail near the cabin.

The cabin in which she lived alone was called "Keewaydin," the Indian name for the Northwest or home wind. She drew the plans for it and helped to build it; designed her furniture and made a number of the pieces.

Anyone with a nose for news would have seen a story in the life of this young woman. When I called to get the story there was more reserve than I expected to find in an art-school graduate.

"I understand that you helped shingle your house," I said, hoping to start her talking concerning building craft.

She smiled and answered: "Yes, the report was out that I shingled as fast as a man, and if it is still circulating it may be faster now!"

Knowing that friends had accused her of loafing—"of wasting her best years homesteading," I asked: "Have you read Stevenson's Apology for Idlers?"

Instantly she flashed up, but with face melting into a smile, replied: "If you really have absorbed it and appreciate it, I'll say 'yes'." And then she added: "But it is not necessary to write a book, create a masterpiece, or evolve some labour-saving device for the recluse to feel justified in separating himself from the affairs of the world. If he values the power that lies in simple things and the height and breadth of vision that comes from a close contact with nature, that is sufficient. An overpowering desire to get away from the superficialities of life can only be satisfied by taking up that unfettered existence where truth is unvarnished and beauty is undefiled. No, it does not require courage to do what you want to do—to homestead, for instance—but it did take courage to say 'no' to the directing advice of relatives and intimate friends."

"And why homestead?" I asked, feeling that she fully appreciated the higher opportunities that go with homesteading.

"Our ancestors," she began, after a few minutes' thought, "who pioneered either through choice or necessity, laboured that their children and their children's children might be 'better off' than themselves. But is it not for each of us to decide anew just what is 'better' for ourselves, and for those with whom and for whom we are living of the present and of the future? Does the 'better off' lie in vainly struggling to outdo our neighbours in accumulating possessions? Or will we find it by holding on to those fine, sturdy, fundamental qualities that make for strength of body and happiness of spirit? The test of all effort should be not how much it gives us, but how deeply it makes us live."

Realizing that she had carefully considered all sides of the subject, I waited for her to continue. Her views of homesteading were convincing, as she disclosed them further:

"A homestead offers infinite opportunities for self-development and enjoyment. Here time is the willing slave rather than the compelling master; here a hobby may be ridden with a reckless abandon or with a prolonged exactitude impossible in the routine of city life. And, if your leaning is along the line of nature study, fortunate are you, indeed, if you have no other companions than those faithful allies of the brain—keen ears and eyes. Who is there who would not enjoy, for a time—at least, the unbroken silences and all-enveloping solitude of a hermit's habitation? Who would not appreciate an opportunity to allow the mind and heart to travel together on limitless journeys into the past and future, gathering facts, creating fancies, that mould and shape new and bigger conceptions of life?"

The warm feelings of this woman, whom the world would regard as a self-exile, again and again reminded me of the words of the exile who wrote: "Life's more than breath and the quick round of blood." She is creative and courageous. Her refreshing enthusiasms are coloured with high ideals. Of course she has definite ideas concerning education. She feels that schools are too much given to memorizing and too little to developing the powers of performance; that the senses are neglected; individuality and the creative faculty suppressed; and the wonderlight of imagination extinguished.

I was thinking that before long she might do something big, so universal were her sympathies, and I finally asked:

"You have become a good mountaineer, you also appreciate the facts and the poetry of natural history, why not become a translator of the great book of nature?"

"For years," she replied, "I have wished that others might have the strange delight from nature that I enjoy. And I have been trying to develop myself so that I might give its appeal to people."

"This can be done," I said, "you are fitted for a guiding career."

The outings which she enjoyed usually were made alone and sometimes they were adventurous. The nearest settlement on the other side of the Continental Divide is thirty miles away. This is reached by trail—a trip across the summit, 12,500 feet above the sea, and then down through fifteen miles of rugged, forested mountains. She resolved to make this journey afoot and without a guide.

She had been on the summit mid-winter, but this snowshoe trip was less eventful than her spring experience. It was a trip that few men had made alone, and local people had concluded

Enos Mills at Elkhorn Lodge, ca. 1902.
Courtesy Estes Park Museum.

that a woman could not make it if she tried. Her success literally startled the natives both sides of the Divide.

It was late spring and the winter accumulations of snow were soft, melting rapidly, and flooding water everywhere. Snow-drifts and soggy places full of flowers covered the steep and dangerously slippery slopes. But she reached the summit by noon. After eating a lunch on these heights, more than a thousand feet above the limits of tree growth, she started down the icy steeps into unknown wilds. She crossed the débris of recent land and snow slides. Everything was slippery, slipping, or ready to slide. But she came down to timberline without starting anything and without a slide herself.

Then for ten miles the trail led through deep snow-drifts and
swollen streams. She crossed on doubtful logs; sometimes with
the logs under water she hitched across astride the log in the
roaring current. In places she waded to her knees. Just as darkness was settling down, all bedraggled, but enthusiastic, she arrived at the end of her journey. She took a longer, less perilous
way returning—a two-day trip that gave her new, though less
rugged, scenes.

This outdoor woman had a purpose—a vision. Daily she accumulated experience and information. These she handled like
an artist. She held on to the essentials only and made these enrich her life. Then, too, she had wide sympathies and in improving her opportunities to learn and grow it was with the idea of
being able to serve others. She had steadily developed since the
day she arrived. She had secured leisure and had used it.

Last summer she was a nature guide—an interpreter of nature—in the Rocky Mountain National Park, licensed by the
Government. Old people gave her their attention, children were
excitedly interested, and everyone was exercising and learning
all at once. A trip with a nature guide is a rare influence for children. Eagerly they look and they listen; they see, they search,
and they think. It is an alluring and most effective way of arousing the child mind so that it wants to know, so that it starts in-
vestigating and exploring, so that it insists on finding out.

This new occupation is likely to be far-reaching in its influences; it is inspirational and educational. Anyone who has a vacation or an outing in contact with nature will have from the
great outdoors its higher values as well as a livelier enjoyment if
accompanied by a nature guide.

Many of the visitors to national parks are nature enthusiasts,
they appreciate having someone out with them who can inter-
pret some of the wealth of local nature lore. There is geology,
the story of the glacial landscapes, the ways of resident birds and
the birds that come from southland for summer and to nest;
beaver houses, Bighorn mountain sheep, brilliant Arctic flowers, the habits of trees, and the romance of everything.

Although everyone has inherited outdoor instincts which
awaken with opportunity, yet, so long have most people been
segregated from contact with the primeval—wild flowers, wild

life, and crumbling, half-vine-concealed cliffs—that they welcome an intelligent and tactful interpreter of nature's ways. Such
a guide enriches the outing, fills it with information, enjoyment,
and vision.

A nature guide is doing the work of the world. Our homesteader had the art and the vision which enabled her to make
these outings permanent, purposeful, growth-compelling experiences. They had none of the movie madness, nor the legend-
diverting magic, but they gave a definite contact with the real
world of life. Nature-guided excursions are educational and
possess astounding possibilities for arousing the feelings and developing the unlimited resources of the mind.

No, this young woman was not wasting her time homesteading; it enriched her life, filled it with eagerness and delight.
"To miss the joy is to miss all," says Stevenson in his immortal
"Lantern Bearers." She is not missing it. The world may not
know it, but she is as happy as Stevenson's boy with the precious hidden lantern on his belt. In the work of nature guiding
she has found her place.

Nature Guiding at Home

Lily Lake, two miles from my cabin, was a large beaver pond which the Arapahoe Indians called Beaver Lodge Lake. There were a number of beaver houses in it. A year before I came into the scene the lake temporarily went dry and the beavers migrated down into Wind River Cañon, to the west of the lake. A high, rocky mountain rose to the north of this lake, a grassy border was on the south, and near the east shore was a forest.

The lake refilled and continued to be a wildlife water hole where birds and animals frequently came, and sometimes gathered in numbers. Often I visited the lake, and among the callers whom I occasionally saw were bears, wildcats, mountain lions, mountain sheep, snow-shoe rabbits, eagles, and many other kinds of birds.

It was a never-ending surprise to me that so many live things came to one place, and that so many different ways of birds and animals could be learned in one little spot.

The animals and birds had fights, feasts, and plays. I saw many of these wild-life exhibitions—real movies. By going frequently to this lake I often saw the beaver inhabitants and I learned a number of lively facts concerning many species of birds and animals.

So interesting was this place that for many years I went to it during every season of the year, and by moonlight as well as by daylight. Early one morning I saw a beaver with an unusually flat back come climbing up out of Wind River Cañon with several other beavers following him. I named him Flattop, and during the eighteen years that followed I occasionally saw him in or by the lake. A number of times I watched him and other beavers cutting trees and dragging them into the lake.

One windy winter day big ice cakes smashed the beaver house and a number of its inhabitants went down to the beaver colony in Wind River Cañon. Three of these were killed on the way, as fur and blood on the snow plainly showed.

One rainy day while I was hidden and watching Flattop cut down a large aspen, a number of mountain sheep came into the scene. The ram leading saw Flattop and walked toward him pretending he was going to butt. Flattop stopped gnawing on the aspen and stood watching the ram, without a move. The ram smelled him, stamped two or three times, then walked away.

By the lake I learned to identify many birds and animals, also flowers and trees. In addition to identification, I learned a number of the ways of each of these living visitors to the lake, and of those who lived in and by it. For several weeks I watched a ground-hog near his den on the west shore, without knowing that he was a ground-hog. I noticed that the aspen grew in moist places, bloomed before its leaves came out, and that it was the favourite tree used by beavers, before I could learn its name and long before I learned its identification marks.

After seeing Flattop around the lake for a number of years I realized that most birds and animals cannot be called gypsies. They have a regular home near which they are ever found. Most of them live and die in the locality in which they are born. They claim a home territory and generally try to keep others of the same species from using this. Even the water birds, and the white-crowned sparrows that nested around the shore, came back to the lake after wintering hundreds of miles south. Three times a white-crown built in the same willow.

A little black bear was swimming in the lake one evening when I arrived. Two claws were missing from the left forefoot print in his track along the muddy shore. Once I saw this little bear tearing a log to pieces near the outlet of the lake; another time he was catching mice in the grass near the south shore. His territory was around this lake. I often tracked him, but never did these tracks lead more than two miles from the lake.

The same lion was three times seen near the lake. A ground-hog was seen so often that he came out and rolled in the sand, or ate dandelions within a few yards of me, only moving enough to prevent my stepping upon him when I walked by his home. After watching the ground-hog for six summers, a coyote who had lived near by for three years at last surprised him too far from his den.

About midway between my cabin and the lake was another ground-hog which I saw occasionally through five summers. In going to and from the lake I often saw the same chipmunk, or the same snowshoe rabbit in its exclusive home territory.

The trees along my trail to the lake I saw every month of the year. I noticed where the gentians lived, that their first bloom was close to the first day of August, and that the first yellow leaves were certain to be on the aspens that stood in the driest spot.

On each trip to the lake I saw tracks, fur, feathers, scratches, and other signs that told me of many of the happenings since I was last along the trail. So many things did I enjoy on the way to and from and around this lake, that if to-day I were thrown on a wilderness island, or should go to a new home, I think I would follow my boyhood habit—would go often to the same spot, and there wait and watch for the numbers of wild folk who were certain to appear each day.

I also played home animal much of the time, and explored and revisited the places all around my home, seldom going far from it. Other places than the lake were frequently visited and watched. One of these I have described in "The Adventures of a Nature Guide." This often was as busy as a three-ring circus. This wilderness waiting place was by a brook in a grassy opening in a tall spruce wood.

One day a lion ran by close to where I sat watching. Not a footfall did I hear. He passed as silently as a shadow. A dead limb broke and fell from a tree. This sound alarmed a squirrel and he peeped from behind a tree toward the supposed danger, without showing himself. A passing coyote stopped at this sound. He did not move for half a minute; then he pointed his nose toward something under the grass, lifted one ear, turned his head, leaped, and picked up a mouse in his teeth together with several grass-blades.

At Lily Lake and other watched places I sat on a log, on the side of a cliff, lay down by a log, squatted in a clump of bushes, and occasionally climbed a treetop. Far above the ground I was not likely to be either seen or scented.

There was no end of nature stories. At each place watched, and often on the way to it, I saw birds or animals, or both, do something that I had not seen before. While I did not have a line of traps out, by visiting places as regularly as though I had, I saw the tracks and other records which wild life had made at each place since the preceding visit; and often these records were almost as exciting as the wild life itself. These signs and the wild life either made a new story or another chapter of a continued story.

A dim trail which I followed to a watched place at timberline crossed a brook on a log that was fifteen or more feet above the water. Once I found a lion lying on this log. Another time, several magpies were playing upon it. Over the south end of the log in summer leaned tall stalks of mertensia, their blue blooms five feet above the earth. Higher still in winter was the top of a snowdrift. One January when I crossed the log this snowdrift showed that during the five preceding days and nights it had been used as a bridge by squirrels, rabbits, porcupines, mice, weasels, and a number of mountain sheep. By the north end of the log, where during September a squirrel had piled pine cones, a coyote had crouched behind a spruce tree and watched for the squirrel. After a long wait he had turned and gone off into the spruce woods to look for something else to satisfy his hunger.

Trailing in the snow nearly always gave me a number of things to think about on each trip made. In following a grizzly for eight days and nights I had a book full of experiences; these, together with what I found to read about this great animal, made him more and more interesting. It was something of interest to know that the bear, dog, and the seal were, a million or so years ago, closely related.

In following one line of tracks I often came to where this was followed, or crossed, by other tracks; often I wanted to follow these new ones, and once I did. This was when, following the trail of a mountain sheep, I came to where it was crossed by the trail of a mother grizzly with only three feet, and her two cubs who stopped now and then to romp and wrestle in the snow.

When a boy, the good plan of learning to identify twenty-five or more birds, flowers, or animals had not been thought of. So I went about doing things in my own way, and by chance it proved a good way at least for me.

This was getting well acquainted with home territory together with specializing on the best spots in it. John Burroughs wrote a number of books concerning experiences on his long-settled New York farm, and Fabre wrote several books about the small wild people in his yard. Many were the ways of trees, birds, and animals that I learned before I could identify anyone of these. At Lily Lake and other beaver colonies I learned twenty-five or more stories about the beaver, and many of the ways of other animals, years before I learned to identify twenty-five birds and animals combined.

Among the numerous things which I had early seen a beaver do were:

Gnaw down trees.
Carry mud in hands.
Sit on his tail.
Carry mud and sticks between tail and stomach while
  swimming.
Dig a canal.
Kill a wildcat.
Run from a wolf.
Dredge mud from the bottom of the pond.
Wrestle and play with other beavers.
Build part of a dam.
Float a tree across a pond.
Scratch himself.
Brush flies off his nose.
Comb his fur with a double claw.
Whack the water with his tail.

These and other things seen in colonies the year round, the work and play of Mrs. and Mr. Beaver and the little beavers, gave me an excellent knowledge of beaver life.

While still a boy, a man came along and wanted someone to show him a beaver colony. I showed him three, and took all day for it. He asked questions about beaver life—I kept track, and it was forty-seven—all but three of which I readily answered, and in addition told him many things that I had seen of beaver life, which he did not ask about.

Two months later this man sent a whole party—men and women, and boys and girls—to me. All wanted to see a beaver colony. We spent the entire day in the Moraine beaver colony. Through the years I kept on going to this colony and on each trip I learned something new concerning it. During the years I have written six magazine articles concerning this one beaver colony.

A little later a New York newspaper man engaged me to guide him to Chasm Lake. This wild lake is on the side of Long's Peak and is about 12,000 feet above sea level. On the way up I asked him why there were pines on the sunny wall of the cañon up which we climbed and spruces on the northerly facing wall; and I also asked why at timberline there were spruces, firs, and willows in the moist places and pines in the near-by dry places. I told him many things concerning glaciers—how they worked and how they dug lake basins and piled up moraines of rocks and soil.

I came to be considered a nature guide. At first I gave my services free, but as I was so often wanted, and had to work for a living, I began to charge for guiding. People wanted to see and hear about rocks, trees, birds, wild flowers, beavers, bears, and everything.

A surprise came when a man took me to Idaho to guide through a region I had not seen. But I knew how to start a fire, and Idaho wood and Colorado wood behaved about the same; Idaho grizzlies had a different bill of fare, but I found that what I had learned of Colorado grizzlies enabled me to understand them without an introduction.

And so it was during my camping trips in Canada, Alaska, and Mexico; the things that I had learned while in sight of my cabin made me more or less at home with the rocks, trees, animals, and beavers a thousand or more miles from home.

In guiding people I found that they cared little for identification marks until they learned how living things made a living, what adventures were their lot, when and where the wild folks

*Enos Mills speaking at the annual Reunion Thanksgiving Dinner,
held at the Community Building in Estes Park Village, ca. 1900.
The Reverend and Mrs. Elkanah J. Lamb (Mills' uncle and aunt)
are in the foreground. Poster on the wall is dated 1899.*
Courtesy National Park Service—Rocky Mountain National Park.

worked and played—especially how they played—and why
each living thing lived in a particular locality. Just as people who
want the story of Robinson Crusoe care little for the name of
the author, or what the book looks like—they want to identify
the book by knowing the story. So it is with the great story of

Natural History: it is not the identification marks and brands of natural history figures that make the outdoors delightful and helpful. Ninety-nine per cent of woodcraft is first-hand experience.

A tree that has more than a single leader or top point probably has had an adventure with wind, porcupine, a falling tree, insects, or something that removed the original single top. So when I see a double-topped tree I wonder what has happened in the treetop. And in treetops I have had adventures numerous and exciting; adventures with ants, with swarms of bees, with two skunks, with a porcupine, with breaking limbs, with two bear cubs, with a black bear under me coming up to see what I was like—who was not frightened, while I was frightened enough for both—and I have watched forest fires, rain- and wind-storms from treetops.

The information found in treetops and elsewhere was useful in guiding. I had climbed Long's Peak more than forty times before I guided anyone up. But I did not know too much about the peak; in fact, I learned something new each time I went to the top as a guide, notwithstanding that before guiding I had climbed it in rain, wind, summer, winter, daytime and at night.

Many people thought that high altitude was harmful and were ever expecting something unpleasant to happen to them. If I hurried them during the climb, or if they had banqueted the night before, something like seasickness did happen. But in due time I learned that altitude generally was helpful and not harmful.

Most people whom I guided thought that the wilderness was full of dangerous animals: that bears, lions, and wolves were waiting for a chance to kill and eat them. All wild animals in America flee at the approach of man. He has been too dangerous an animal himself for the wild animals to allow close approach, or for them to take any chances on coming close to him. Fear of man has developed wildness in most animals and caused them the world round to find safety first in wild retreat on his approach. Exceptions are rare, and there are more men likely to kill a man than there are wild animals likely to do so.

A wolf has never offered to attack me, but several tame dogs have. Any animal, and perhaps even a worm, will fight in defense of its life, but only when it cannot run away from the danger. The few cases of wild animals attacking people appear to have been those of animals mentally deranged.

I have been surprised and delighted in many out-of-the-way places by wild animals who were not afraid of me, but who came up for a friendly look, and to find out what sort of a new model of an animal I might be. In a side cañon of the Grand Cañon, a number of mountain sheep who evidently had not before seen man looked at me with intense, curious interest, then came up to smell of me.

In the Yellowstone Park, and in other wild-life refuges, birds and animals are tame, though wild. The grizzlies, except where they have been teased and overfed on garbage, are not even cross. And thus it is with wild life under many environments; it is ever responding—ever doing something interesting.

It is this understanding of the wilderness and its hundreds of inhabitants that makes it a wonderland; and this understanding a nature guide can speedily enable others to acquire and enjoy.

The giving of most attention on each trip to one species of tree, bird, or animal, while gathering incidental information, is a good plan to practise. This idea may be extended over several trips. The nature guide should be a good all-round guide in natural history, and he may also be an expert concerning tree life, the beaver, butterflies, or geology.

The essential of nature guiding is a thorough understanding of something, and the ability to transfer this information clearly, entertainingly, to others. A guide must be able to talk—not too much—and in talking, say things in the right way. A guide, if he really knows principles, will be able to talk to one person in the field, or to many; he will rapidly learn to address those who listen around the camp-fire, or in a hall; or to write so that his ideas will be read by thousands.

Several times I have gone along as a nature guide in a region that I did not know, and received three times the wage of the other guide who knew only the way, and how to camp. People of all ages enjoy hearing the real facts concerning outdoor things. In Kansas City years ago a boy who was the son of a millionaire guided me among the bluffs and along the river. He did not charge for guiding. He was planning to be a farmer; he was a live, happy boy, and what he had learned outdoors had done more to develop him than all other experiences.

Often I have had people who were naturalists guide me through some place of interest. John Muir kindly showed me the Redwoods, and a celebrated geologist allowed me to camp with him for two weeks in and along the Grand Cañon.

On the other hand, I have been fortunate in having a number of people who are famous, each in a particular line, allow me to guide them afield.

Already there is need for one or more nature guides in every locality. In many of these the need is for expert guides who charge for their services. Every boy who knows the wild places near his home, or who understands intimately some one thing in the outdoors—why a living thing is where and what it is—will have many advantages that no other knowledge can give him. Outdoor experiences are educational and they are lastingly useful. Fortunate the boy who, like the bear, knows every nook and corner of his home territory.

The most likely places for paid nature guides are the National Parks, National Forests, State Parks, and wilderness spots in the mountains by the sea, where people come to rest and exercise.

A nature guide who plans to continue in this for a life work, or for some years, will need to prepare thoroughly for guiding. He needs to camp in wild places, and there study the trees, flowers, birds, rocks, animals, and insects, and supplement this with books and with talks with people who know. It requires as much preparation to become a top-notch guide as an author, lawyer, or engineer who is in class A. But I feel that guiding is more fun.

Nature—that is, the rocks with their stories, the streams, and wild life—is ever interesting. No matter what one's occupation, he wants, now and then, a vacation outdoors. If, as a boy, he was well enough acquainted with the wild life to be a guide, he will ever have something that will delightfully guide him during these vacations. And this wilderness lore will enable him a thousand times during his happy years to give a lively enjoyment to others.

On Wild Life Trails

A skunk passed by me going down the trail. In sight was a black bear coming up. Which of these wilderness fellows would give or be forced to give the right-of-way? There must be trail rights. I sat near the trail an innocent and concealed by-stander—a bump on a log—wondering about the wilderness etiquette for the occasion.

The black bear is happy-go-lucky. This one was pre-occupied until within two lengths of the skunk. A three-length side-leap and he stood watchful and ready to escape. The solemn, slow-moving skunk held the right-of-way and passed by without a turn of his head toward the curious and watching black bear. The skunk ever has his own way. His influence is most far reaching.

The wilderness has a web of wild life trails. Many of these are dim. The unobserved of all observers, I often sat in hiding close to a worn, much-trampled wild life trail—a highway—where it crossed a high point.

Before me just at sunrise a grizzly and a mountain lion met. The grizzly—the dignified master of the wilds—was shuffling along, going somewhere. He saw the lion afar but shuffled indifferently on. Within fifty feet the lion bristled and, growling, edged unwillingly from the trail. At the point of passing he was thirty feet from his trail-treading foe. With spitting, threatening demonstration he dashed by; while the unmoved, interested grizzly saw everything as he shuffled on, except that he did not look back at the lion which turned to show teeth and to watch him disappear.

It was different the day the grizzly met a skunk. This grizzly, as I knew from tracking him, was something of an adventurer. His home territory was more than forty miles to the southeast. He had travelled this trail a number of times. On mere notion sometimes he turned back and ambled homeward.

But this day the grizzly saw the slow-walking skunk coming long minutes before the black and white toddler with shiny plume arrived. The skunk is known and deferred to by wild folk big and little. Regardless of his trail rights the grizzly went on to a siding to wait. This siding which he voluntarily took was some fifty feet from the trail. Here the grizzly finally sat down. He waited and waited for the easy-going skunk to arrive and pass.

The approaching presence of the solemn, slow-going skunk was too much and the grizzly just could not help playing the clown. He threw a somersault; he rolled over. Then, like a young puppy, he sat on an awkwardly held body to watch the skunk pass. He pivoted his head to follow this unhastening fellow who was as dead to humour as the log by the trail.

Along the trail friend meets friend, foe meets enemy, stranger meets stranger, they linger, strangers not again. The meetings may be climaxes, produce clashes, or friendly contact; and in the passing high-brows and common folks rub elbows. To meet or not to meet ever is the question with them.

One old trail which I many times watched was on a ridge between two deep cañons. At the west the ridge expanded into the Continental Divide and the trail divided into dimmer footways. The east end terraced and the trail divided. Stretches of the trail were pine shadowed, spaces were in sunlight.

Where the trail went over a summit among the scattered trees travellers commonly paused for a peep ahead. Often, too, they waited and congested, trampling a wide stretch bare and often to dust. On this summit were scoutings, lingerings, and fighting. Lowlanders and highlanders, singly, in pairs and in strings, stamped the dust with feet shod in hoofs or in claws and pads.

One of the meetings of two grizzlies which I witnessed was on this ridge trail. A steady rain was falling. Each saw the other coming in the distance and each gave the right-of-way as though accidentally, by showing interest in fallen logs and boulder piles away from the trail. Each ludicrously pretending not to see the other, finally a passing was achieved, the trail regained without a salute.

A meeting of two other grizzlies revealed a different though a common form. Each saw the other coming but each held to the trail. At less than a length apart both rose and roared—feigned surprise—and soundly blamed the other for the narrowly averted and well-nigh terrible collision. But no delay for the last word. Each well pleased with the meeting hastened on, too wise to look back.

One day nothing came along this highway and I looked at the tracks in the wide, dusty trail. The multitude of tracks in it overlapped and overlaid each other. A grizzly track, like the footprint of a shoeless primitive man, was stamped with deer tracks, stitched and threaded with mice tails and tracks and scalloped with wolf toes. But its individuality was there.

For three days I had been a bump on a log by this place and no big travellers had passed. The birds, chipmunks, and a squirrel were entertaining as ever, but I had hoped for something else. I had just started for camp when dimly through the trees I saw something coming down the trail.

A dignified grizzly and a number of pompous, stiff-necked rams met and were so filled with curiosity that everyone forgot reserve and good form. They stopped and turned for looks at one another and thus merged a rude, serious affair into a slowly passing, successful meeting.

I sometimes sat at a point on this ridge trail so that the passing animal was in silhouette. The background was a lone black spruce against the shifting sky scenery. Horns and whiskers, coats of many colours, and exhibits of leg action went by. Horned heads, short-arched necks, and held-in chins abundantly told of pride and pomposity. But the character topography was in each back line. From nose tip to tail, plateau, cañon, hill, and slope stories stood against the sky.

The tail, though last, was the character clue to the passing figure. Regardless of curve, kink, or incline, it ever was story revealing: sometimes long and flowing, but the short tail attitude incited most imaginative interest in the attached individual.

From treetop I watched one trail where it was crossed by a stream. Generally deer and sheep went through the stream without a stop. In it bears often rolled. Sometimes they used the wilderness bridge—the beaver dam, and occasionally they splashed through the pond. Coyotes, porcupine, squirrels, rabbits, and lynx used the dam. A porcupine backed a lynx off this into the water, the lynx threatening and spitting. But the lynx met a rabbit near the other end and the rabbit went back with the lynx.

A grizzly was about to cross when three fun-loving grizzly cubs appeared. He stood aside and watched, perhaps enjoyed, their pranks in the water before coming across. On the bank the cubs hesitated for a moment before passing a sputtering squirrel who was denouncing them for youthful pranks. A few inches of the first snow was on the ground. I went back along the trail and examined tracks. At one point a lion had come out of the woods and given the cubs a scare; and still farther back they had stood on hind feet one behind the other, evidently watching a black bear go well around them.

Two flocks of bighorn mountain sheep passed by in single file like two lines of proud, set wooden figures. One of these flocks was down from the heights to visit a far-off salt lick. The other evidently was returning to its local territory on the high range by a circuitous route after being driven off by hunters. A few days later I saw these flocks meet on a high plateau. They stopped to visit. Then one flock turned back with the other and both edged over to an outlook rim of the plateau where I left them, racing and playing in the on-coming darkness.

In numberless places I saw a single wild fellow meet his species. Two coyotes advanced bristling and passed snarling. Another time two coyotes met, eyed, and then turned off in the woods together. Two wild cats advanced with declaration of war, made the forest aisles hideous with whoops and threats, struck attitudes which go with blood and gore—but nothing happened. Two squirrels approached, each loudly demanding the right-of-way. They blustered, backed-up, threatened, raced tempestuously up and down trees, and finally boastingly passed.

Many a time two rabbits speeded silently by without a slowing, a signal, or a look. Others kicked as they passed. One mid-winter day two rabbits leaped to meet mid-air; then like bucking bronchos they leaped high for action and like miniature mules turned here and there to kick at the target with two feet. If this was fight or frolic only rabbits know.

It often happened that the breeze was favourable and I watched the passing processions from my camp. Near camp two otters met and turned aside and later I followed their trail to the otter slide. Two woodchucks met by a boulder on which I sat quietly. They counter-marched in half war-like half circles. A pause, then with apparently friendly negotiations progressing, they discovered a coyote slipping toward them.

Many times through the years I waited for odd hours, and days, at a promising place on a trail a few miles from my cabin. The tracks along this showed it to be in constant use, but never have I seen a traveller pass along it. My being at many a meeting elsewhere was just coincidence. Years of wilderness wanderings often made me almost by chance an uninvited guest—I was among those present.

Dull fellows well met were skunk and porcupine. These dull-brained but efficiently armed fellows are conceded the right-of-way by conventional wilderness folk. They blundered to head-on clash. Never before had this occurred. Each was surprised and wrathy. There was a gritting of teeth. Each pushed and became furious. Then the skunk received several quills in the side and in turn the porcupine a dash of skunk spray. Both abandoned the trail, sadder but not wiser.

Deer, bear, beavers, and wolves travel because they need to do so, or for the fun of it. Deer shift for miles from a summer to a winter range, travelling a regular migration route. A number of enemy wolves may follow this moving food supply. Beavers may be seeking a home in new scenes and a bear may be off on an adventure.

Wild life trails were worn by generation after generation of wild animals using the same route, the line of least resistance long followed from one territory to another. Trampling feet assisted by wind and water maintained a plain trail. Indian trails often were wild life trails. Stretches of buffalo trails on the plains and bear trails in Alaska were abandoned because so deeply worn and washed.

From a low cliff by a mountain stream I watched the wild life along the trail on the other side of the stream. The cañon was wooded but the trail immediately opposite was in the open.

Two packs of wolves met on the trail across the river. The leaders rushed to grips and a general mix-up was on. But this was surprisingly brief. There was an outburst of snarling and the gangs passed with but little loss of time and with but one limping.

Often as these travellers passed out of sight after a meeting I wondered what and when would be their next adventure. Around a turn of the trail within five minutes after the black bear met the skunk he clashed with a lion, so tracks by the trails showed.

I often wondered, too, what experience an animal had been through immediately before he trailed into my sight. The peevish lion was just from her fat, safe, happy kittens. One of the two cross grizzlies was from a row with another grizzly, while the other had been playing along the trail and was on good terms with himself and the world.

When a skunk and mink—the more offensive of the smelly family—meet in contest, then smells to heaven their meeting. Driven into a corner, the mink will spread high-power musk in the only avenue of advance. He then is in an impregnable position—no fellow has nose sufficiently strong to pass. Or, if the mink place a guarding circle of musk around a prize kill this makes a time lock and will hold his prize for hours against all comers.

A skunk and mink clashed by the trail across the river. The skunk was leisurely advancing to seize a flopping, misguided trout on the bank when a mink rushed as though to close with the skunk. The skunk hesitated—and lost the fish. The mink in the delay of action made musk screen near the trout. The skunk went into action and drove the mink off with vile skunk spray. The musk of mink caused his advance to pause, he edged around to the other side, but too much, gave up the fish, and walked off gritting his teeth.

Beavers commonly leave stuffy house and spend summer vacation miles up or down stream. They travel by water. The swift water of a rapids forced two companies of beaver travellers to use the trail of land-lubbers on the bank. Here the company going up visited with another company going down. They mingled, smelled, and rubbed noses. The company going up turned back and both went off to frolic in a beaver pond. Later one company went on down and the other up the stream. Tracks showed that ten left the pond going down; this company had numbered twelve when it met the other company. The upbound company numbered fourteen at the meeting. Late that day I counted those going up stream as they left the trail and took to the water at the head of the rapids. They had increased their number to sixteen.

Two droves of deer met one October on the trail by stream and a beaver pond. They stopped, mingled, visited, and then laid down together. One drove was migrating from summer range on the peaks and high plateaus to winter range miles below. It was following along a trail generations old. The other drove was home-seeking. A forest fire with smoke still in the sky had laid barren their home territory.

From my treetop observation tower I saw a single coyote coming, and wondered what would be his attitude concerning the blockading of the trail by superior numbers, and also how these superior numbers would receive a single ancient enemy. But the deer were indifferent to the lone little wolf. They utterly ignored him.

The coyote walked leisurely around the vast assemblage with an air of ownership. Then he sat down before them and eyed them with a display of cynical satisfaction. He turned from this inspection and with a leisurely, contented air walked by with, "I haven't time to-day—but I should worry."

I had my camp by a cliff a short distance up stream and of mornings birds were numerous. A waterfall was at its best in the night. I had planned to watch this place another day or two but the wind was from the wrong quarter—it would carry my scent and warn travellers that a possible killer was in ambush. So I travelled away on this trail.

Many a time in the wilds I "met up" unexpectedly with wild life. And as I recall these meetings I plan again to be among those present. Unexpected meetings and near meetings were had with most large and leading species of animals on the Continent.

The alert grizzly, realizing I was one of the superkiller species, generally avoided me. I travelled alone and unarmed, and before I had satisfied myself that the grizzly is not a ferocious animal I most unexpectedly met one. I was his bogie—both acted on the impulse.

In the wilds one may meet a skunk or a bear. Either gives concentration—one's every-day faculties take a vacation, and the Imagination has the stage. A bear adventure is telling. You meet the bear, he escapes, and eager listeners hear your graphic story.

The skunk is a good fellow—a good mixer. His policy is to meet or be met—the other fellow will attend to the running. The war-filled wilderness of tooth and claw ceases to be aggressive in the pacifying process of the little black and white skunk. When a skunk goes into reverse thus runs the world away. From the met skunk you absorb story material—local colour, carry off enduring evidence; your friends scent the story, they shrink from you; from registered fragments their creative faculties have restored a movie scene.

The Mountain Lion

Raising my eyes for an instant from the antics of a woodchuck, they caught a movement of the tall grass caused by a crawling animal. This presently showed itself to be a mountain lion. He was slipping up on a mare and colt on the opposite edge of the meadow. The easy air that was blowing across my face—from horse to lion—had not carried a warning of my presence to either of them.

I was in Big Elk Park, seated on a rock pile, and was nearly concealed by drooping tree limbs. Behind me rose the forested Twin Peaks, and before me a ragged-edged mountain meadow lay in the forest; and across this meadow the lion crawled.

The colt kicked up its heels as it ran merry circles round its mother. This beautiful bay mare, like her colt, was born in unfenced scenes and had never felt the hand of man. She had marked capability and the keenness exacted by wilderness environment.

I watched the bending grass as the lion crept closer and closer. Occasionally I caught a glimpse of the low-held body and the alert raised head. The back-pointing, sensitive three foot tail, as restless as an elephant's trunk, kept swinging, twitching, and feeling. Planning before the lion was within leaping distance to warn the mare with a yell, I sat still and watched.

The well-developed and ever-alert senses of the mare—I know not whether it was scent or sight—brought a message of danger. Suddenly she struck an attitude of concentration and defiance, and the frightened colt crowded to her side. How capable and courageous she stood, with arched neck, blazing eyes, vigilant ears, and haughty tail! She pawed impatiently as the lion, now near, watchful and waiting, froze.

Suddenly he leaped forward, evidently hoping to stampede both animals and probably to seize the separated colt. Instantly the mother wheeled, and her outkicking heels narrowly missed the lion's head. Next the lion made a quick side-leap to avoid being stamped beneath the mare's swift front feet.

For half a minute the mare and lion were dodging and fighting with all their skill. A splendid picture the mare made with erect tail and arched neck as she struck and wheeled and kicked!

Again and again the lion tried to leap upon the colt; but each time the mother was between them. Then, watching his chance, he boldly leaped at the mare, endeavouring to throw a forepaw round her neck and, at the same instant, to seize and tear the throat with his savage teeth. He nearly succeeded.

With the lion clinging and tearing at her head, the audacious mare reared almost straight on her hind legs and threw herself backward. This either threw the lion off or he let go. She had her nose badly clawed and got a bite in the neck; but she was first to recover, and a kick landed upon the lion's hip. Crippled, he struggled and hurried tumbling away into the woods, while the bleeding mare paused to breathe beside the untouched colt.

The mountain lion is called a puma, catamount, panther, painter, or cougar, and was originally found all over North America. Of course he shows variations due to local climate and food.

The lion is stealthy, exceedingly cunning, and curious in the extreme; but I am not ready, as many are, to call him cowardly. He does not have that spectacular rash bravery which dashes into the face of almost certain death; but he is courageous enough when necessity requires him to procure food or to defend himself and his kind. He simply adapts himself to conditions; and these exact extreme caution.

The mountain lion may be called sagacious rather than audacious. Settlers in his territory are aware of his presence through his hogging the wild game and his occasional or frequent killing of colts, horses, cattle, sheep, and chickens. But so seldom is he seen, or even heard, that, were it not for his tracks and the deadly evidence of his presence, his existence could not be believed.

Though I have camped in his territory for weeks at a time, and ofttimes made special efforts to see him, the number of lions I have seen—except, of course, those treed by dogs—is small.

When a mountain lion is frightened, or when pursued by dogs, he is pretty certain to take refuge in a tree. This may be a small tree or a large one. He may be out on a large limb or up in the top of the tree.

The lion is a fair runner and a good swimmer. Often he has been known to swim across lakes, or even arms of the sea, more than a mile wide. And he is an excellent tree climber, and often uses a living tree or a dead leaning one as a thoroughfare—as a part of his trail system on a steep mountain side. Twice I have seen him on a near-by limb at night watching me or my fire. Once I woke in the night and saw a lion upon two out-reaching tree limbs not more than eight feet above me. His hind feet were upon one limb, his forefeet upon a lower limb, and he was looking down, watching me curiously. He remained in this position for several minutes, then turned quietly, descended the tree on the opposite side, and walked away into the woods.

It is probable that lions mate for life. Sometimes they live year after year in the same den and prowl over the same local territory. This territory, I think, is rarely more than a few miles across; though where food is scarce or a good den not desirably located, they may cover a larger territory.

Lions commonly live in a den of their own making. This is sometimes dug in loose sand or soil where its entrance is concealed among bushes. Sometimes it is beneath a fallen log or a tree root, and in other places a semi-den, beneath rocks, is enlarged. In this den the young are born, and the old ones may use it a part of each year, and for year after year.

Though occasionally a mother lion may raise as many as five kittens, rarely does she succeed in raising more than two; and I think only two are commonly brought forth at a birth. These kittens probably remain with the mother for nearly a year, and in exceptional cases even longer. As I have seen either kittens or their tracks at every season of the year, I assume the young may be born at any time.

The mountain lion is a big-whiskered cat and has many of the traits possessed by the average cat. He weighs about one hundred and fifty pounds, and is from seven to eight feet long, including a three-foot tail. He is thin and flat-sided and tawny in colour. He varies from brownish red to grayish brown. He has sharp, strong claws.

Mr. Roosevelt once offered one thousand dollars for a mountain lion skin that would measure ten feet from tip to tip. The money was never claimed. Apparently, however, in the state of Washington a hunter did succeed in capturing an old lion that weighed nearly two hundred pounds and measured ten and a half feet from tip to tip. But most lions approximate only one hundred pounds and measure possibly eight feet from tip to tip.

The lion eats almost anything. I have seen him catching mice and grasshoppers. On one occasion I was lying behind a clump of willows upon a beaver dam. Across the pond was an open, grassy space. Out into this presently walked a mountain lion. For at least half an hour he amused or satisfied himself by chasing, capturing, and eating grasshoppers. He then laid down for a few minutes in the sunshine; but presently he scented something alarming and vanished into the thick pine woods.

One evening I sat watching a number of deer feeding on a terrace of a steep mountain side. Suddenly a lion leaped out, landing on the neck of one. Evidently the deer was off balance and on a steep slope. The impact of the lion knocked him over, but like a flash he was upon his feet again. Top-heavy with the lion, he slid several yards down a steep place and fell over a precipice. The lion was carried with him. I found both dead on the rocks below.

The lion is a master of woodcraft. He understands the varying sounds and silences of the forest. He either hides and lies in wait or slips unsuspected upon his victim. He slips upon game even more stealthily than man; and in choosing the spot to wait for a victim he usually chooses wisely and, alert waits, if necessary, for a prolonged time. He leaps upon the shoulders and neck of horse, deer, or sheep, and then grabs the victim's throat in his teeth. Generally the victim quickly succumbs. If a lion or lioness misses in leaping, it commonly turns away to seek another victim. Rarely does it pursue or put up a fight.

A friend wished a small blue mule on me. It had been the man's vacation pack animal. The mule loitered round, feeding on the abundant grass near my cabin. The first snow came. Twenty-four hours later the mule was passing a boulder near my cabin when a lion leaped upon him and throttled him. Tracks and scattered hair showed that the struggle had been intense though brief.

Not a track led to the boulder upon which the lion had lain in wait, and, as the snow had fallen twenty-four or more hours before the tragedy, he must have been there at least twenty-four hours, and he may have waited twice as long.

Another time I frightened a lion from a cliff where he was waiting for a near-by flock of bighorn sheep to come within leaping distance. Though it was nearly forty-eight hours since snow had ceased falling, not a track led to the lion's watching place or blind.

The lion probably is the game hog of the wilds. Often I have read his red records in the snow. On one occasion he killed nine mountain sheep in one attack. He ate a few pounds of one of them and never returned to the kill. On another occasion he killed eleven domestic sheep in one night. Inside of twenty-four hours a lion killed a doe, a fawn, a porcupine, a grouse, and was making a try for a mountain sheep when I appeared on snowshoes. He seems to prefer colts or horses for food.

Mr. J. A. McGuire, editor of *Outdoor Life,* who has made special investigations concerning the killings of mountain lions, estimates that a lion will kill a deer every week if he has the opportunity to do so. From personal experience I have known him to kill four deer in a single week.

On one occasion, when I was hidden and watching the carcass of a deer which a lion had killed to see what carnivorous animal might come to the feast, a mountain lion walked quietly and unalertly to it and commenced to eat. After a few minutes the lion suddenly bristled up and spat in the direction from which a grizzly bear presently appeared. With terrible snarling and threatening, the lion held on to the prize until the grizzly was within a few feet. He then leaped toward the grizzly with a snarl, struck at it, and dashed into the woods. The grizzly, without even looking round to see where the lion had gone, began eating.

From many experiences I believe that much of the killing of domestic and wild animals attributed to bears is done by lions. The lion prefers warm blood and fresh meat for each meal, and will kill daily if there is opportunity. I have known bears to follow mountain lions evidently for the purpose of obtaining food. One day I came upon the recently killed carcass of a cow. Only mountain lion tracks led to it and from it. The following night I spent at a near-by ranch house, and the rancher informed me that on the previous day he had discovered a bear eating the carcass of this cow which he accused the bear of killing. The lion is a most capable raider of ranches, and colts, horses, sheep, pigs, and poultry are his prizes.

In northern New Mexico one day I saw a lion bounding across an opening carrying a tame sheep in its mouth. On another occasion I saw a lion carrying off a deer that apparently weighed much more than the lion itself. The lion appeared to have the deer by the shoulder, and it was resting on the lion's shoulders in such a way that I do not believe it touched the ground.

I suppose when the lion makes a kill in an out-of-the-way place, where he may eat with comparative safety, he does not take the trouble to carry or to drag the victim off. Often, of course, the kill is made for the benefit of the young, and hence must be transported to the den.

It is quite true that he will sometimes wander back to his kill day after day and feast upon it. It is also true, when food is scarce, that lions will eat almost anything, even though they have nothing to do with the killing. They have been trapped at the bait that was out for bears: and so, though a lion prefers blood and warm meat, he will return to his kill to feast, or, if food is scarce, gladly eat whatever he can obtain.

From many observations I judge that after eating he prefers to lie down for a few hours in some sunny or secluded spot, or on a many-branched limb generally well up toward the top of the tree but sometimes not more than ten feet above the earth.

The lion has extreme curiosity. He will follow travellers for hours if there is opportunity to keep out of sight while doing so. Often during long snowshoe trips I have returned over the route first travelled. Lion tracks in the snow showed that I was repeatedly followed for miles. In a number of places, where I had taken a long rest, the lion had crept up close, so that he could easily watch me; and on a few occasions he must have been within a few feet of me.

While walking through a forest in the Medicine Bow Mountains I was startled and knocked down by a glancing blow of a tree limb. This limb had evidently broken off under the weight of a lion. The lion also came tumbling down but caught a claw on a limb and saved himself from striking the earth. Evidently in his curiosity to see me he had leaned out too far on a weak limb. He fled in confusion, perhaps even more frightened than myself.

The mountain lion is not ferocious. Mr. Roosevelt, in summing up its characteristics, concluded that it would be no more dangerous to sleep in woods populated with mountain lions than if they were so many ordinary cats.

In addition to years of camping in the wilds in all sorts of places and under all conditions of weather I have talked with careful frontiersmen, skillful hunters and trappers, and these people uniformly agreed with what I have found to be true—that the instances of mountain lions attacking human beings are exceedingly rare. In each of these cases the peculiar action of the lion and the comparative ineffectiveness of his attacks indicated that he was below normal mentally or nearly exhausted physically.

Two other points of agreement are: Rarely does anyone under ordinary conditions see a lion; and just as rarely does one hear its call. Of the dozen or more times I have heard the screech of the lion, on three occasions there was a definite cause for the cry—on one a mother frantically sought her young, which had been carried off by a trapper; and twice the cry was a wail, in each instance given by the lion calling for its mate, recently slain by a hunter.

During the past thirty years I have investigated dozens of stories told of lions leaping upon travellers from cliffs or tree limbs, or of other stealthy attacks. When run down each of these proved to be an invention; in most cases not a lion or even lion track had been seen.

Two instances of lion attacks are worth mentioning. One night in California a lion leaped from a cliff, struck a man, knocked him down, and then ran away. Out of this incident have come numerous stories of lion ferocity. The lion was tracked, however, and the following day the pursuing hunter saw it crossing an opening. It suddenly clawed and hit at a boulder. Then, going on, it apparently ran into a tree, and fought that. As it started on the hunter shot it. This beast was badly emaciated, had a swollen face from an ulcerated tooth, and was nearly, if not entirely, blind.

Another instance apparently was of a weak-minded lion. As though to attack, it came toward a little ten-year-old girl in Idaho. She struck it over the head with a bridle she was carrying. Her brother hurried to the rescue with a willow fishing pole. Together they beat the lion off and escaped with a few bad scratches. Yet had this been a lion of average strength and braveness he must have killed or severely injured both.

The mountain lion rivals the shark, the devilfish, and the grizzly in being the cause of ferocious tales. The fact that he takes refuge on limbs as a place of lookout to watch for people or other objects, and that he frequently follows people for hours through the woods without their ever seeing him—and, I suppose, too, the very fact that he is so rarely seen—make him a sort of storm centre, as it were, for blood-curdling stories.

Through years I investigated plausible accounts of the ferocity of mountain lions. These investigations brought little information, but they did disclose the fact that there are a few types of lion tales which are told over and over again, with slight local variations. These tales commonly are without the slightest basis of fact. They are usually revamped by a clever writer, a frightened hunter, or an interesting story teller, as occasions offer. One of the commonest of the oft-told tales that have come to me through the years is as follows:

"Late Saturday evening, while Mr. and Mrs. Simpson were returning from the village through the woods, they were attacked by a half-starved mountain lion. The lion leaped out upon them from brush by the roadside and attempted to seize Mr. Simpson. Though an old man, he put up a fight, and at last beat off the lion with the butt of the buggy whip."

Sometimes this is a family and the time of day is early morning. Sometimes the lion is ferocious instead of half-starved.

Sometimes it is of enormous size. Once in a while he leaps from a cliff or an overhanging tree limb. Generally he chews and claws someone up pretty badly, and occasionally attempts to carry off one of the children.

Many times my letter addressed to one of the party attacked is returned unclaimed. Sometimes my letter to the postmaster or the sheriff of the locality is returned with the information: "No such party known." Now and then I ask the sheriff, the postmaster, or the storekeeper some questions concerning this attack, and, commonly their replies are: "It never happened"; "It's a pipe dream"; "A pure fake"; or "Evidently whoever told you that story had one or two drinks too many."

One day I came out of the woods in the rear of a saw-mill. I was making my way to the living room of the place, between logs and lumber piles. Right round the corner of a slab heap I caught sight of a mountain lion just as it leaped at me. It missed me intentionally, and at once wheeled and rose up to play with me. In the two or three seconds that elapsed between the time I had my first glimpse of it and when I realized it was a pet I had almost concluded that, after all, a lion may be a ferocious animal.

On one occasion, when I was on a cliff at the edge of a grassy opening, I was astonished to see a coyote trot leisurely across and just before he disappeared in the woods a lion appear on the opposite side of the opening, following contentedly along the trail of the coyote. The next day I again saw this friendly pair, but on this occasion the lion was leading and the coyote following. Afterward I saw their tracks a number of times.

Just why they were associated in this friendly manner we can only conjecture. It will be readily seen that the coyote, which has all the wisdom of a fox, might follow a game-hog lion about and thus, with little effort, get a substantial and satisfactory food supply. But why the lion should willingly associate with a coyote is not quite clear. Perhaps this association proved to be of some advantage to the lion in his killing, or it may have been just one of those peculiar, unaccounted-for attachments occasionally seen between animals.

In any discussion concerning the mountain lion, or, for that matter, any living animal, hardly can the last word be said concerning the character of the individual of the species. Individuals vary, and now and then a mountain lion, as well as a human being, shows marked and peculiar traits. These may be the result of unusual alertness and sheer curiosity, or they may be subnormal, and cruel or murderous.

Notes

Notes are keyed to the page and line numbers. For example, 1:18 means page 1, line 18. For the spelling of place-names I have been guided by Louisa Ward Arps and Elinor Eppich Kingery, *High Country Names: Rocky Mountain National Park and Indian Peaks* (Boulder: Johnson Books, 1994).

Colorado Snow Observer

1:18. Louis George Carpenter (1861–1935), a native of Michigan, joined the faculty of Colorado Agricultural College in Fort Collins (now Colorado State University) in 1888 as professor of Engineering and Physics to teach irrigation engineering and to conduct irrigation experiments at the Colorado Agricultural Experiment Station. At CAC Carpenter earned a national reputation by organizing the first systematic instructional and research program in irrigation engineering, a subject of major importance to the water-starved West. In 1899 Carpenter was appointed director of the Colorado Agricultural Experiment Station. 1903 and 1905, he served as state engineer of Colorado and it was in this capacity that he engaged the services of Enos Mills as snow observer. For a number of years the Carpenter family had a summer cabin close to Longs Peak Inn, built on land purchased for Mills.

3:24. The town of Crested Butte is located in west central Colorado, some 22 miles north of Gunnison.

4:11. Lead Mountain (12,537 feet) is located on the Continental Divide to the west of Rocky Mountain National Park. It was apparently named by prospectors during the 1870s.

5:9. Mount Lincoln (14,284 feet), located in central Colorado, 12 miles northeast of Leadville, is the highest peak in the Park Range.

6:34. The 16-mile trail from Estes Park over the "bleak heights" of Flattop Mountain to Grand Lake by way of the North Inlet Trail was blazed by Fred Sprague (1857–1922), who with his brother Abner Sprague (1850–1943) had homesteaded in Moraine Park, and by surveyor Franklin I. Huntington. Mills made this journey in February 1903.

10:39. In 1905 Wyoming's Medicine Bow National Forest was extended to include the area now embraced by Rocky Mountain National Park. Five years later, in 1910, the year after the volume containing this essay, *Wild Life on the Rockies,* appeared, the section of this forest reserve in Colorado was renamed the Colorado National Forest. In 1932 it became the Roosevelt National Forest.

Faithful Scotch

13:1. Enos Mills received Scotch as a puppy in 1902, and the dog soon became his constant companion and a fixture at Longs Peak Inn. Mills taught Scotch to put out fires, and his death in 1910 occurred because the dog tried to extinguish the fuse on a charge of dynamite being used by a local road crew.

17:5. The "young lady from Michigan" was Victoria Broughm, or Brougham, who had been staying at Longs Peak Inn. Three of the four guides whom Enos Mills dispatched in search of Miss Broughm were his younger brother Enoch "Joe" Mills (1880–1935), William S. Cooper (1884–1978), who pioneered in the exploration of Wild Basin south of Longs Peak Inn, and went on to become a leading ecologist at the University of Minnesota, and local mason Carl Piltz (186?–1926). Mills expanded this chapter, retelling the Victoria Broughm rescue story, into a magazine article, "The Story of Scotch," which he published in the May 1, 1912, issue of *Country Life in America* and then into book form, *The Story of Scotch* (Boston: Houghton Mifflin, 1916). Joe Mills includes his own version of the event in his fictionalized autobiography *A Mountain Boyhood* (New York: J. H. Sears & Company, Inc., 1926).

20:21. The allusion is to the small tin-roofed homestead cabin that Enos Mills built in the Tahosa Valley in 1885–86.

Kinnikinick

26:33. The Blackfoot Indians were the largest and most powerful of the tribes inhabiting the northern plains. The Piute (or Paiute) Indians, mentioned below, were a small tribe inhabiting the Great Basin east of the Sierra Nevada, encompassing parts of California, northwestern Nevada, and eastern Oregon. The Alaska Indians, also mentioned below, were members of one of several small tribes inhabiting what was then a U.S. Territory.

Besieged by Bears

28:14. Geneva Park is located southwest of Geneva Mountain in northern Park County. Mills visited the area in the winter of 1902–1903 during a six-day, 120-mile inspection trip of the headwaters of the Platte River. Presumably it was on this occasion that he encountered the two old prospectors, Sullivan and Jason, and heard their bear story of two decades earlier.

The Forest Fire

35:17. Now called the Never Summer Range.

36:4. The Grand River is the former name given to the upper portion of the Colorado River, which has its source in what is now the northwestern corner of Rocky Mountain National Park and flows south through Middle Park. Its name was officially changed in 1921.

Little Boy Grizzly

51:2. Mt. Meeker (13,911 feet), which lies directly to the south of Longs Peak, is named for Nathan Meeker (1817–1879), the agricultural editor of Horace Greeley's *New York Tribune* and a social reformer, who in 1869 came west to Colorado to organize and run the Union Colony, the agricultural cooperative which became the town of Greeley. Meeker himself was killed by Utes during the White River Massacre in September 1879.

52:6. Both Enos Mills and his younger brother Joe claimed exclusive credit for the 1903 capture and rearing of the two bear clubs Jenny and Johnny and their subsequent relocation to the Denver Zoo. Enos Mills told the story here and again in his book, *The Grizzly: Our Greatest Wild Animal* (Boston: Houghton Mifflin, 1919). Joe Mills told the story of Jenny and Johnny in "My Friend the Grizzlies," *St. Nicholas* (February 1914) and in his autobiographical *A Mountain Boyhood* (1926).

The fact that neither brother mentions the other is attributable to the quarrel that irreparably estranged them in 1908. (See Alexander Drummond, *Enos Mills: Citizen of Nature* [Niwot, CO: University Press of Colorado, 1995], pp. 213–220.) The truth of the matter, undoubtedly, is that the original capture of the bear cubs was a joint enterprise that became parochial only in retrospect. As a writer for the *Denver Post* noted in his July 22, 1936, story of Jenny's death:

> Jennie [sic] was born in the wilds of what is now Rocky Mountain National Park in January 1903. The late Joseph [sic] and Enos Mills, longtime residents of the region and Colorado naturalists, had a set of traps out for coyotes. Jennie, a cub, was caught.
>
> What became of the mother is a mystery, but Jack, her brother, refused to desert her and was captured with her. He died ten years ago [1925]. Both bears were sold to the zoo, and, according to the late Joe Mills's story of the catch, as told to Hill [Clyde E. Hill, whose father Alfred E. Hill (1850–1918) worked for the Denver Zoo from 1890 to 1912, the greatest part of the time as superintendent], the

$225 they brought went toward Mills's education at the University of Colorado. (p 16)

In his *A Mountain Boyhood* the younger Mills reported that the mother bear had been caught in the steel bear trap he had set and that "her two cubs, of about fifteen pounds each, had lingered near by, until, growing hungry, they had ventured to their mother, and one had been caught in a coyote trap set to protect the bait." The mother bear, he confesses, was "about spent, and easily dispatched." That Joe Mills' version of the story stands closer to the truth is validated by the photograph taken that day and reproduced in this volume, which shows Joe posing, knife in hand, engaged in "mortal combat" with the already-dead mother bear which has been propped up and posed for the occasion. The money from the Denver Zoo may well have been spent on education, for Joe Mills entered the University of Denver (not the University of Colorado) in the fall of 1903, where he quarterbacked the football team.

On the other hand, how or why Jack became Johnny remains unclear.

57:18. Joe Mills in *A Mountain Boyhood* tells about visiting the two bears in the Denver Zoo, and being saved by Johnny from the attack of a black bear who had bitten him on the left knee.

Working Like a Beaver

68:5. The Jefferson River in southwestern Montana rises in the Granelly Range near Yellowstone National Park.

Transportation Facilities

71:2. Lily Lake, two miles north of Longs Peak Inn, lies at the foot of Lily Mountain (9,786 feet) on the road to the Estes Valley and the village of Estes Park at an elevation of 9,000 feet. It was named for the lily pads which once were abundant on the small lake. Lily Lake drains into the Big Thompson River by way of Fish Creek.

72:5. Wind River is a small stream northwest of Lily Lake. Today it flows past the entrance of the YMCA of the Rockies to empty into the Big Thompson River.

77:8. Mills describes the Spruce Tree Colony as "the most active" of the 16 colonies of beaver that made their home along the Roaring Fork which flows out of Chasm Lake below the East Face of Longs Peak and then east along the southern flank of Mills Moraine.

Beaver Pioneers

90:7. Willow Creek was the early name of Fish Creek, the outlet stream of Lily Lake.

91:12. Windham Thomas Wynham Quin (1841–1926), the fourth Earl of Dunraven, was the wealthy Irish-born, Oxford-educated lord who visited Estes Park on a hunting expedition in late December 1872, and subsequently launched an ambitious scheme to gain control of the valley for his own private uses. Though Dunraven's grand design was foiled by the militancy of early settlers, he did succeed in gaining effective control of upwards of 10,000 acres. In 1877 he built the three-story, fifty-room Estes Park Hotel on lower Fish Creek, the first luxury resort in Estes Park. It was rumored at the time, and since, that Dunraven intended to make Estes Park a private game preserve for himself and his aristocratic friends, an undertaking that in view of the fact that Estes Park was even then a well-known and increasingly much-visited place of summer refuge seems unlikely.

Going to the Top

99:16. Mills' initial reputation was as a Longs Peak guide. A career in which he excelled and which he carried on through the summer of 1906, when his busy life as a writer, lecturer, and innkeeper caused him to turn over that activity to other, younger men whose training Mills personally supervised.

101:29. Mills' allusion is to the ailment—perhaps an allergy to wheat—that brought him to Estes Park from his native Kansas in 1884.

102:18. Trampas is the famous villain of Owen Wister's 1902 novel *The Virginian,* and the recipient of one of the most famous lines in all of western American literature: "When you call me that, *smile.*" But the statement quoted—"In gatherings of more than six there will generally be at least one fool; and this company must have numbered twenty men"—belongs to Wister's unnamed narrator, not to any of the novel's characters.

104:16. Clarence King, *Mountaineering in the Sierra Nevada* (1872). The quotation is from the chapter titled "The Descent of Mount Tyndall." King (1842–1901) had been in charge of the Fortieth Parallel Survey, which scientifically explored a hundred mile strip from eastern Colorado to the border of California between 1867 to 1872. As part of that survey King mapped the northern portion of the Estes Valley during a visit in 1871.

105:7. The Narrows is the ledge midway along a rock wall some 2,000 feet high on the south face of Longs Peak that climbers must traverse on their way to the summit.

105:23. The practice of refusing tips extended to Longs Peak Inn, which the fastidious Mills ran strictly as a "non-tip house."

105:27. The Keyhole is the jagged opening at the head of the rock-strewn Boulder Field on Longs Peak through which climbers bound for the top must pass on their ascent.

107:29. As noted above, Mills' last season of guiding occurred in 1906.

108:9. See "Climbing Long's Peak," *Wild Life on the Rockies* (Houghton Mifflin: 1909), pp. 99–111. Mills identifies her home as "the 'big' end of the Arkansas River," presumably in the state of Arkansas where it joins the Mississippi. The Arkansas River, however, also flows through the states of Colorado, Kansas, and Oklahoma. See also "Harriet—Little Mountain Climber" in this volume.

108:17. The source of Mills' allusion is found in John Tyndall's *Hours of Exercise in the Alps* (1871). Tyndall (1820–1893), the noted British scientist and mountaineer, was especially interested in glaciation. Tyndall Glacier, below Hallett Peak in Rocky Mountain National Park, at the suggestion of Enos Mills, now bears his name.

108:34. The source of the quotation is John Muir's *Our National Parks* (1901), a book that Mills later emulated in a book of his own, *Your National Parks* (1917). Mills had accidentally met the great naturalist and mountaineer (1838–1914) on the beach in San Francisco's Golden Gate Park in December 1889, an event which he later called the turning point of his life. "You have helped me more than all the others," he wrote Muir in 1913; "but for you I might never have done anything for scenery."

The Grizzly Bear

109:1. The northernmost of the three great parks, or valleys, that lie north to south across north-central Colorado. North Park lies in Jackson County, between the Medicine Bow Mountains, an extension of the Front Range, and the Park Range.

112:16. See Note 52:6, above.

114:25. The Selkirk Mountains of Canada lie mostly in southeastern British Columbia but extend into Idaho and Montana.

116:38. Battle Mountain (12,044 feet), one of the near neighbors of Longs Peak to the northwest, was so-named by Enos Mills because it so obviously bore the scars of the forces of nature, including an early forest fire.

118:19. The Bitterroot Mountains are a range of the Rockies extending along the Montana-Idaho line.

The Rocky Mountain National Park

120:5. Ferdinand Vandiveer Hayden (1829–1887), as head of the U.S. Geological and Geographic Survey of the Territories (better known as the Hayden Survey), visited the Estes Park–Rocky Mountain National Park region in 1873.

120:15. When William S. Cooper (1884–1978) surveyed and mapped Wild Basin in 1908, he initiated an unsuccessful campaign to change the name of Copeland Mountain (13,176 feet) to Mt. Clarence King in honor of the leader of the 40th Parallel Survey (see above) who became the first head of the U.S. Geological Survey. The original—and current name—honors rancher John C. Copeland, who homesteaded near what became Copeland Lake at the entrance to Wild Basin.

122:4. Stones Peak was named after Professor George H. Stone (1841–1917), a professor of geology at Colorado College in Colorado Springs, who explored the area during the 1880s.

122:14. David Starr Jordan (1851–1931) and Vernon L. Kellogg (1867–1937) were among those who enjoyed the famous hospitality of Longs Peak Inn. Jordan, a distinguished natural scientist, served as president of Indiana University (1885–1891) and Stanford University (1891–1913). Kellogg, a zoologist, served as professor of entomology at the University of Kansas (1890–1894) and at Stanford (1894–1920). The two men co-authored a number of books, including *Animal Life* (1900), *Animals* (1902), *Animal Studies* (1903), *Evolution and Animal Life* (1907), and *The Scientific Aspects of Luther Burbank's Work* (1909). Kellogg, who had camped in Moraine Park during the summer of 1889 with a group of fellow Kansas students that included William Allen White, the future Emporia, Kansas, journalist, contributed an illustrated article titled "Parks and Peaks in Colorado," focusing on the Estes Park region, to the February 1901 issue of the *Sierra Club Bulletin*.

122:15. Edward L. Orton, Jr. (1865–1932), as a member of the Ohio State University Department of Chemistry, carried out a geological survey of Mills Moraine and the Longs Peak region during the summer of 1908. Mt. Orton (11,724 feet) in Wild Basin to the south is named after his father, Edward Orton, Sr. (1829–1899), the president of both Antioch College and the Ohio State University between 1882 and 1889.

122:20. Moraine Park, located near the eastern boundary of Rocky Mountain National Park, takes its name from the two lateral glacial moraines to the north and south responsible for its creation. Between the two flows the Big Thompson River. It was originally known as Willow Park.

122:21. Glacier Gorge, which contains both Loch Vale and Mills Lake, lies to the northwest of Longs Peak. Mills elsewhere notes that it "probably has the most magnificent scenery in the Park."

122:21. Loch Vale (10,180 feet), located between Otis Peak and Thatchtop Mountain is one of the most spectacular in Rocky Mountain National Park. "Loch" is, of course, the Scottish word for lake.

122:24. Bierstadt Moraine, like nearby Bierstadt Lake, was named for the German painter Albert Bierstadt (1830–1902), known for his romantic landscapes, who came to Estes Park in the autumn of 1876 to paint a landscape for the Earl of Dunraven. That five-by-eight-foot painting, "Long's Peak, Estes Park, Colorado," now hangs outside the Western Room of the Denver Public Library.

122:28. Chasm Lake lies in the glacial cirque at the base of the rugged East Face of Longs Peak.

122:37. Shoshone Peak was the name briefly given to Mt. Alice (13,310 feet) in Wild Basin. For a short period, which began in May 1914 and included the date in which this essay was published, Ellsworth Bethel (1863–1925), a retired Denver botany teacher, led a campaign to have many of the mountains in what would become Rocky Mountain National Park named or renamed after Indian tribes or their original Indian names. The U.S. Board of Geographic Names, to which Bethel had applied, ultimately rejected five of his names, including Shoshone. Mt. Alice was thus destined to remain Mt. Alice.

123:2. Otis Peak (12,586 feet) is named after Dr. Edward Osgood Otis (1848–1933), a Boston physician with an interest in climatology who for many years served on the faculty of Tufts College. Otis was one of the members of the Appalachian Mountain Club who climbed with Frederick Chapin in 1887 (see below).

123:3. Hallett Peak (12,713 feet) was named after William Hallett (1851–1941), one of Estes Park's pioneering mountaineers. A native of Massachusetts and an engineer by training, Hallett came to Estes Park in 1878 and returned a year later on his honeymoon. In 1881 Hallett took up ranching in the Park and built a summer home, Edgemont, just northwest of Marys Lake. When not ranching, Hallett climbed the nearby peaks and guided summer visitors.

123:9. Green Mountain (10,313 feet) is situated north of Grand Lake in Middle Park along the western boundary of Rocky Mountain National Park.

123:32. Fall River originates below Fall River Pass (which sits at 11,796 feet) in the Mummy Range, and flows eastward through Horseshoe Park and into the town of Estes Park where it empties into the Big Thompson.

123:32. According to tradition, the Cache la Poudre River, which flows northeast out of Poudre Lake to the east of the Continental Divide at Milner Pass, was so named in 1836 by a party of French trappers from St. Louis who over the course of one winter safely deposited some of their supplies, including a quantity of black gunpowder, close by its banks.

123:33. Densely timbered Forest Canyon, originally known as Willow Canyon, from which the Big Thompson empties, runs northwest to southeast below Trail Ridge.

124:10. The allusion is to William Cullen Bryant's poem "To the Fringed Gentian," written in 1829.

124:34. Specimen Mountain (12,489 feet) and the adjacent Crater to the southwest (both of which lie immediately north of Milner Pass and the Poudre Lake) were once believed to be part of an extinct volcano. Geologists have now established that both features were formed of ash and other volcanic material from an eruption that took place elsewhere.

126:10. Fall River Road, whose lower portion was constructed by convict laborers from the Colorado Penitentiary beginning in 1913, was officially opened on September 14, 1920, after nearly eight years of work. The original road follows the course of Fall River, ascends to the top of Fall River Pass, then descended a thousand feet to cross the Continental Divide at Milner Pass, proceeded to the floor of the Kawuneeche Valley by switchback, and ran south to Grand Lake. When Trail Ridge Road opened in 1932, the eastern section of Fall River Road below Fall River Pass was restricted to one-way traffic west as it is today.

126:20. Boulder Canyon is located west of the city of Boulder. It is bisected by Colorado Highway 119 linking Boulder and Nederland.

126:20. Left Hand Canyon, northwest of Boulder, contains the road to the old mining camps of Ward and Jamestown. The canyon and its creek were named for Ni-Wot (Left Hand), an Arapaho Indian chief who befriended early settlers and propectors.

126:21. The St. Vrain River rises in two branches near Mount Audubon (13,223 feet) in the Indian Peaks Wilderness Area, and flows east and northeast through canyons past Lyons and Longmont respectively before entering the South Platte.

126:36. Bierstadt did not, in fact, visit Estes Park until 1876.

126:37. Isabella Lucy Bird (1831–1904), a plucky Englishwoman, recorded her adventures in Estes Park, climaxing in the October 1873 ascent of Longs Peak in the company of the legendary "desperado" "Rocky Mountain Jim" Nugent (ca. 1828–1874), in her book *A Lady's Life in the Rocky Mountains* (1879).

126:37. Anna Dickinson (1842–1932), a well-known author and lyceum lecturer, on September 13, 1873, became the first woman to climb to the top of Longs Peak, when she made the ascent with members of a party from Ferdinand V. Hayden's United States Geological and Geographical Survey of the Territories which included William N. Byers, editor of the Rocky

Mountain News who later reported her trip. Dickinson recalled her experiences in A Ragged Register (of People, Places and Opinions) (1879).

126:38. Helen Hunt (1830–1885), or Helen Hunt Jackson as she became following her second marriage in 1875, a native of Amherst, Massachusetts, earned a minor reputation as a writer of popular poetry and fiction, which included the novel *Ramona* (1884). Her enthusiastic essays about the scenic wonders of the American West and her new life in the Colorado Territory, where she moved for reasons of health in 1873, were collected and published in 1878 as *Bits of Travel at Home.* Helen Hunt Jackson later became the champion of the displaced American Indian in *A Century of Dishonor* (1881) and in the series of letters and essays which she wrote for newspapers and magazines.

126:38. As Mills notes, Connecticut druggist Frederick Hastings Chapin (1852–1900) celebrated his 1888 visit to Estes Park (as well as his two previous visits in 1886 and again in 1887) in *Mountaineering in Colorado: The Peaks About Estes Park,* published at Boston by the Appalachian Mountain Club in 1889. This book has been reissued by the University Press of Colorado as *Frederick Chapin's Colorado: The Peaks About Estes Park and Other Writings* (1995), with introduction and notes by the present editor.

127:14. The quotation is from Ferdinand V. Hayden's *Ninth Report of the United States Geological and Geographical Survey* (1875). Hayden led expeditions into the Yellowstone region in 1871, 1872, and 1877.

127:22. The quotation is from Frederick Chapin's *Mountaineering in Colorado: The Peaks About Estes Park* (1889).

127:37. Storm Peak (13,326 feet) is located just north of the Keyhole on Longs Peak and west of Mount Lady Washington.

128:27. Scenic Fern Lake (9,530 feet) lies below Odessa Lake (10,020 feet) at the foot of the Odessa Gorge.

128:31. Mt. Meeker (13,911 feet) and Mt. Lady Washington (13,281 feet) flank Longs Peak to the south and north.

128:36. Long Lake, covering an area of nearly 40 acres, is located in the Indian Peaks Wilderness Area to the south of Rocky Mountain National Park.

128:36. Black Lake, located at 10,620 feet, lies to the west of Longs Peak above Mills Lake in Glacier Gorge.

128:37. Mills Lake (9,940 feet), at the head of Glacier Gorge, was named by Estes Park pioneer Abner Sprague, its original owner, after the naturalist-author.

129:1. Mills is nearly correct. Of the lakes in Rocky Mountain National Park only Arrowhead Lake (11,130 feet), lying among the remote and difficult-to-reach Gore Lakes above Forest Canyon is larger.

130:2. The original recommendation to establish Rocky Mountain National Park was made in January 1913 by Robert B. Marshall of the U.S. Geological Survey who had come to the Estes Park region the previous fall to conduct a feasibility study. His recommendation called for setting aside a wilderness area of some 700 square miles, subsequently reduced by congressional legislation to 358.5 square miles.

130:3. North Arapaho Peak (13,502 feet) and South Arapaho Peak (13,397 feet) surround Arapaho Glacier.

130:4. Mills is referring to Twin Sisters Mountain (11,428 feet), located in the Tahosa Valley across from Longs Peak Inn. In 1917 Mills got his wish when Rocky Mountain National Park was enlarged to include the top of the Twin Sisters as well as Deer Mountain and Gem Lake, some 25,000 acres.

130:5. The Rabbit Ears Range, part of the Park Range of the Rockies, is located along the Continental Divide in north-central Colorado just east of Steamboat Springs. It takes its name from the peculiar rock formation on top of Rabbit Ears Peak (10,719 feet).

130:15. The Lincoln Highway was the much-applauded coast-to-coast road completed in 1915. Its name was suggested by Henry B. Joy, president of the Packard Motor Car Company, who happened to be a friend of Enos Mills and guest at Longs Peak Inn.

Why We Need National Parks

150:1. See 26:33.

151:15. The quotation is from Act III, Scene IV of William Shakespeare's *King Lear* (ca. 1605).

152:11. The statement, slightly adapted, comes from Robert Louis Stevenson's (1850–1894) book of travels, *An Inland Voyage* (1878): "There should be nothing so much a man's business as his amusements." The source of the quotation that follows, from "some one else," however, is unclear.

153:19. World War I.

154:23. Mills is quoting from "A Man's A Man for a' That" by Scottish poet Robert Burns (1759–1796).

154:35. See 108:34.

A Day with a Nature Guide

175:36. Liberty Hyde Bailey (1858–1954), a graduate of Michigan Agricultural College (today's Michigan State University), became one of the leading botanists of his generation, teaching at both his alma mater and at Cornell University where he established a new curriculum in practical and experimental horticulture and with the help of state funding began a program to teach nature study in rural schools. Mills' thinking on nature guiding was greatly influenced by Bailey's 1903 book *The Nature-Study Idea.*

178:22. As with John Muir below, Enos Mills very much admired his older contemporary John Burroughs (1837–1921), who established his reputation as an essayist by writing about the nature he observed in and around his home, "Slabsides," near Esopus, New York. Among Burroughs' best-known books are *Wake Robin* (1871), *Locusts and Wild Honey* (1879), *Fresh Fields* (1884), and *Signs and Seasons* (1886).

Harriet—Little Mountain Climber

179:1ff. Harriet Peters made a lasting impression on Enos Mills and came to represent a model of how nature could be appreciated by the very young. As he notes below, their climb occurred in September 1905, when Mills, still very much a bachelor, was 35. The following year he gave up guiding and turned to other activities. Later, Mills concludes his essay, "I heard that Harriet graduated from a girls' college in Texas. I often wonder what has become of her." Had Mills not died prematurely in 1922, he would have known considerably more, for three years later, in 1925, Harriet Peters, by then living in Denver, opened the Green Roof Tea Room close to the Estes Park country club where she specialized in providing breakfast for golfers and picnic lunches for tourists. By 1930, she was working as a clerk at the Elkhorn Lodge where she became friends with local artists Dave Stirling and Richardson Rome with whom she published *The Infamous Dude Dictionary: Rocky Mountainania* in 1934. Clearly aimed at the tourist trade, the amusing and slightly irreverent definitions ("Naturalist: A Nature Fakir" and "Alabi: Where you were when you were NOT where you were accused of being.") were the work of Harriet herself. In January 1946, Harriet Peters, again living in Denver, married Roger Taggart, founder of what later became Greyhound Bus Lines.

The Development of a Woman Guide.

186:6. The woman, whose name Mills omitted "at her request" was Esther Burnell (1889–1946), a young woman from Kansas and a graduate of Lake Erie College in Ohio whom Mills met during the summer of 1916 when she arrived at Longs Peak Inn with her sister Elizabeth to recuperate from a nervous breakdown suffered while working as a consulting decorator for the Sherwin-Williams Paint Company. (Esther apparently had heard Mills lecture in Cleveland the previous year.) At the end of the season, during which Esther did some part-time secretarial work for Mills, Elizabeth returned to California to teach, while Esther took up a homestead claim off Fall River Road near the pass between MacGregor Mountain and Castle Mountain west of the village of Estes Park. As Mills indicates below, she named her homestead cabin, to which she took formal title in 1918, "Keewaydin," an Indian name for the Northwest or home wind. The relationship between Mills and Esther ripened over the winter, and the following summer, when Elizabeth returned from California, the sisters moved to Longs Peak Inn where they trained under Mills' direction to be nature guides in the national park. Both girls returned to the Inn once again in the summer of 1918. On August 12, 1918, Enos Mills and Esther Burnell were married in a simple ceremony that took place across the road at Mills' homestead cabin. On April 27, 1919, their only child, a daughter named Enda, was born. Following Enos Mills' death in September 1922, Esther Mills ran Longs Peak Inn until 1945, when she sold it and moved into a small house not far from the homestead cabin. Longs Peak Inn burned to the ground on June 9, 1949.

187:5. The name Mrs. Pond, like Mrs. Samuel and Mr. Pond below, is fictitious.

190:2. The other homesteader was undoubtedly Katherine Garetson (1877–1963), who had discovered Estes Park during the summer of 1909 when she came west from St. Louis with her sister and brother-in-law Ella and William Dings and ended up staying at Longs Peak Inn. Smitten by the area, Katherine decided to take up a homestead not far from the Inn on Big Owl Road. Her first fall and winter, in the company of her friend Annie Adele Shreve and a 200-pound Great Dane named Gypsy, are charmingly remembered in *Homesteading Big Owl*, published posthumously by her sister in 1989.

191:6. The allusion is to Robert Louis Stevenson's essay of 1877, written at the age of 25, in which he defends the kind of life and lifestyle he had chosen for himself. Idleness, he contends, does not consist of doing nothing but rather in doing those things that the world generally does not value.

195:15. The climactic line from the short story which Stevenson wrote while recuperating at Lake Saranac in New York's Adirondacks. It was published in *Scribner's Magazine* in February 1888.

Nature Guiding at Home

200:6. See 178:22.

200:8. Presumably a reference to the writings of French naturalist Jean-Henri Fabre (1823–1915).

202:3. The famous 1720 novel by Daniel Defoe (1660–1731) about a castaway who lives a solitary island existence for 24 years.

The Mountain Lion

214:8. Big Elk Park lies directly south of Twin Sisters Mountain.

217:5. Theodore Roosevelt (1858–1919) was well known for his enthusiasm for hunting and the out-of-doors.

218:25. *Outdoor Life,* devoted to outdoor sports and recreation, particularly to hunting and fishing, was one of the popular magazines in which Mills published. It was founded in January 1898 by J. A. McGuire, who continued to edit the magazine until 1931. Mills' first magazine article appeared in *Outdoor Life* in 1902.

Select Bibliography

Abbott, Carl. "The Active Force: Enos Mills and the National Park Movement," *Colorado Magazine,* 56, No. 1 and 2 (1979): 56–73.

_____. "The Literary Career of Enos Mills," *Montana: The Magazine of Western History,* 31 (April 1981): 2–15.

Buchholtz, Curt W. *Rocky Mountain National Park: A History.* Boulder: Colorado Associated University Press, 1983.

Drummond, Alexander. *Enos Mills: Citizen of Nature.* Niwot, Colo.: University Press of Colorado, 1995.

Mills, Esther Burnell (with Hildegarde Hawthorne). *Enos Mills of the Rockies.* New York: Houghton Mifflin, 1935.

Pickering, James H. *America's Switzerland: Estes Park and Rocky Mountain National Park, The Growth Years.* Boulder: University Press of Colorado, 2005.

_____. *In the Vale of Elkanah: The Tahosa Valley World of Charles Edwin Hewes.* Estes Park: Alpenaire Publishing Inc. and the Estes Park Area Historical Museum, 2003.

_____. *Mr. Stanley of Estes Park.* Kingfield, Me.: The Stanley Museum, 2000.

_____. *"This Blue Hollow"; Estes Park, The Early Years, 1859–1915.* Niwot, Colo.: University Press of Colorado, 1999.

Wild, Peter. *Enos Mills.* Boise, Id.: Boise State University, 1979.

_____. "Enos Mills: Propagandist of the Rocky Mountains," *Pioneer Conservationists of Western America.* Missoula, Mont.: Mountain States Publishing Company, 1979, pp. 71–79.

About the Author

James H. Pickering, a long-time summer resident of Estes Park, is a professor of English at the University of Houston, where he has also served as dean, senior vice president for academic affairs and provost, and president. He has written or edited seventeen books on Colorado history, including four volumes of Enos Mills' nature essays.